YUGOSLAVIA'S BLOODY COLLAPSE

CHRISTOPHER BENNETT

Yugoslavia's Bloody Collapse

Causes, Course and Consequences

NEW YORK UNIVERSITY PRESS
Washington Square, New York

First published in the U.S.A. in 1995 by
NEW YORK UNIVERSITY PRESS
Washington Square
New York, N.Y. 10003

Library of Congress Cataloging-in-Publication Data
Bennett, Christopher.
    Yugoslavia's bloody collapse : causes, course and consequences /
Christopher Bennett.
        p.   cm.
    Includes bibliographical references and index.
    ISBN 0-8147-1234-7
    1. Yugoslavia—History.   2. Yugoslav War, 1991–   I. Title.
DR1246.B46   1995
949.7—dc20   94–30170
                                                                      CIP

Printed in Hong Kong

CONTENTS

PREFACE

As I was on a train in the London underground one Saturday night a couple of years ago a deranged man grabbed me by the neck and slammed me against the window before charging on into the next carriage. It was the kind of incident which is not uncommon and was over in a flash. But I was left stunned and upset. I had been reading at the time of the attack and felt that I could not have provoked my assailant in any way. Yet when he turned on me, the compartment I had been sitting in, which had been relatively full, emptied in an instant. My assailant was at least six feet tall, muscular and clearly disturbed, and nobody wanted to help me. He was my problem, not theirs, and, in the event, I was simply fortunate that he did not have a knife.

The peoples of Bosnia-Hercegovina and Croatia have not been so lucky. Since 1991, they, too, have been assaulted by a powerful and deranged assailant, wielding not only a knife but also an array of sophisticated weaponry. Moreover, in Bosnia-Hercegovina and Croatia the assailant has refused to let go. At the same time, onlookers in the international community have made themselves scarce, leaving the assailant to get on with his assault unimpeded, and have virtually abetted the assault with a series of measures to prevent the victims from acquiring the means with which to defend themselves.

Since the outbreak of hostilities in June 1991, events in the former Yugoslavia have been impossible to ignore. Yet, despite saturation media coverage in most of the Western world, understanding of the conflict among the public at large is generally poor. This is hardly surprising. Yugoslavia's complexity has never translated well into journalism and, in any case, the media were not especially interested in the country until war actually broke out. Indeed, during the critical years leading up to the war television cameras were conspicuous by their absence. Media coverage of Yugoslav affairs was as minimalist before fighting broke out as it has been maximalist during the past three years.

Everybody who writes about the war in Yugoslavia brings his or her own preconceptions to the task, and in this respect I am no

vii

exception. I start from the premise that a Yugoslav state with a genuine commitment to national equality was the best living arrangement for the lands of the south Slavs. It was also the only practical settlement. I consider the Titoist experiment to have been a qualified success on a political level, especially where relations between Yugoslavia's peoples are concerned, though disastrous economically. However, that experiment was dead and buried by 1989 when Serbia used force to crush Kosovo's autonomy. Moreover, Yugoslavia in any meaningful form was irretrievably destroyed as soon as the Yugoslav People's Army moved against Slovenia. In addition, I refuse to accept that there was anything inevitable about Yugoslavia's disintegration, that Balkan peoples are somehow predisposed to violence, or that the international community was powerless to halt the killing. Instead, I believe that there are rational explanations for everything which has taken place, and I have tried to condense them into this book.

While centuries of Habsburg and Ottoman rule gave the Balkans their enduring character, the key events in Yugoslavia's disintegration took place not in the distant past, or in the Second World War, or even during Tito's rule, but in the years immediately preceding the outbreak of war. It is a tale not of 'ancient hatreds', centuries of ethnic strife and inevitable conflict, but of very modern nationalist hysteria which was deliberately generated in the media. Indeed, Yugoslavia's disintegration is largely a testimony to the power of the media in the modern world.

The real Yugoslav tragedy is the demise of the very Yugoslav idea — that is, the political philosophy that all south Slavs should live, and feel that they belong, in a single state. The beauty of Yugoslavism was that it prevented the various Yugoslav peoples from falling out with each other over rival claims to ethnically-mixed territory, and although Yugoslavia could never entirely satisfy the nationalist ambitions of every Yugoslav nation, it was infinitely preferable to the alternative, which is today's carnage. In Bosnia-Hercegovina, for example, Serbs, Croats and Muslim Slavs could either live together within some form of Yugoslav framework or they would wipe each other out in the attempt to create ethnically pure states. However, although Yugoslavism emerged out of both the First and the Second World Wars as the best formula for national coexistence, the concept has been shattered by the present conflict and a Yugoslav state cannot now be resurrected.

My interest in Yugoslavia stems from my mother who was born

and brought up in Slovenia. As a child I visited the country most years, grew to love it and, as an adolescent, made a great effort to learn both Slovene and Serbo-Croat. I can remember Yugoslavia's good years—and there really were good years—and am especially pleased that I knew Serbia before Milošević's rise to power. Since my early contact with Yugoslavia was generally with Slovenia, I assume that this is reflected in my basic attitudes towards Yugoslav affairs, although my opinions have also been shaped by exceptional individuals from throughout the former country, as well as by my experiences there both as a student in the 1980s and as a journalist in the 1990s.

I was in Ljubljana when war broke out in June 1991 and remained in the former Yugoslavia for the next fourteen months. In that time I covered the wars in Slovenia and Croatia in their entirety, as well as the formative events in the Bosnian war. In the intervening couple of years I have continued to follow Yugoslav developments closely, but believe that little of substance has changed since August 1992 and the London Conference. By that stage, the Serb offensive in Bosnia-Hercegovina had already gound to a halt and, following media revelations of the horrors of ethnic cleansing, the great powers were threatening some form of intervention to end the conflict. However, though the London Conference promised a new dawn, the international community failed to deliver any of the commitments it made. The war continued, albeit at a lower intensity, and it continues today.

Writing this book has in one sense been therapeutic for me, since I too have had to come to terms with the demise of Yugoslavia. I am under no illusion that it will have any influence upon international attitudes or, critically, policy towards the former Yugoslavia, since that policy has been determined in advance and is based on the domestic political considerations of the great powers, not an analysis of Yugoslav affairs. I have simply tried to explain as concisely as possible what has taken place, and to suggest what the implications are and where events are likely to lead, on the assumption that there will be no change in the international strategy towards the conflict. I can only hope that my book will contribute to a better understanding of events in Yugoslavia among those who read it and perhaps intensify their compassion for the innocent victims of the war.

The months I spent in the former Yugoslavia as a war correspondent are, without doubt, the most exciting period of my life and I hope that the book conveys some of the passion I feel and the excitement I experienced at that time. Nevertheless, I chose to write a history of Yugoslavia rather than a more personal account of events, since I believe that one of the best ways to distort the past is to focus on those events you have witnessed yourself. The book is largely based on existing literature in English, Slovene and Serbo-Croat, much of which I originally read as part of an undergraduate history course at London University, taught by Mark Wheeler of the School of Slavonic and East European Studies. It is supplemented by interviews with as many key figures as possible throughout the former Yugoslavia, which helped me piece together a picture of how the country disintegrated.

I am grateful to all the Yugoslavs who allowed me to pick their brains, and especially to those members of the Association for a Yugoslav Democratic Initiative (*Udruženje za Jugoslovensku demokratsku inicijativu* or UJDI) who gave me their time. UJDI was a truly remarkable organisation, founded by the Croat intellectual and committed Yugoslav, Branko Horvat, on the eve of the disintegration of communist rule, and it contained many of the country's greatest minds. It was designed to be a forum for debate to analyze the best way forward as Yugoslavia evolved out of communism, and UJDI members are an unrivalled source of information on the events leading to the outbreak of war and the destruction of their common country. Moreover, although UJDI members come from throughout the former Yugoslavia, they are generally agreed on the causes of the country's disintegration and I am happy to acknowledge that I have borrowed much of their analysis. Ultimately, the individual who has had the greatest influence on my outlook is Vesna Knežević, with whom I shared a flat in Zagreb during 1991 and 1992. Vesna, who is a Serb Jew from Priština, was Radio Belgrade's correspondent in Croatia between 1984 and 1991. Her appointment pre-dated Milošević's purge of the media in Serbia, and until she too was sacked in October 1991, Vesna's reports were a beacon of light in the Serbian media. At the time we moved in together Vesna was receiving death threats. Though it was a desperate period for her, she helped me greatly and I only hope my presence proved as beneficial to her.

In Britain I have called on the expertise of Christopher Cviić, Mark Wheeler and Branka Magaš and am grateful for the help they each gave me. I am also grateful to my father who put in more hours than he could really afford improving my style, and my mother who contributed her ideas. Sandrine Bardouil also deserves special mention since she has faithfully read my work, offered constructive criticism and put up with my moods during the past year as I have struggled to write this book. In attempting to condense much into little space there are inevitably gaps. In a bibliographical note I suggest further reading on specific areas.

London   CHRISTOPHER BENNETT
November 1994

ABBREVIATIONS

Derived from Serbo-Croat names of institutions:

NDH Independent State of Croatia, the Croatian state set up by the Ustaša movement under the aegis of Germany and Italy (*Nezavisna Država Hrvatske*)

HDZ Croat Democratic Union (*Hrvatska demokratska zajednica*)

HOS Croat Defence Forces (*Hrvatske odbrambene snage*), the military wing of the Party of Right

HSP Croat Party of Right (*Hrvatska stranka prava*)

HVO Croat Defence Council, the Bosnian Croat army (*Hrvatsko vijeće odbrane*)

JNA Yugoslav People's Army (*Jugoslovenska narodna armija*)

KNS Coalition of National Agreement (*Koalicija narodnog sporazuma*)

SDS Serb Democratic Party (*Srpska demokratska stranka*)

SDA Muslim Party for Democratic Action (*Stranka demokratske akcije*)

UJDI Association for a Yugoslav Democratic Initiative (*Udruženje za Jugoslovensku demokratsku inicijativu*)

ZNG The Croatian National Guard (*Zbor narodne garde*)

Derived from English names of institutions:

CNN Cable News Network

CPY Communist Party of Yugoslavia

EC   European Community

EU   European Union

LCY League of Communists of Yugoslavia

UN   United Nations

GUIDE TO PRONUNCIATION

In Serb-Croat,

c is pronounced 'ts' as in 'mats'

č is 'ch' as in 'chore'

ć is 'tj' of 'tu' as in the British-English pronunciation of 'tune'

dj and dž are like the 'j' in 'jeans'—the difference in value between each being imperceptible to the alien ear

j is 'y' as in 'yes'

lj is 'liyuh' like the middle sound of 'million'

nj is 'ny' as in 'canyon'

š is 'sh' as in 'shore'

ž is like the 's' sound in 'pleasure'

All vowels are short. Other letters are pronounced much as in English. Short words are stressed on the first syllable and longer words are generally stressed on the third syllable from the end.

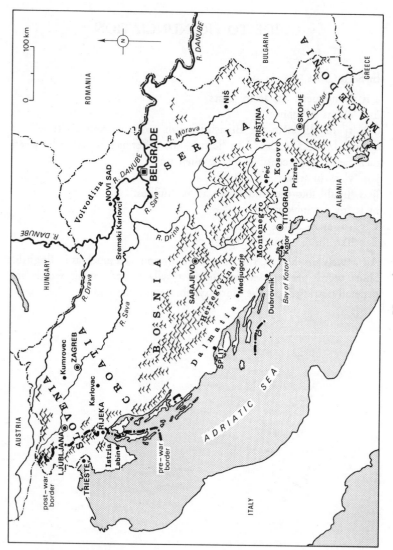

All the three maps were drawn by Mr A.S. Burn of the Geography Department, University of Southampton.

xiv

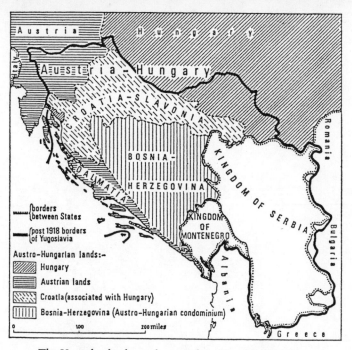

The Yugoslav lands on the eve of the First World War.

The federated units of Yugoslavia since the Second World War.

xv

1

INTRODUCTION

'Yugoslavia had tourism, heavy industry; it was a food-surplus nation. Its new freeways linked the rest of the European Community with Greece, Turkey, and the export markets of the Middle East. The totems of an emerging consumer society were everywhere: new gas stations, motels, housing developments, and discos and sidewalk cafés in the villages. Most impressive were the large private houses covering the roadside hills. Before the killing started practically everybody, it seems, was just finishing a new house, or had just bought a new car.' — T.D. Allman.[1]

The Yugoslav Killing Fields

When the Berlin Wall, that ultimate symbol of the Cold War and the division of Europe, came crashing down in November 1989 it appeared to herald the dawn of a new age of peace, prosperity and optimism. However, less than two years later a war erupted in Yugoslavia which has shattered visions of a New World Order and cast a long, dark shadow across the entire European continent. Since the outbreak of hostilities on 27 June 1991, events in the former Yugoslavia have been impossible to ignore. The conflict has so dominated the news agenda that Balkan leaders have seemingly become household names the world over, and it is difficult to open a newspaper or switch on a television without being confronted by images of destruction and heart-rending scenes of misery. The phrase 'etničko čišćenje' (ethnic cleansing) has passed from Serbo-Croat into English and many other languages to encapsulate the brutality of a conflict in which the principal aim has been to erase all trace of alien culture, while the name Bosnia-Hercegovina, in particular, has become synonymous with killing, cruelty and human suffering on an unprecedented scale.

Yugoslavia formally ceased to exist on 15 January 1992 when all twelve members of the European Community officially recognised

[1] T.D. Allman is a foreign correspondent for *Vanity Fair*, New York, and covered part of the war in Yugoslavia.

1

Slovenia and Croatia as independent states. For Croats, Yugoslavia's demise could not come soon enough and many celebrated by shooting wildly in the air, relieved that their struggle for independence was over. Three months later, in an attempt to halt the escalating fighting in Bosnia-Hercegovina, the United States followed the European Community, recognising Slovene, Croatian and Bosnian independence. Recognition signified a major shift in US policy towards the former Yugoslav republics. Just ten months earlier, days before Slovenia and Croatia intended to declare their independence, the then Secretary of State, James Baker, visited Belgrade to make his country's position categorically clear and declared that the United States would not recognise Slovenia or Croatia 'under any circumstances'.

Like most international statesmen Baker did not wish to see Yugoslavia disintegrate, since he feared for the future stability of the Balkans. Despite a number of shortcomings, Yugoslavia had enabled its many peoples, cultures and traditions to live side by side in peace for more than forty years. Indeed, the Yugoslav state had already emerged twice in the 20th century at the end of protracted wars as the best formula for national coexistence in that part of the world. It appeared absurd that, at a time when other European countries were voluntarily giving up much of their sovereignty to forge lasting bonds with each other, Yugoslavia's republics should be heading in the opposite direction. However, more than six months of fighting made further attempts to hold the country together pointless.

The international community became directly involved in the Yugoslav conflict as soon as war broke out in Slovenia, when the European Community set itself up as mediator. Three months later, as war engulfed Croatia, the United Nations joined the diplomatic search for a settlement. However, diplomacy alone had no impact on the bloodshed, and fighting continued to escalate amid increasing reports of atrocities. Without the war, international recognition for Slovenia and Croatia was unthinkable. But as cease-fires came and went to no avail, pressure to recognise the two republics, widely seen as the victims of aggression, soared. When eventually the EC member-states did recognise Slovenia and Croatia, albeit with misgivings, they were merely bowing to the inevitable and acknowledging that Yugoslavia was no more. Yet, as most diplomats were aware, recognition was not a magic wand which would overnight restore stability to the Balkans.

The year 1992 was scheduled to be a milestone on the road to

European unity. Instead, it will probably be remembered as the year in which a European civilisation and people were very nearly exterminated, while the European powers sat and watched. In April 1992, Serb forces set out to ensure that Bosnia-Hercegovina remained part of the rump Yugoslav state, irrespective of the wishes of the republic's non-Serb majority and even of much of the Serb population. In the process they laid waste much of the republic and massacred untold numbers of innocent and defenceless people simply on account of their national origins. Survivors of the initial Serb offensive were herded into concentration camps, where their ordeal continued. During the months of April, May, June and July 1992 thousands more Bosnians were systematically raped, tortured and executed, and, but for the courage of a handful of journalists who exposed some of the horror, and the ensuing public outrage throughout the world, this level of killing might have continued for much longer. Nevertheless, despite what can only be described as attempted genocide, the international community chose not to intervene militarily to protect the victims, and more than two years later the war in Bosnia-Hercegovina goes on.

The Yugoslav wars are to the 1990s what Lebanon's civil war was to the 1970s and 1980s. But in the former Yugoslavia the numbers killed are larger, the extent of destruction is greater, and media coverage has been more comprehensive. Estimates of the dead range from about 200,000 to more than 300,000, but until some form of order returns and a formal census is carried out, there is no way of knowing exactly how many people have lost their lives. Moreover, the killing is far from over. Even if a settlement could be found in Bosnia-Hercegovina to satisfy all parties to the war, it would not, by any means, end all conflict in the former Yugoslavia. Further bloodshed in regions which do not receive the same media attention as Bosnia-Hercegovina remains very much on the cards—in Kosovo, in the Sandžak, in Macedonia, in Vojvodina, in Croatia again and even in Serbia.

Advance teams of UN peacekeepers began arriving in Croatia in March 1992 after the 17th cease-fire of the Croatian war had held for two months. UN forces, or UNPROFOR as they are called in the former Yugoslavia,[2] came as part of a peace agreement ending that war which had been signed in Sarajevo on 2 January 1992, when the Bosnian capital was still at peace. Under the terms of the Sarajevo

[2]UNPROFOR stands for United Nations Protection Force.

Accord, 14,000 peacekeepers were to be deployed in Croatia to police regions with a significant Serb population and to create the conditions for the negotiation of an overall settlement in Yugoslavia. Since then, following the spread of war to Bosnia-Hercegovina, UN activities have mushroomed to such an extent that UNPROFOR has become the organisation's largest and highest-profile peacekeeping operation. As of May 1994 more than 30,000 UN personnel were permanently deployed on the territory of the former Yugoslavia, in the republics of Croatia, Bosnia-Hercegovina and Macedonia. The first two years of peacekeeping[3] cost the United Nations $1.74 billion as well as the lives of eighty soldiers, while UNPROFOR's annual budget has spiralled above $1 billion.

In addition to its peacekeeping operations, the United Nations is helping to feed more than 4 million people in the former Yugoslavia, 2.7 million in Bosnia-Hercegovina alone, through its aid agencies. This humanitarian effort is also extremely costly. In 1993, the United Nations High Commission for Refugees' operations alone cost more than $505 million, of which the United States contributed $128 million and the United Kingdom another $45 million. Moreover, in the period up to May 1994 eleven relief workers lost their lives.

Despite more than three years of war the prospects of an end to violence and a return to something resembling peace are poor. Though the Balkans no longer have the explosive capacity to trigger a world war, Yugoslavia's successor states are set to remain a significant trouble-spot and diplomatic headache for the foreseeable future. As long as there are the physical means — that is, the weaponry — and as long as aggression appears to yield dividends, the Balkans will remain prone to violent conflict. The hatred spawned by the recent fighting and fanned by jingoistic local media will not die away quickly, nor will the desire for revenge. The only certainties are that very many lives have been, are being and will be destroyed, that UN operations in the former Yugoslavia will continue to be extremely costly and that the entire international community will have to pick up the bill.

It was not always like this. Until very recently Yugoslavia was generally viewed as the acceptable face of communism. Yugoslavs were able to travel abroad freely and, in contrast to the rest of eastern Europe, grew accustomed to a reasonably high standard of living. With the exception of Slovenia no republic can seriously claim to have

[3] From 1 March 1992 to 1 March 1994.

benefited from Yugoslavia's demise. As a result, coming to terms with the break-up will be critical to all its former peoples as they set about building new futures. Though a balanced understanding of the past does not automatically aid recovery, an especially distorted interpretation of history can only add to the scar tissue and hamper reconstruction.

How and why Yugoslavia fell apart are burning questions in every former Yugoslav republic. With rare exceptions, however, Yugoslavs are the worst possible sources of information about the country they used to share and the manner in which it broke up. The passion and apparent expertise with which so many talk so often and at such length about Yugoslavia and especially its history conceal a depressing lack of balance and understanding. Opinions are almost invariably based on prejudice and conditioning. Indeed, almost every Yugoslav will insist that the ethnic group or republic to which he or she belongs was forever being exploited by all the others in Yugoslavia, which patently could not be the case. But this should come as no surprise to anyone who has watched a Yugoslav news bulletin or read a Yugoslav newspaper in recent years. For, as Yugoslavia disintegrated, the media of the various republics served not to inform their respective publics but to bolster support for the stances taken by their respective leaderships. Years before the first shots were fired the media were already at war and the journalists who deliberately fanned the flames of national hatred must bear a heavy responsibility for the carnage.

An Inevitable Disintegration?

Prophets of doom began to speculate about Yugoslavia's future as soon as Josip Broz Tito, 35 years its uncrowned monarch, died in 1980. They argued that deep, historical fault-lines divided the country. The north was comparatively wealthy, the south poor, and the gap between rich and poor enormous.[4] Serbs, Montenegrins and Macedonians were Orthodox and had lived under Ottoman rule, while Croats and Slovenes were Catholic and had lived within the Habsburg Empire. Moreover, during the Second World War, fanatical Croat and Serb nationalists had done their best to wipe each other out. Yugoslavia was supposedly an artificial creation plagued by atavistic

[4] *Per capita* income in Slovenia, the richest federal unit, was about six times greater than in Kosovo, the poorest.

and irrational hatred, and, in the absence of Tito's charismatic leadership and unifying presence, the country would surely not survive.

The outbreak of war appeared to confirm the above point of view, as if fighting was part of the culture and it was only been a matter of time before Yugoslavia fell apart in war. It was also an opinion which has been heard again and again from the lips of Western politicians and statesmen opposed, on principle, to any form of military intervention. As accounts of atrocities and massacres from the war in Croatia, especially the attack on Dubrovnik and the siege of Vukovar, made newspaper headlines throughout the world, most commentators agreed that Yugoslavia had been a historical mistake. The gulf between Serb and Croat claims and counter-claims and the intransigence of all sides at the negotiating table appeared to confirm this image of an irrational conflict steeped in seemingly unfathomable historical animosity. But was it really so unreasonable to join Ottoman and Habsburg traditions? And was war in Europe in the last decade of the 20th century really unavoidable?

The Balkans are lands of historical myths—myths which may have kept national identities alive during centuries of alien rule but are, nevertheless, myths. However, not all Balkan myths are ancient. Take, for example, the myth of centuries of Serb-Croat animosity. Try as they might, contemporary propagandists cannot seriously claim that Serbs and Croats have been at each others' throats from time immemorial. Serb-Croat rivalry is in an entirely different league from, say, that of the French and Germans, which now seems to have been resolved, for its history is comparatively brief. Indeed, until this century, most Serbs and Croats had had virtually no contact with each other. For centuries, Serbs were engaged in a fight for independence from Turkey, and if they had an historical enemy, it was the Ottomans. At the same time, Croats were struggling against Habsburg over-lords and fending off predatory Hungarian, German and Italian nationalisms. Even when Serbs fought Croats in two world wars this century this was not the result of any inherent enmity, but, to a large extent, because extreme circumstances, over which both peoples had little control, had pitted them against each other.

This is not to say that there is no historical dimension to today's conflict. There certainly is. However, in the former Yugoslavia, popular perceptions of the past are infinitely more important than what may or may not actually have taken place. Moreover, those perceptions are based not on the works of respected historians but on the Yugoslav media, which have deliberately fostered crude and distorted interpretations of the past—interpretations which may serve contemporary political needs, but which contribute nothing to an understanding of Yugoslav history. Nevertheless, the scars of this century and especially the Second World War are real and could only be healed by responsible and sensitive government, and a lot of time.

The Yugoslav experiment lasted just over seventy-three years with two separate incarnations; the first a kingdom, generally referred to as Royal Yugoslavia, the second a communist dictatorship, indelibly linked to the person of Tito. Both incarnations had their good points and there were periods when Yugoslav optimism and ambitions appeared limitless. Though hampered by an ideological commitment to Marxism-Leninism, the communist Yugoslavia which emerged out of the Second World War was a genuine attempt to reconcile the interests of all the country's peoples. The system of government was intricate and complex, but designed to be manifestly fair. It should be remembered that Yugoslavs managed to get along with each other. Moreover, the killing of the Second World War, which had not, by any means, been confined to Serbs and Croats, ceased to be a matter of contention.

Despite the claims of contemporary propagandists, the second Yugoslavia was not an unmitigated failure in which national tensions were simply swept under the carpet. Indeed, only a few years ago Yugoslavs could, and did, walk tall in the world boasting of the cultural diversity which made their common country unique. Thanks largely to the country's geopolitical position, sandwiched between East and West and yet independent, and Tito's enormous prestige abroad, Yugoslavia had many friends. It hosted a number of notable international competitions, including the 1984 Winter Olympics in Sarajevo, and each year hundreds of thousands of foreign tourists flocked to its many holiday resorts, especially those on the Adriatic coast.

Considering the great differences between Yugoslavia's many regions, it is hardly surprising that republics regularly fell out over development strategies and the allocation of scarce resources. Nevertheless, until the late 1980s, republican alliances were fluid. Yugoslavia was certainly not divided into two naturally hostile camps, one of former Habsburg republics and the other former Ottoman republics. On the contrary, if a traditional alliance did exist it was between ex-Habsburg Slovenia and ex-Ottoman Serbia, the two republics with least to fall out over. But all republics had to indulge in horse-trading with each other and to make compromises to see part of their own programmes accepted at the federal level.

It is, in fact, remarkably difficult for any state, no matter how oppressive or corrupt, to fall apart. The disintegration of a country is rarely in the interest of its people and is invariably opposed by the international community, which, ultimately, has to deal with the consequences. Many countries with regimes far more despicable than Yugoslavia's ever was, nevertheless remain together. The Habsburg Empire was also a multinational state which appeared anachronistic to most commentators in the 19th century and whose break-up was frequently predicted. Yet it managed to survive, and even to adapt when necessary to changing circumstances. Moreover, it eventually took four years of the greatest war the world had known to destroy it forever, and its passing has hardly proved to be in the long-term interests of its many peoples.

Despite the complexity of the decision-making process in the second Yugoslavia, the country notched up several successes at home. Living standards rose to historically unprecedented levels. The health and life expectancy of Yugoslavs improved dramatically, schooling became universal and illiteracy was virtually wiped out. Urbanisation after 1945 radically altered the country and its ethnic map. Workers migrated to cities in search of jobs and a generation was growing up which was more aware of its urban roots than its national origins. Inter-marriage had become common and the undeniably Yugoslav offspring of mixed marriages were increasingly a feature of Yugoslav society. Indeed, contrary to nationalist expectations, Yugoslavia's last census, which was carried out months before fighting broke out, registered a jump in the numbers of people who considered themselves primarily Yugoslav, rather than Croat, Serb or any other nationality. In many ways, nationalism should no longer have been an issue.

Though prosperity was shortlived and Yugoslavia lacked a sound economic base, the country was, nevertheless, in far better shape than much of the rest of eastern Europe as it abandoned communism to make the painful economic transition to the free market. Moreover, the last Prime Minister, Ante Marković, was an honest and able politician, respected both at home and abroad, whose radical economic stabilisation programme was producing impressive results. Clearly, Yugoslavia's disintegration was not inevitable, nor, sadly, can it simply be put down to an unfortunate series of events and misunderstandings.

Guilt

While all the peoples of the former Yugoslavia have been profoundly affected by their country's demise, the greatest losers, to date, are, without doubt, Bosnia-Hercegovina's Muslim Slavs, whose society has been all but destroyed. Vojvodina's Hungarians, Kosovo's Albanians and the Macedonians have also fared extremely badly and face an especially uncertain future, though their plight has not been as spectacular as that of the Muslim Slavs and has not received as much media attention. Yet Muslim Slavs, Hungarians, Albanians and Macedonians had virtually no say in the events leading to Yugoslavia's disintegration, which was essentially a private affair between Slovenes, Croats and Serbs, with a little assistance from abroad.

The decision to recognise Slovenia, Croatia and Bosnia-Hercegovina as independent states was a major step towards apportioning war-guilt, since it implied that Serbia, which claimed to be fighting to hold Yugoslavia together and to protect Serb communities throughout the country, was actually to blame for the conflict. In addition, Serbia has repeatedly been singled out for condemnation in the many reports into the war compiled by international organisations, including those of the War Crimes Commission which was set up by the UN Security Council in October 1992 to gather evidence of rapes, tortures and murders perpetrated in the former Yugoslavia. However, any examination of guilt must also take into account events before fighting broke out. Essentially, there are three issues to consider: how Yugoslavia came to the brink of war; how war broke out; and why the fighting has been so bitter and protracted.

How far back to look to determine culpability is perhaps inevitably a matter of contention. But to attribute developments in the 1990s to events which took place half a century earlier, as some propagandists would, is surely far-fetched. By the same logic the whole of Europe should be in a permanent state of war. Since Yugoslavia's complexity did not translate easily into journalism and since in-depth coverage of protracted inter-republican squabbling was unlikely to sell more newspapers or boost television ratings, the international media had largely neglected Yugoslav affairs until war broke out. As a result, the Yugoslav conflict was initially examined from the propaganda positions of the belligerents. However, contemporary events require contemporary explanations, and rather than attempting to piece together the tenuous link between one historical half-truth and another, it is necessary to consider where this unhealthy obsession with distorted interpretations of the past came from.

Slobodan Milošević and his rise to power in Serbia are critical to Yugoslavia's disintegration, for Milošević changed the face of both Serbian and Yugoslav society. Before Milošević's rise, Serbia was, in many ways, the most liberal and progressive of Yugoslavia's republics. The Serbian media were remarkably open by the standards of eastern Europe, and political opposition was tolerated, if not encouraged. But as soon as Milošević installed himself in power, Serbia changed beyond recognition. Serbian society was systematically purged, all opposition was crushed and the media were brought firmly under political control. As early as 1987, four years before the shooting war began, the Serbian media were already on a war-footing, spewing out a barrage of ethnic hatred. Moreover, the propaganda offensive was so intense that ordinary Serbs rapidly came to believe that they were permanently under siege and surrounded by blood enemies whose only desire was to wipe them out.

The media had always played a critical role in Yugoslav society but had, hitherto, been employed to bring Yugoslavia's peoples together in the Titoist spirit of 'brotherhood and unity', and to smooth over national disputes, not to create ethnic conflict. By revamping communist authority with nationalism Milošević came to enjoy enormous popularity at home, but set Serbia on a collision course with the rest of Yugoslavia which rapidly led to bloodshed. For Kosovo's Albanians, the Yugoslav wars began not in June 1991, but more than two years earlier in March 1989, when they were forcibly stripped of their autonomy and rose up in defence of the constitutional order Tito had bequeathed Yugoslavia. The Albanian uprising failed and was brutally put down with somewhere between 120 and 140 deaths. However, its significance was not lost on the rest of Yugoslavia's non-Serbs. For, by the time Kosovo fell to Milošević, the Titoist vision of Yugoslavia as a home to all its many peoples was no more.

Having presided over Yugoslavia's destiny for more than three times as long as the country subsequently survived without him, Tito, too, must share some responsibility for the manner of Yugoslavia's demise. In essence, Titoism amounted to a system of checks and balances designed to make sure that all peoples were treated equally and that no individual was able to acquire as much power as Tito himself had possessed. However, when confronted by a determined challenge from within the League of Communists, Titoism was found wanting. The

failings of the Titoist state were primarily economic and it was against
a background of declining living standards that Milošević launched
his assault against the federation. But economic failure rapidly bred
political crisis, and, in Tito's absence, Titoism proved incapable of
organising effective resistance to a political philosophy which would
ultimately destroy the Yugoslav state as well as the lives of many
millions of its citizens.

Milošević's clamp-down in Kosovo pushed Slovenia's then communist leadership reluctantly to stand up to Serbia, and it was this
rift which developed between Slovenia and Serbia, not events in
Croatia or Bosnia-Hercegovina, which led to Yugoslavia's break-up.
Spurred forward by an increasingly confident and vociferous opposition, Slovenia's communists worked to extricate their republic from
the Yugoslavia which Milošević was building, irrespective of the
impact of their actions on the rest of the country. In the event,
Slovenia was spared a similar fate to that of Croatia and Bosnia-
Hercegovina by the fact that it was the only Yugoslav republic without
an indigenous Serb community, and had thus never formed part of
the Greater Serbian vision of Yugoslavia.

By the beginning of 1989 Yugoslavia was already in an advanced
state of decay, but monumental developments abroad exacerbated the
country's crisis and hastened its demise. As communism collapsed in
the rest of eastern Europe and the threat of Warsaw Pact invasion
disappeared, Yugoslavia lost the unique geopolitical position it had
occupied in world politics for more than four decades. Diplomatic
activity and foreign investment shifted away from Yugoslavia towards
eastern Europe's emerging democracies, and, without the Eastern
bogey to bind the country together and Western money to bail out
the economy, Yugoslavs found themselves for the first time entirely
on their own. As long as Yugoslavia's internal quarrels did not spill
over into neighbouring countries, the international community no
longer cared what happened.

Since the Yugoslav communists had come to power with a
minimum of Soviet support and Yugoslav communism was an
indigenous creation, Yugoslavia was in a somewhat different position
from eastern Europe's other communist states. Nevertheless, the
economic and political failings of Marxism-Leninism were as great in
Yugoslavia as anywhere else in the communist world and Yugoslavia's
home-grown communism could not survive the demise of communist
authority in the Soviet Union and the rest of eastern Europe. In

January 1990 the League of Communists of Yugoslavia broke up and
three months later the Slovene and Croatian communists were defeated
by newly-formed nationalist coalitions in multiparty elections. The
result was a further polarisation of Yugoslav society and the creation
of a two-speed community. Slovenia and Croatia were governed
by non-communists[5] professing a commitment to liberal democracy,
while communists remained firmly entrenched in power in Serbia and
its provinces, Kosovo and Vojvodina, as well as in Montenegro. In
addition, Bosnia-Hercegovina and Macedonia were caught in the
middle, unsure which way to turn, and the picture was complicated
by the military, which remained committed to hardline communism
and took the opportunity to disarm the territorial defence forces of
both Slovenia and Croatia before the formal hand-over of power.

Though Yugoslavia remained a single entity in the eyes of the
world, communism had helped to hold Yugoslav society together for
almost forty-five years, and its demise made a major reorganisation of
the state unavoidable. In effect, the debate which had preoccupied
Yugoslav politicians during the 1920s as to the best form of government for their common state had been reopened. Future inter-
republican relations were ostensibly negotiable, and in a climate
of goodwill it would certainly have been possible to erect a third
Yugoslavia out of the ruins of the communist state. However, in the
seventeen months between the break-up of the League of Communists
and the outbreak of war, talks never got off the ground.

Since the best time for a negotiated settlement in any conflict is
before it escalates into war, the period immediately prior to the outbreak of hostilities is critical to an understanding of the Yugoslav wars.
Indeed, events in the months leading up to independence declarations
in Slovenia and Croatia and the decision of the Yugoslav People's
Army (*Jugoslovenska narodna armija* or JNA) to use force to crush those
republics, were of a far greater magnitude than the more spectacular
events which followed the outbreak of war. Yet this is precisely the
period of Yugoslav history about which least is known abroad. For,
at the very time when Yugoslavia was breaking up, events in the
Middle East — Iraq's invasion of Kuwait and the subsequent Gulf
War — eclipsed all others, and monopolised the news agenda.

---

[5] Since almost everybody with any political ambitions in Yugoslavia had belonged
to the Communist Party at some stage in their career, the non-communists who came
to power in both Slovenia and Croatia were themselves generally former communists.

At the inter-republican talks on Yugoslavia's future which preceded the outbreak of war all non-Serbian leaders had the same goal, namely a settlement to protect them from Serbia. However, the various republics had very different options open to them. For Bosnia-Hercegovina and Macedonia, the integral Yugoslav state provided an unprecedented level of security. For them the critical issue was that Yugoslavia should remain a unitary state. While the leaders of both republics hoped to prevent Serbia from dictating terms to the rest of the country, they were prepared to accept greatly reduced autonomy in the interests of continued Yugoslav union. By contrast, Slovene leaders were not prepared to accept second best, and, as war loomed in Croatia and Bosnia-Hercegovina, came increasingly to view Yugoslavia simply as a liability in which they had little to gain and a great deal to lose, and took steps to extricate themselves from the quagmire. Moreover, Slovene decisions had serious implications for Croatia. Croatian leaders were reluctant to give Serbia any cause for intervention in Croatia, but calculated that the risks of remaining part of a Serb-dominated Yugoslavia in Slovenia's absence were greater than those of following Slovenia towards some form of independence.

In December 1990 Slovenes voted overwhelmingly to declare independence from Yugoslavia if, during the next six months, they could not reach a new working arrangement with the rest of the federation. At the time, the threat of independence was to be used as a bargaining counter in the inter-republican discussions, but as the date came closer and there were no signs of progress, Slovenia chose to press ahead with a declaration, followed cautiously by Croatia. For all the rhetoric about sovereignty and statehood, the independence declarations were essentially symbolic. Slovenia and Croatia were not seceding from Yugoslavia, but from Milošević's vision of Yugoslavia. Moreover, nothing whatsoever changed in Croatia and the only difference in Slovenia after its 25 June declaration was that the republic stopped paying excise duties to the federal government in Belgrade and hoisted a single Slovene flag whose design had only been agreed the night before. To put the declarations into context, according to the existing constitution all Yugoslavia's republics were already sovereign and independent, and Serbia, which claimed to be aiming to preserve Yugoslavia's integrity, had stopped paying those same excise duties to the federal government eight months earlier. Neither Slovenia nor Croatia viewed the independence declaration as a definitive break with the rest of the federation. Indeed, it could not be, as both republics remained within Yugoslavia's monetary and even security systems.

The fundamental reason for the lack of progress at the negotiating table was that one side, namely Serbia, had no need to negotiate. Whereas Slovenia and Croatia had been disarmed and were essentially defenceless, Serbia could count on the support of the JNA and the huge arsenal it had built up during the previous forty-five years. Milošević was in a position to achieve his own vision of Yugoslavia, irrespective of anybody else's wishes, and the negotiating process was over-shadowed by his attempts to extend his authority throughout the country, by the on-going repression in Kosovo and the actions of militant Serbs in Croatia and Bosnia-Hercegovina. In an attempt to restore some equilibrium to the Yugoslav equation, Slovenia and Croatia looked abroad for support, but to no avail.

The Slovene and Croatian envoys who lobbied world capitals during spring 1991 found themselves cold-shouldered and ordered back to the negotiating table in Yugoslavia. The international community wanted a unitary state and was not prepared to listen to, let alone consider, the Slovene and Croatian points of view. This was tantamount to backing Serbia and the Serbian vision of Yugoslavia, and misguided and counter-productive attempts by Western politicians to hold the country together in the days preceding the independence declarations only made war more likely.

When the JNA High Command decided to intervene in Slovenia, it did so in the belief that the United States was prepared to turn a blind eye to intervention, provided the operation was rapid and efficient, in the interest of holding Yugoslavia together. Whether or not the US Secretary of State, James Baker, had intended to give the JNA such an impression when he made his eleventh-hour visit to Belgrade, he had certainly opted for bullying Slovenia and Croatia out of their independence declarations rather than exerting comparable pressure on Serbia and the JNA to moderate their respective stances, and the JNA chose to interpret this as a green light for intervention. While Baker's visit was presumably well-intentioned, the outcome could not have been worse, and Yugoslavia in any meaningful form was finished as soon as the JNA moved against Slovenia.

The recourse to violence shattered the Yugoslav equation and hardened attitudes on all sides. Before the conflict escalated into war, a negotiated settlement remained a possibility. Indeed, even the instigators of the independence declarations were unclear what precisely independence entailed. However, military intervention made up their minds, and, once the JNA opted for a military solution, it rapidly became clear that the future shape of the Balkans would be decided on the battlefield, and not at the negotiating table. As the tanks rolled, everything appeared to be up for grabs and nationalist fanatics were able to act out their wildest fantasies, oblivious to attempts at mediation, until their territorial ambitions were checked by force. Nevertheless, for the destruction and killing to have been so brutal and on so great a scale as in Croatia and especially Bosnia-Hercegovina, it has required the complicity of many parties to the conflict, including the international community.

Given the imbalance in firepower in the former Yugoslavia, the war was not going to come to a rapid conclusion unless either the JNA was triumphant, or the international community took measures to address the causes of the conflict. Moreover, the longer fighting continued, the more difficult it would be to halt. Nevertheless, instead of attempting to neutralise the military imbalance, the international community chose simply to contain the conflict within the former Yugoslavia. Mediation rapidly descended into a policy of, on the one hand, appeasing the aggressors, and, on the other, bullying the victims into accepting their defeat. The approach has failed either to resolve the conflict or halt the bloodshed with the result that, more than three years since war broke out, the fighting continues and the prospects of a lasting peace agreement remain bleak.

2

THE SOUTH SLAVS: LANGUAGE, CULTURE, LANDS

'The history of the Balkans is the history of migrations—not just of peoples, but of lands.'—Ivo Banac[1]

The Myths of History

Even the least observant traveller who journeyed across what used to be Yugoslavia rapidly discovered that history and geography divided the lands of the south Slavs. From Slovenia in the north to Macedonia in the south every region was distinct, each fiercely proud of its own traditions, culture and past. Wars, especially the Turkish thrust through the Balkans, and multinational empires have shaped the destinies of the south Slavs and the evolution of their lands—lands in which, even today, several cultures and peoples live side by side, where east meets west, Islam confronts Christianity and Catholicism comes up against Orthodoxy.

Most travellers could make out the key cultural influences within minutes of arrival in any Yugoslav city simply by glancing around. First impressions were usually a good guide to the past and confirmed the proverbial diversity and turbulent history of the Balkans. Each empire left its own architecture, each religion its own places of worship. Indeed, one may wonder how such contrasting territories ever formed one country. Yet, at the same time, there were few obvious borders and the transition from one region to another was often imperceptible. To the observer who came to know the south Slavs intimately, differences which may have, at first, appeared so great were easily outweighed by the many similarities, the language, the humour, the life-style.

Even in war, as Yugoslavs fought and killed one another and political leaders claimed the struggle was a clash between irreconcilable

---

[1] Ivo Banac teaches Yugoslav history at Yale University and is author of several books, including *The National Question in Yugoslavia: Origins, History, Politics*, Cornell University Press, Ithaca, 1984.

cultures, they could not conceal their similarities. When soldiers in the front lines tried to boost morale by singing traditional battle songs, Serbs, Croats and Muslims on opposing sides often sang the same tunes. Sometimes, during battles, in between shelling, rival commanders chatted over walkie-talkies with their opposite numbers trading insults and black jokes. And on some bizarre occasions, usually the exchange of dead bodies, where former friends found themselves fighting against each other the two sides actually sat down together to drink themselves silly as they reminisced about happier times.

All today's south Slavs, Slovenes, Croats, Serbs, Muslims and Macedonians, are descendants of the hordes which began migrating into Europe from Asia in the sixth century in the wake of the disintegration of the Roman Empire. They spread throughout the Balkans and in the course of the seventh century settled down. Non-Slav observers first distinguished between Croats and Serbs in the ninth century as their tribal associations evolved into primitive states. Croats settled west of the line Roman Emperor Theodosius had drawn in AD 395 to divide his Empire into eastern and western halves, Serbs settled to the east. In time, this brought Croats within Rome's orbit and made them Catholic, and Serbs under the influence of Byzantium, making them Orthodox.

Though the great difference between Serbs, Croats and Muslim Slavs is their religion and the traditions which accompany each faith, these distinctions were not always clear-cut. Slav conversion to Christianity was a lengthy and complicated process and separate national identities evolved slowly over many centuries. Serbs retained contact with the Papacy long after Rome and Byzantium parted ways in 1054. Indeed, in 1217, Serbia's first king, Stefan Prvovenčani[2] was crowned by a Papal legate, while Catholics in Dalmatia and Dubrovnik maintained close links with Byzantium for many centuries and even borrowed some religious rites from the Orthodox Church. Moreover, in Bosnia the Bogomils, a heretical church which was independent of both Rome and Byzantium, attracted a large following long before the Ottoman invasion.

Ancient Serbian, Bosnian and Croatian states all existed for brief periods. The contours of these states, in common with most in Europe at the time, were forever changing and depended largely on the fortunes of each on the battlefield. The early Serbian state was centred

---

[2] The name *Prvovenčani* means 'first crowned.'

on what is today the Sandžak and included Montenegro and Kosovo. For a brief period in the 14th century the Serbian Empire extended across most of today's Greece, Albania and Macedonia as well as Serbia, Kosovo, the Sandžak and Montenegro. But advancing Turks routed the Serbian Army in 1389 at the battle of Kosovo Polje and conquered all of Serbia by 1459. The Bosnian principality was also at its height during the 14th century with a population which, it seems, was already divided between three Churches, Catholic, Orthodox and Bosnian. By 1463 Bosnia, too, had fallen to the Turks. Thirty years later it was Croatia's turn to confront the might of the Turkish Army. Since 1102, after a brief independent existence, Croatia had been a semi-autonomous province of Hungary. At the battle of Krbava in 1493 the Croatian nobility was defeated and stripped of its lands. In 1526 when most of Hungary fell to the all-conquering Turks and the King was killed at the battle of Mohacs the Habsburgs inherited the Hungarian throne. Croatia, though largely under Ottoman occupation, came as part of the settlement.

The impact of the Turkish thrust through the Balkans and 500 years of intermittent warfare cannot be overestimated. In the wake of the Ottoman invasion, the Balkans' Christian peoples sought refuge by fleeing north and westward. Some made it into German-speaking lands and even today the ancestors of those refugees still live in Austria speaking an archaic dialect of Serbo-Croat. As peoples migrated and some Slavs adopted the creed of the conqueror, the religious map of the Balkans was altered forever. The Ottoman advance was eventually halted, leaving an uneasy military frontier running through the heart of what was to become Yugoslavia. The lands declined, war became fundamental to the economy and the people living on the fault-line grew backward and wild.

Though independent statehood was short-lived and national consciousness hardly existed before the Ottoman invasion, centuries of foreign rule have made that time appear something of a golden age and lent it mythical qualities. Even today, Croats proudly recount tales of their dashing 10th century King Tomislav, while Serbs love to recall the might of the 14th–century Serbian Empire of Stefan Dušan. In the 19th and 20th centuries Serb and Croat nationalists have placed great emphasis on the continuity of the early Serbian and Croatian states. However, modern identities evolved under alien rule and reflect deep frustration at what might have been. The trauma of the Ottoman invasion lives on. Few visitors to Serbia get away without hearing the boast that Serbs were eating with a knife and fork while our ancestors were still using their hands! Both Serbs and Croats insist that only their blood sacrifice and heroic defence of Christendom saved western Europe from a similar fate. But that sacrifice came at great cost to their early, flourishing civilisations.

The only south Slavs free of foreign overlords at this time were citizens of the Dubrovnik Republic.[3] Dubrovnik remained independent until the beginning of the 19th century by paying a tribute to the Ottomans, and many other protectors, including both Hungary and the Venetian Republic, whenever the aristocratic families which dominated the city-state considered it in their interests to do so. The Dubrovnik Republic grew wealthy on banking and trade and boasted a thriving cultural life. Many of the greatest early Slav writers came from there, so that, as a beacon of freedom during centuries of foreign rule, Dubrovnik holds a special significance for all south Slavs.

Until the end of the 18th century Dalmatia and Istria were part of the Venetian Republic. The population of the coastal cities was largely Italian in feeling, the descendants of Roman settlers, while the surrounding lands and most of the islands were populated by Slavs. After the Napoleonic Wars in 1815 Dubrovnik, Dalmatia and Istria, as well as the rest of the Venetian Republic, became provinces of an enlarged Habsburg Empire.

During the centuries of Ottoman rule many Slavs in Bosnia-Hercegovina[4] and the Sandžak[5] converted to Islam, as well as large numbers of the Balkans' original inhabitants, the Albanians. While the Turks did not pursue a policy of forced conversions, Bosnia was fertile ground for the spread of Islam on account of its heretical traditions. After Bosnia fell to the Turks the Bogomil Church was rudderless. In the chaos of defeat and the absence of alternative spiritual guidance, the economic and political benefits of conversion, which included exemption from the poll tax, were sufficient incentive for the surviving

---

[3] At this time Dubrovnik was generally known abroad by its Latin name, Ragusa.

[4] Bosnia and Hercegovina became linked at the beginning of the 14th century. The name Hercegovina is derived from *Herceg*, the title of the region's medieval ruler, which corresponds roughly to Duke.

[5] The name *Sandžak* is part of the Ottoman legacy in the Balkans. The Empire was divided into sanjaks, or military districts, and the region which is today known as the *Sandžak* was formerly the Sanjak of Novi Pazar, that being the principal town in the district.

nobility as well as most Bogomils to become Muslims. Arguments between Serb and Croat nationalists as to the origins of the Muslim Slavs are academic for, whatever their roots, they developed a truly separate identity. As a result, both Bosnia-Hercegovina and the Sandžak enjoyed a privileged, self-governing status within the Ottoman Empire.

Slavs who did not convert to Islam under Ottoman rule lived within semi-autonomous communities, or *millets*. This was a form of government based around religious entities in which non-Muslims were ruled by their spiritual leaders and, in return for tributes, were free to practice their own religions. People were defined by their faith, with the result that, over the centuries, religion and national identity became indelibly linked. The *millet* system was especially central to the evolution of a Serb national identity for the Ottomans entrusted the Serbian Patriarch of Peć, today a city in Kosovo, with authority over all Orthodox subjects as far to the north and west as Slovakia. By this measure the Ottomans hoped to create an ally against the common Catholic enemy. Instead, they enabled a state church to spread its influence over a huge geographic area and over many Orthodox communities which had not belonged to the early Serbian state. The Serbian Orthodox Church was thus able to nurture a distinct Serb national consciousness in all Orthodox communities during Ottoman rule, based around legends of former rulers from Serbia's medieval past, most of whom were canonised and worshipped.

As the borders between Christian and Muslim Europe solidified, both the Habsburgs and the Ottomans stimulated migration into frontier regions to bolster the economic and military strength of the two Empires. The settlers on both sides were predominantly Orthodox, although Catholics and Muslims also moved in to take advantage of the incentives both Empires were offering. The Habsburgs built a so-called military frontier, or *vojna krajina*, governed from Vienna in which the inhabitants were granted the status of free peasants exempt from feudal dues as well as the freedom to practice their own religion in return for military service. In effect, until its abolition in 1881, the military frontier was one huge army camp, providing the Habsburgs with an inexhaustible and loyal source of cheap, high-quality soldiers.

The Ottoman Empire was already in decline when in 1683 its armies swept through the Balkans for the last time to lay siege to Vienna. After repelling this final major Turkish offensive with the help of the Polish Army, the Habsburgs began reconquering their occupied lands.

By 1688 they had expelled the Turks from the Hungarian plain—this included what is today Slavonia and Vojvodina—and appeared on the verge of driving them out of Europe altogether. Encouraged by Habsburg military successes Serbs rose against their Ottoman masters, but their revolt was crushed and then savagely put down, forcing large numbers to flee reprisals into Habsburg lands.

The Serb exodus of 1690 emptied Kosovo[6] and parts of Macedonia,[7] the so-called Old Serbia. Three centuries of intermittent warfare left the liberated Hungarian plain depopulated. As both the Habsburgs and the Ottomans sought to repopulate these regions, the ethnic composition of the Balkans changed again in the 18th century. Albanians moved into Kosovo and parts of Macedonia to fill the void left by fleeing Serbs. Peoples from all over the Habsburg lands—Germans, Hungarians, Czechs, Slovaks, Croats—as well as Serb refugees from Old Serbia colonised the extremely fertile reconquered Habsburg lands. Economic prosperity returned and, under the influence of the Enlightenment, Habsburg southern Hungary, now called Vojvodina,[8] became the centre of Serb cultural life.

National Revivals

The pattern of national awakening and the nature of modern nationalisms in the Balkans were clear by the beginning of the 19th century. For Serbs, the path to national emancipation was relatively straightforward; for Croats, it was far more complicated. Serbs lived under a decaying, alien power—the Ottoman Empire stagnated in the 17th century and was in terminal decline by the 19th. They had a clear enemy and knew they could win their freedom by armed struggle. By contrast, Croats were part of an Empire which, despite many faults, was not in any real danger of collapse. Moreover, the Habsburgs had been their benefactors against the Turks and more recently against the Hungarians.

[6] Kosovo is short for Kosovo Polje which literally means the field of the blackbird.

[7] The name Macedonia predates the Slav arrival in the Balkans and has historically been a geographical, not a political entity. Today's Macedonians are mainly Slavs who took their name from the land they lived on.

[8] The name Vojvodina comes from the Serb word *vojvoda* meaning duke. The Habsburg Emperor Leopold I had promised Serb settlers a whole host of privileges including the right to elect their own leader or *vojvoda*. Though most of the promises failed to materialise, the name stuck.

Tales of the epic struggle for national liberation pervade Serbian literature. In these, the heroes are often Cetniks[9] whose courage, cunning and sacrifice as guerrilla fighters lead inexorably towards the freedom of the entire Serb nation. Here, Montenegro,[10] thanks largely to its inhospitable terrain, led the way. Guided by warrior bishops, the sparsely-populated, mountainous land won effective independence by 1718 and within a century the Serbs of what is today Serbia also rose up against Ottoman rule. Led first by Karadjordje Petrović in 1804 and then Miloš Obrenović in 1815, the founders of Serbia's two royal families, the insurgents forced the Sultan to recognise Serbia as an autonomous principality in 1830. This, however, was but the beginning of the struggle for national liberation.

Serbian national aims in the 19th century were set out in a paper called *Načertanije* (Outline) drawn up in 1844 by Ilija Garašanin, the young principality's Interior Minister. *Načertanije* was a seminal document regarded by Western diplomats in Belgrade of sufficient significance to be required reading in 1991. In Garašanin's opinion, Serbia had a national mission to expand to include all areas in which Serbs lived and to resurrect the short-lived 14th-century Empire of Stefan Dušan. To achieve this Garašanin had to turn Serbia into a powerful state with an efficient centralised administration and standing army. While Garašanin aimed to unite all Serbs in one country, his definition of who was a Serb was rather broad and certainly included Macedonians as well as Muslims who were prepared to convert to Orthodoxy. Other Serb nationalists went even further. Vuk Karadžić, the language reformer who standardised literary Serb, for example, considered all who spoke a similar dialect, including the Croats of Hercegovina, parts of Dalmatia around Dubrovnik and parts of Slavonia, within his definition of Serbs.

As Serbs from throughout the Ottoman lands flocked to join the national crusade, both Serbia and Montenegro expanded. By 1878, four years after Garašanin's death, Serbia's rising star appeared sufficiently threatening to set alarm bells ringing in Vienna. The Habsburgs had already been stung twice in the previous twenty years by the expansion of national states in Germany and in Italy and were not about to let Serbia become the 'Piedmont of the South Slavs'. At the Congress of Berlin, called to end the Russo-Turkish war, which had

---

[9] Četnik literally means member of a *četa*, or unit.

[10] Montenegro, or Crna Gora in Serbo-Croat, means the Black Mountain.

also seen widespread revolt throughout the Ottoman-held Balkans, the Habsburgs moved to occupy Bosnia-Hercegovina, though formally it remained within the Ottoman Empire.

The occupation and in 1908 annexation of Bosnia-Hercegovina came as a great blow to Serbian territorial aspirations as it had been the obvious area for expansion. Bosnia-Hercegovina bordered on Serbia and, at the time, Serbs, not Muslims, were numerically preponderent. According to the Austro-Hungarian census of 1910 they made up 43 per cent of the population while 32 per cent were Muslim and 24 per cent Croat. Furthermore, the Russo-Turkish war had been precipitated by widespread uprisings against Ottoman rule throughout the Balkans, not least among the Serb peasantry of Bosnia-Hercegovina. However, instead of unification with Serbia, the Serbs of Bosnia-Hercegovina found themselves trading one set of foreign overlords for another. Worse still, they were swapping a power which was clearly on its last legs for one which they could never, realistically, hope to defeat. If there was a silver lining from the Congress of Berlin, it was international recognition for both Serbia and Montenegro in expanded borders and complete independence from Turkey. Four years later, in 1882, Serbia declared itself a kingdom.

Until 1903 Serbia was ruled by the Obrenović dynasty and was effectively a client state of Austria-Hungary. That year the King was killed in a military *coup d'état* and replaced with the Karadjordjević pretender to the throne. The new monarch introduced a parliamentary democracy, forged an alliance with Russia and embarked anew upon an aggressive foreign policy. Since Bosnia-Hercegovina was in Habsburg hands, Serbian ambitions shifted southwards towards lands which, though at the heart of the medieval Serbian Empire, no longer had sizeable Serb populations. In the Balkan Wars of 1912 and 1913 the new direction bore fruit. In the first, Turkey was finally expelled from Macedonia, Kosovo and the Sandžak by an alliance of Balkan states. In the second, Serbia and Greece took the lion's share of the spoils at the expense of Bulgaria and only Habsburg opposition prevented Serbia acquiring an outlet on the sea. The victories doubled the territory and population of the country, but also dragged in large numbers of non-Serbs, too many either to assimilate or to eliminate.

All these wars were characterised by immense brutality aimed especially against the Muslim populations. Ethnic cleansing, the neologism of the present conflict, is not a new phenomenon. That inner Serbia, that is Serbia without Vojvodina, Kosovo and the Sandžak is as ethnically homogeneous as it is today is the direct result of 19th-century ethnic cleansing. Atrocities, the destruction of mosques and mass expulsions accompanied each Serbian victory in an attempt to wipe out all traces of Ottoman rule. But ethnic cleansing is by no means unique to Serbia. It was standard practice in Greece and Bulgaria which also spent several hundred years under Turkish rule. Indeed, even in the 1980s, under the aged communist dictator Todor Živkov, Bulgaria was still expelling its Turkish minority and forcing those who remained to Slavicise their names.

As in today's conflict, much of the fighting was carried out by irregulars who, apart from participating in the national crusade, had the added incentive that they could expect to inherit and colonise whatever land they captured. The fewer indigenous Serbs who lived on the land the more savage the fighting, the more hostile the population and the more difficult the task of making it Serbian. This was especially the case in Kosovo and Macedonia where occupation, terror and colonisation spawned terrorist organisations. Nevertheless, national euphoria in Serbia reached unprecedented levels with the capture of Kosovo, the so-called 'cradle of the Serb nation', in 1912. After more than five centuries, it seemed that finally the defeat of Kosovo Polje had been avenged.

Serbian victories did not pass unnoticed in Croatia. Far from being perennial enemies, there were times when Croat admiration for Serb achievements knew no bounds. Croat nationalists were frustrated in the Habsburg Empire. To them Serbia's dynamic expansion was, at the same time, a cause of envy and a source of inspiration. In the years leading up to the First World War, this virtual Croat love affair for everything Serb found its most eloquent expression in the arts, especially in the works of the sculptor Ivan Meštrović. Though a Croat from Dalmatia, Meštrović drew much of his early inspiration from Serb folklore, especially the legends surrounding Kosovo. But while Serb achievements spawned a following in Croatia among artists and intellectuals, there was no reciprocal movement of comparable size and influence in Serbia. Whereas Croats looked to Serbs to help achieve their national goals, Serbs were doing very well on their own and had no comparable psychological or political need for Croat support.

The Yugoslav idea itself was born in Croatia in the 1830s with the

Illyrian movement, which formed its own political party in 1841.[11] The Illyrianists believed fervently in the ethnic, linguistic and cultural unity of all south Slavs. They also provided an intellectual explanation for the very real physical need among Croats for unity with Serbs and even Slovenes in the face of aggressive, non-Slav nationalisms. For, while Serb nationalism developed within the context of armed struggle against Ottoman rule, Croat nationalism evolved as a reaction against predatory German, Italian and in particular Hungarian nationalisms.

In addition to the Croats of Bosnia-Hercegovina, Croats were divided between three separate Habsburg lands: Croatia and Slavonia which were tied to Hungary; Dalmatia and Istria, which after centuries as part of the Venetian Republic became part of the Austrian half of the Empire; and the military frontier which was ruled directly by Vienna. For a brief period during the Napoleonic Wars these provinces and much of what became Slovenia were joined together in the French province of Illyria. While French government stimulated Slav national consciousness, the return of Habsburg rule curbed nationalist ambitions. As a result, the Illyrianists concentrated on questions of culture and language reform.

Despite the exaggerated claims of today's nationalists and a deliberate campaign to differentiate between Croat and Serb in Croatia since 1990, what most Serbs and Croats actually speak, especially after seventy-three years living in one country, is very similar. That said, two separate, literary languages exist and, since 1991, the BBC World Service has been careful to broadcast in both Serb and Croat. The literary languages are artificial 19th–century creations devised by linguists. The obvious, visible difference is that Croat uses the Latin alphabet while Serb uses Cyrillic. That the two languages are so similar is largely due to Ljudevit Gaj, the most prominent Illyrianist, and reflects his overwhelming desire for south Slav unity. For the dialect Gaj chose as the base for literary Croat was, in fact, that which Karadžić had chosen for literary Serb and was closer to that spoken by a majority of Serbs than that which most Croats spoke.

Linguistic frontiers are of course less clear-cut than international ones. Dialects vary throughout the Slav lands and languages blend together around political borders. All the original Slav colonists spoke

[11] The name was derived from Illyricum, the Roman province which roughly corresponded to Yugoslavia.

something similar which over the centuries has developed into several modern Slav languages. Across the Balkans dialects change gradually. At the extremes, on the Croatian border with Slovenia and the Serbian border with Bulgaria, for example, dialects are extremely pronounced and borrow heavily from neighbouring languages. But what people actually speak depends on geography, not national origins. Serbs who live in Croatia speak the same dialect as their Croat neighbours, just as Croats who live in Serbia speak the same as their Serb neighbours. As a result, outsiders have lumped the two languages together calling them Serbo-Croat. The official name before Yugoslavia's break-up was Serbo-Croat or Croato-Serb, or Serb or Croat (*Srpsko-Hrvatski ili Hrvatsko-Srpski, ili Srpski ili Hrvatski*), but not necessarily in that order.

While Illyrianism and later Yugoslavism were influential movements in Croatia in the 19th and early 20th centuries, Croat nationalism had another significant strand, one which demanded independence as a historic and legal right. In the Habsburg Empire such arguments were common among nationalists since the Habsburgs had accumulated their vast domains over many centuries and largely by inheritance. Each acquisition, the nationalists argued, was a separate entity united with the rest of the Habsburgs' territories only in the person of the Emperor. Each land had differing rights and degrees of autonomy based on the legal terms with which it joined the Empire.

In the 18th century, as soon as the Turkish threat receded, the Croatian nobility attempted to reassert control over its former lands, including the military frontier, using such legalistic arguments, but to no avail. In the 19th century Ante Starčević's Party of Right, that is Croatian state right, clung to the fiction of the legal continuity of an independent Croatian state, but again failed to win any concessions from the Habsburgs. Nevertheless, the Party of Right became the most influential opposition party in Croatia in the last decades of the 19th century.

Though today's Croat fascist party of Dobroslav Paraga also calls itself the Party of Right and even named its Zagreb headquarters after Starčević, the 19th-century Party of Right was not necessarily anti-Serb. Starčević himself was the child of a mixed marriage and his ideology was that of a nationalist with no chance of achieving his goals, confused and forever shifting. He laid claim to all Croat lands in the name of the Croat nation, to which all south Slavs, including Slovenes and Serbs, belonged. For, according to Starčević, Serbs were but Orthodox Croats. Inevitably, the Party of Right spawned many splinter groups, some liberal others extreme.

While the pseudo-historians who today have free rein in both the Croatian and Serbian media have striven to dredge up a history of hatred between Serbs and Croats, in truth they have failed to come up with much before the First World War and the creation of Yugoslavia. Though a potential for conflict appears to exist wherever rival Churches live side by side, relations between the communities were remarkably tranquil. The only event which stands out is four days of anti-Serb riots in Zagreb in August 1902. The catalyst for these was an article in a Serb newspaper called *Srbobran* (the Serb Shield) belittling Croat culture and national aspirations and warning prophetically of a struggle 'to your annihilation or ours'. But even in this case nobody was killed. Furthermore, the cause of the friction was not innate Serb-Croat animosity; rather it was the result of a concerted attempt by the Hungarian authorities to drive a wedge between the two communities.

From 1867 until the collapse of the Habsburg Empire Croatia was governed from Hungary, or, to be precise, by a ruler or *Ban*[12] appointed in Budapest. This was the result of a major reorganisation of the Empire following military disasters in Italy and Germany. To bolster his authority the Habsburg Emperor chose to ally with the strongest opposition group, namely the Hungarians, and effectively divide his Empire into two halves, one ruled by Vienna the other by Budapest. While traditionally the Habsburgs had endeavoured not to favour one nation above another and to suppress all nationalisms equally, the new Austro-Hungarian Empire, as it was now called, became dominated by Germans and Hungarians. Budapest set out to hold Croatia down in the same way that the Habsburgs had earlier held Hungary down with a policy of divide and rule.

The obvious potential division in Croatia, especially after 1881 when the military frontier with its large Serb population was reincorporated into Croatia, was between Serbs and Croats. The Hungarian *Bans*, in particular the notorious Károly Khuen-Hédérvary who ruled Croatia between 1883 and 1903, worked to exploit this by favouring the Serb minority at the expense of the Croat majority. The newspaper

---

[12] The best translation for *Ban* is viceroy. It is an ancient title which was originally given to the office-holders who ruled medieval Croatia on behalf of the Hungarian crown.

Srbobran, for example, was subsidised by Khuen-Hédérvary and during the last two decades of the 19th century relations between Serbs and Croats deteriorated steadily. Nevertheless, following the 1902 riots, Serb and Croat politicians of the Habsburg lands decided they were better off uniting against their common enemy, rather than squabbling among themselves. In 1905 they founded the Croat-Serb Coalition which dominated Croatian politics until the First World War.

The First World War

Without the disappearance of Austria-Hungary the Yugoslav state formed in 1918 could never have come into existence. Frustrated south Slav nationalists in the Habsburg Empire may have dreamed of a Yugoslav state, but they had no clear vision of the form that state might take. Most Slavs in Austria-Hungary were loyal to the Habsburgs and the most that Yugoslav nationalists could, realistically, aspire to was a third, south Slav tier to the Empire. In 1914 the Habsburg Empire was not about to collapse and seemed destined to stumble on in its inimitable way indefinitely. Unification with Serbia and Montenegro appeared out of the question. However, four years of the most dreadful war the world had experienced changed that.

Unification came at high speed in the wake of the spectacular disintegration of Austria-Hungary and was a reflex reaction to avert chaos. Habsburg authority was being replaced by anarchy across parts of Croatia and Bosnia-Hercegovina, while the Italian army was threatening to hive off Dalmatia from the debris of the Habsburg Empire and the new states of Austria and Hungary also claimed lands with a large south Slav population. Predominantly Serb regions of Austria-Hungary spontaneously declared themselves for Serbia and the advancing, reconstituted Serbian Army reconquered all of Serbia and Montenegro. Rapid union with Serbia appeared to offer salvation to south Slav politicians from the Habsburg lands who had formed a National Council in Zagreb. However, no groundwork had been prepared for a common state.

During the war attempts were made by *émigré* Habsburg south Slavs to forge a common policy with Serbia, but they foundered on diverging visions of the post-war settlement. While the *émigrés* had rather vague hopes for a common south Slav state, Serbian war aims were specific and achievable without recourse to an alliance with the Habsburg south Slavs. Serbia was fighting to liberate all Serb lands and had no intention of annexing any purely Croat or Slovene territories. As a result, Nikola Pašić, the veteran Serbian Prime Minister, was careful not to agree anything with Habsburg politicians before he was sure of victory. Negotiations were further complicated by Britain and France who had bribed Italy into entering the war against Germany and Austria-Hungary with promises of territorial gains in Istria and Dalmatia and who, before 1918, hoped to maintain some form of diminished Habsburg state. When, at the end of the war, Serbian politicians met in Geneva with their counterparts from the Habsburg Empire as part of wider post-war talks on the future of Europe, they failed to reach a satisfactory agreement.

Time, however, was working against the Habsburg politicians, whose grip on power was insecure. As a result, while the Geneva talks stalled, the National Council despatched a twenty-eight-man delegation to Belgrade to negotiate with the Serbian monarch. The National Council was headed by the Slovene Anton Korošec and included Slovenes, Croats and Serbs. Ultimately, the most influential politician was Svetozar Pribičević, a Serb Vice-President of the National Council and leader of the Croat–Serb Coalition. On 1 December 1918 Prince Alexander granted them an audience and, in Pašić's absence, accepted the union of Serbia with the former Habsburg territories. Details were left for later. Only one Habsburg politician present opposed the union, Stjepan Radić, deputy of the minor Croat Peasant Party but soon to become tribune of all Croats.

Unification on these terms, or rather lack of terms, was Pribičević's triumph. It suited neither the non-Serbs from the Habsburg lands, nor the Serbs from Serbia proper. It did, however, ensure that the Serbs of the Habsburg lands ceased to be a minority and became the most numerous nationality in the new country. Pribičević's desire to look after the interests of the Habsburg Serbs enabled him to believe fervently in national unity (*narodno jedinstvo*), the political philosophy that Serbs and Croats were one people. However, he overlooked the fact that two separate national identities had already evolved with two separate focal points in Zagreb and Belgrade.

In Croatia, where Yugoslavism had a long history and genuinely attempted to embrace all south Slavs, it was a Yugoslavism which, nevertheless, considered Zagreb the natural centre of a south Slav state. Zagreb was home to the Yugoslav Academy and culturally and economically it was the most advanced Yugoslav city. Even Croats committed to Yugoslavism were disappointed to see the city's status diminished in the new Yugoslavia. From being the capital of Croatia-Slavonia with its own parliament, Zagreb's status was reduced to that of a provincial city, albeit a large one, in a highly centralised state with its capital in Belgrade. While the Serbs and Croats of Croatia and the Serbs and Croats of Bosnia-Hercegovina had a lot in common with each other, the Croats of Croatia had a very different historical experience to the Serbs of Serbia.

It is tempting to view Serbia before the First World War as a backward state with an enormous and disproportionate military capacity bent on territorial expansion. Indeed, comparisons with Prussia, the German kingdom whose armies forged the German Empire, are not unreasonable. Serbia was landlocked, economically backward and surrounded by potentially hostile neighbours. Merely to win independence and to survive Serbia had needed to evolve a huge military, to the extent that in 1914 the country was able to put 400,000 men in the field out of a total Serb population of under 3 million. While the world's great multinational empires were decaying, Serbia was actually in the process of creating another. As a result of Serbian territorial gains in the Balkan Wars, the Kingdom was already inherently unstable. Though the non-Serb populations annexed in 1913 were extremely backward, the evolution of hostile Albanian and Macedonian nationalisms was inevitable in a unitary state which based its legitimacy on a mythical medieval empire and territorial conquest.

Nevertheless, there was another side to Serbia, one which was liberal way beyond the impoverished Kingdom's level of economic and cultural development. Since 1903 Serbia had been a constitutional monarchy with a parliament elected by universal male suffrage. In addition to the system of government, members of the Kingdom's elite had begun sending their children abroad to be educated in western Europe. On account of hostility towards the Habsburg Empire, this essentially meant France, though many also went to Germany and some were even educated in Britain. For example, Prince Paul, who became regent in 1934 after his cousin King Alexander was assassinated, had attended Oxford University. As a result, a tiny but influential section of Serbian society was genuinely imbued with liberal ideas.

Though the proverbial shot which triggered the First World War was fired by a Serb in Sarajevo, the south Slavs had no real influence over the war, which pitted them against each other. The origins of the Great War are many and complex but the outbreak of fighting was largely the result of a series of miscalculations, great power alliances and inflexible German military tactics. The assassination of Archduke Franz Ferdinand, heir to the Habsburg throne, on 28 June 1914 was merely the event which precipitated the slide to war. To an extent Franz Ferdinand was tempting fate when he decided to visit Sarajevo that day, for 28 June was Saint Vitus' Day, the anniversary of the battle of Kosovo Polje, and his presence in a territory claimed by Serbia offended Serb nationalists. While the assassin Gavrilo Princip and his *Crna Ruka* (Black Hand) gang accomplices certainly had links high up in the Serbian military, the assassination did not represent official Serbian policy. Nevertheless, Austria-Hungary issued Serbia with an ultimatum whose terms were so strong that the Kingdom found it impossible to comply with them.

In the aftermath of Franz Ferdinand's assassination anti-Serb sentiment ran high throughout the Habsburg Empire and in Croatia and Bosnia-Hercegovina it boiled over into anti-Serb pogroms. Though these pogroms were clearly incited by the Habsburg authorities, it eventually took Hungarian intervention to prevent relations between Croats and Serbs within the Empire getting totally out of hand. Though, strictly speaking, the First World War in the Balkans was fought between states, it was also, in many ways, a civil war since it pitted south Slav against south Slav and Serb against Serb. Indeed, an oft-recounted tale from the early days of the war is that of a Serbian officer shouting to his opposite number demanding that he surrender only to hear the Habsburg officer answer: 'What kind of a Serb ever surrenders?'

After initially holding its own against the Habsburg Army with almost suicidal bravery and massive casualties, Serbia was overwhelmed in 1915 by a combined Habsburg-German-Bulgarian offensive. The remnants of the Serbian Army retreated through Albania to the sea from where they were evacuated by the British and French to Greece. For the next two and a half years Serbia was occupied and under Austro-Hungarian military administration. In 1918 the reconstituted Serbian Army pushed forward with British and French support from Salonika as Austria-Hungary disintegrated. Total casualties during the war were enormous, though more died of disease than in the fighting. Altogether about 900,000 people perished, 750,000 from pre-war Serbia and Montenegro (largely the result of a particularly virulent outbreak of typhus in 1915) and 150,000 from the Habsburg lands.

Although south Slavs in the Habsburg Army began to mutiny in

1917 and *émigré* politicians attempted to force units of Habsburg Slavs to join the Serbian Army, Serbian politicians avoided any military cooperation. When it came, victory was Serbia's because Serbia had fought on the right side in the war. It was not a south Slav victory. When the south Slavs came together to create the Kingdom of Serbs, Croats and Slovenes, as Yugoslavia was initially called, it was not a union of equals. Instead, they came together as victors and vanquished.

3

FROM CREATION TO COLLAPSE TO REBIRTH

'The union of 1 December 1918 was a shotgun wedding; the honey-moon was as short as the hangover was long.' — Mark Wheeler[1]

The First Yugoslavia

The first Yugoslavia was not an unmitigated disaster doomed to end in the slaughter of the Second World War. That it did has more to do with foreign intervention and the exceptional circumstances of 1941, than any innate desire of Serbs and Croats to wipe each other out. At times, enthusiasm for the new state was overwhelming in Zagreb and Ljubljana as well as in Belgrade. When, for example, King Alexander visited Zagreb in 1925 to commemorate the 1000th anniversary of the coronation of the Croatian King Tomislav, tens of thousands of Croats turned out to greet their monarch, who named one of his sons Tomislav as a mark of respect. Indeed, the new state gave Slovenes and Croats many tangible benefits. The language of administration ceased to be German or Hungarian, and ambitious Slovenes and Croats no longer needed to send their children to be educated in Vienna or Budapest if they wanted to secure their future.

Unification would have been a difficult process under any circumstances, but after four years of war the task proved well beyond the new country's political leaders. Three separate approaches to governing the country were tried between the wo world wars, though the first Yugoslav incarnation failed to win over its many peoples or to develop any framework for national coexistence. The first was the Greater Serbian option; the second was an attempt by the monarch to impose, from above, an artificial 'Yugoslav' identity on all Yugoslavia's peoples; and the last approach entailed coming to terms and making a deal with the state's most vociferous opponents, the

[1] Mark Wheeler teaches Yugoslav history at London's School of Slavonic and East European Studies and is author of *Britain and the War for Yugoslavia, 1940–43*, Westview Press, London and Boulder, CO, 1980.

Croats. In the event, the Greater Serbian option poisoned relations between Serbs and Yugoslavia's other peoples and soured the prospects of any future south Slav state. The second managed to alienate all Yugoslav peoples, including Serbs, and the third approach was over-taken by events as the onset of the Second World War never gave it a chance to succeed.

Given the separate traditions and identities of Yugoslavia's consti-tuent peoples, a highly centralised state was possibly the least appropriate form of government. Yet it was the preferred option as far as most Serb politicians, whether from the Kingdom of Serbia or the Habsburg lands, were concerned. Serbia's pre-war leaders aimed to rebuild their own war-shattered country and to continue to guide the destiny of the new state, while Serb leaders from the Habsburg lands hoped to integrate themselves into the new ruling élite. Though Serbs never formed an absolute majority of Yugoslavia's population, they were the country's most numerous nation[2] and centralism was part of Serbian state tradition. Indeed, Serbia's military capacity and territorial expansion were due in no small part to its centralised state apparatus. As Serbia sucked in large numbers of non-Serbs in the course of the 19th and early 20th centuries no attempt was made to modify the state's structure to accommodate them, and even in the Kingdom of Serbs, Croats and Slovenes few Serbian politicians were initially prepared to make sufficient concessions to Slovenes and Croats to win them over to the new state.

While the Serbian parliament was asked to ratify unification, such an option was not given to any Croatian body for fear of reversal. A provi-sional government was appointed from Zagreb's National Council and the Serbian parliament. It governed the country for the next twenty-one months until the final post-war territorial settlement was agreed in Paris and elections could be organised. The first provisional cabinet included thirteen Serbs, four Croats, two Slovenes and one Muslim. No other nationalities were represented. It was a pattern which continued throughout the inter-war period, in which time only one non-Serb, the Slovene Anton Korošec, became Prime Minister.

[2]The precise ethnic break-down of Yugoslavia in 1918 is perhaps inevitably a mat-ter of some dispute. In the interwar period Yugoslavs were classified according to their religion, not their ethnicity. According to the 1921 census 46.7 per cent of the population was Orthodox (Serbs, Macedonians and Montenegrins), 39.2 per cent Catholic (Croats, Slovenes, Germans, Hungarians and Italians), and 10.8 per cent Muslim (Albanians, Turks and Muslim Slavs).

Bad blood between Serbs and Croats is not centuries old but dates from the early Croat experience in a Serb-dominated Yugoslavia which disillusioned even the most Yugoslav-oriented Croats. No attempt was made to combine governing systems. Instead, the Habsburg bureaucracy, infrastructure and military were completely dismantled and replaced with the Serbian state machinery and army. Moreover, in addition to the police, the Serbian gendarmerie was introduced into the former Habsburg territories and about 12,000 men recruited for the task, the vast majority of whom were Serbs.

Yet more galling to Croats were the economic terms on which they joined Yugoslavia. A certain amount of financial gerrymandering was only to be expected: whereas in most countries the economically advanced regions are also politically dominant, in Yugoslavia the situation was reversed. However, the scale of the transfer of wealth from the Habsburg lands to the former Serbian Kingdom was so great that Yugoslavia's former Habsburg subjects were effectively paying war reparations to Serbia. The best example of this is monetary union since the four currencies which were legal tender in different parts of the country at unification had to be replaced with a single currency.[3] To distinguish 'Yugoslav' Habsburg crowns from those circulating in the rest of the former Empire the currency was withdrawn and stamped, and in the process 20 per cent was confiscated and used to repay the Serbian national debt.

The first Yugoslavia did not have an obvious Tito or even a Bismarck or Cavour who imposed himself upon the new state. The man whom most Yugoslavs would acknowledge as the architect of the Kingdom of Serbs, Croats and Slovenes is Svetozar Pribičević, the leader of the Habsburg Serbs. Pribičević had been the driving force behind south Slav unification during November and December 1918 and became Interior Minister in the new country's first cabinet. As a Habsburg Serb he was convinced that his Serb communities who lived in a sea of Croats and/or Muslims would be most secure in a highly centralised Yugoslav state. To this end, he presided ruthlessly over the administrative extension of pre-war Serbia across the entire country. Perhaps it is ironic that having done more than anyone to make the country into what can only be described as a Greater Serbia, Pribičević later became Yugoslavia's fiercest critic in exile.

---

[3] The four currencies were Serbian dinars, Habsburg crowns, Bulgarian leva and Montenegrin perpers.

Serbian politicians were relying on Pribičević as the most senior Habsburg politician, though a Serb, to keep them informed about public opinion in the former Habsburg lands. However, Pribičević's overwhelming desire to integrate his Serb communities into Serbia proper blinded him to the excesses of centralism and encouraged him to rush through a programme which was deeply offensive to the country's non-Serbs. His error was to mistake Great Serbism for Yugoslavism though, in fact, the arrangement was exactly what the Serbian leaders had hoped to achieve and only a parliamentary boycott by the main Croat party made it possible.

That Croats did so badly out of unification was largely the fault of the Croat political leaders themselves, especially Stjepan Radić, the enigmatic leader of the Croat Peasant Party. While all Yugoslavia's non-Serb peoples aimed to obtain as much autonomy as possible and to protect and maintain what rights they had, only the Croats had the political muscle to secure their aims by democratic means. However, instead of working for a better deal in parliament, Radić chose to boycott the parliamentary process during the country's formative years.

Before the First World War Radić had been a relatively minor figure at the head of a tiny party since only a very small proportion of Croatian society was able to vote. His position changed when Croatia joined Yugoslavia and Croatia's peasant masses were enfranchised. Radić had been the only Habsburg politician to oppose the original union of Yugoslavia and believed that joining the parliamentary process would be condoning that union. Instead, like the leaders of Slovenia, Croatia and Bosnia-Hercegovina in the 1990s, Radić put his faith in the European powers, hoping they would intervene to create an independent Croatian state. From prison, where Pribičević had interned him for his opposition to unification, Radić lobbied the post-war peace conference in Paris and even appealed directly to the French government for support. However, as in the 1990s nobody had any desire to become entangled in the Balkans. After his release from prison, Radić maintained his opposition and eventually took his case abroad in person to London, Paris and even Moscow, all to no avail.

Yugoslavia's highly centralised state apparatus was enshrined in the St Vitus' day, or *Vidovdan*, constitution of 1921.[4] In the absence of

---

[4] It became known as the *Vidovdan* constitution because it was promulgated on 28 June, St Vitus' day. Vitus, an obscure saint martyred at the beginning of the fourth century, had no obvious connection with Yugoslavia. However, the tumultuous

the Croat political parties, the Serb parties made a deal with a party representing the interests of Bosnian Muslim landowners and pushed through a centralist constitution virtually unopposed. They had no intention of making concessions to territories with which they had been at war, and which they were not, in any case, desperate to possess. However, the fact that the Croats, the second most numerous people in the country, completely rejected the settlement boded ill for the new state.

Since no nationality formed an absolute majority in the new Yugoslav state and no political party could ever win a parliamentary majority on its own, government was of necessity by coalition. Despite his mishandling of the early parliaments Radić's popularity grew rapidly as a result of Croat disillusionment within the new state. By the early 1920s he and his party commanded almost universal support among Croats and today the square in Zagreb which houses Croatia's parliament is named after him. When Radić finally came into parliament, just as before the First World War in Austria-Hungary the Croat bloc used its parliamentary muscle to filibuster, block legislation and make government farcical. The result was parliamentary deadlock. Gradually, all the Serbian parties came to accept that for the new state to prosper Croatia had to be accommodated.

To break the deadlock, first the Serbian opposition and then the ruling Radical Party under the leadership of the veteran Prime Minister, Nikola Pašić, attempted to bring Radić into coalition with them. The will to reform the new state to make it work existed on both sides. However, though Radić joined Pašić's government as Education Minister in 1925, the gulf between basic positions was too great. The Serbian parties considered the 1921 constitution as the basis of the state and that it could be altered or reformed but not scrapped, while Radić insisted on a renegotiation of the terms of unification.

The great loser out of this political realignment was Pribičević who felt that the Serbian parties had sacrificed him and the former Habsburg Serbs to come to terms with Radić. In 1927 Pribičević made a dramatic volte-face and began to espouse federalism as the answer to the

---

events which have taken place on his day make it the most emotionally-charged date in Yugoslav history. It was the date of the battle of Kosovo Polje in 1389 and of the assassination of Franz Ferdinand in 1914. Moreover, it cropped up again in Tito's Yugoslavia when on 28 June 1948 Cominform expelled Yugoslavia from the international communist movement.

country's problems and he too formed a parliamentary alliance with Radić, the man he had imprisoned eight years earlier. It was the political union of the Serbs and Croats of the former Habsburg Empire against the Serbs of the former Kingdom of Serbia. The political stalemate continued and relations between Serbia and the former Habsburg lands deteriorated until on 20 June 1928 a Montenegrin deputy shot Radić and four other members of the Croat Peasant Party in parliament.[5] When Radić died of his wounds on 8 August Pribićević withdrew the opposition from parliament. It left the new Prime Minister, the Slovene Korošec, presiding over a half-empty chamber, an ailing economy and a discontented country. When Korošec resigned on 30 December, King Alexander dissolved parliament and took the reins himself in a desperate attempt to hold his Kingdom together.

Dictatorship

Historically, dictatorships have repeatedly failed to solve anything and, in this respect, King Alexander's was no exception. Alexander hoped to reconcile both Serbs and Croats to their common state within his own vision of Yugoslavism. To this end, he renamed the country Yugoslavia, broke it up into administrative units which bore minimal resemblance to historic or ethnic entities, and, in 1931, introduced a new constitution designed to avoid conflict between ethnically-based political parties and ensure that real power remained with the monarch. However, Alexander's timing was inauspicious as Yugoslavia began feeling the effects of the Great Depression, with the result that he succeeded only in alienating all groups; Croats feared he was trying to create a Greater Serbia by the back door, while Serbs objected to the loss of their political liberties.

Soon after Alexander imposed the dictatorship Pribićević went into political exile in Prague, where he died seven years later. In Pribićević's absence Vlatko Maček, who had already succeeded Radić as head of the Croat Peasant Party, became the most influential opposition leader. Meanwhile, Ante Pavelić, then a minor figure, founded the Ustaša-

---

[5] Three of the Croat Peasant Party deputies died and two survived. The assassin, Puniša Račić, got off lightly with a custodial sentence served in an open prison but was executed in 1945 by Tito's communists for collaboration during the Second World War.

Croat Revolutionary Organisation[6] committed to the creation of an independent Croatia by any means. The Ustašas fled to Italy where Mussolini took them in and provided them with financial help, military training and weaponry as part of his wider scheme to undermine Yugoslav security. Pavelić's most famous victim was King Alexander himself who was gunned down while on a state visit to France in 1934.[7] The assassination had been intended to destroy Yugoslavia, but it had the opposite effect and united all Alexander's subjects in mutual condemnation of the outrage.

Since Alexander's son and heir was aged only ten at the time, his Oxford-educated cousin Prince Paul became regent. Before the assassination Paul had never shown any political ambition and would probably have been happier to live his life in relative obscurity studying and collecting the works of art which were his real passion. However, a sense of duty compelled him to take over where Alexander had left off and there was no return to the failed parliamentary democracy of the 1920s. Instead, Paul maintained Alexander's 1931 constitution and renewed efforts to reconcile Croats to Yugoslavia, a task made more urgent by the rise of Nazi Germany and the deteriorating European security position.

Ironically, relations between Serbs and Croats were never better than in the late 1930s as their political leaders cooperated with each other against the dictatorship. Though the electoral system was designed to ensure victory for the monarch's supporters, the vote of the United Opposition, a Serb-Croat coalition headed by Maček, increased with every election. At the same time, Prince Paul made a genuine attempt to integrate Croatia into Yugoslavia, including negotiations with the Papacy to regulate relations with the country's Catholic population.[8]

Direct negotiations were held between Prince Paul's representative, Prime Minister Dragiša Cvetković, and Maček, but behind the back of the Serbian parties, eventually bore fruit in 1939. The outcome was the so-called *sporazum*, or Cvetković-Maček Agreement, which set up an autonomous province, or *Banovina*, of Croatia within Yugoslavia,

[6] *Ustaša* literally means insurgent in Serbo-Croat.

[7] Though the Ustašas had planned the assassination, the hitman himself was actually a Macedonian terrorist. In the shooting the French Foreign Minister Louis Barthou was also killed.

[8] A Concordat was negotiated in 1935 but the agreement was scuppered in 1937 by determined opposition from the Serbian Orthodox Church and Serb nationalists.

governed by a crown appointee or *Ban*. In many ways, the settlement resembled the dualism obtaining in the Habsburg Empire after 1867 when Franz Joseph divided his lands into Austrian and Hungarian halves. However, it was not necessarily a solution to Yugoslavia's national question. Serbian and Slovene political parties resented the settlement because Croatia appeared to have won a privileged position for itself. Maček remained Yugoslavia's Vice Premier and Croatia's politicians retained a say in Yugoslav affairs, even though Croatia had effectively become autonomous and Serbian and Slovene politicians had no reciprocal say in Croatian affairs. In the event, the deal lasted less than two years and was never fully implemented.

The *sporazum* had been rushed in to counter support for the Ustašas and only attempted to satisfy Yugoslavia's two largest peoples. It did nothing for the country's other nationalities. Of a population of about 12 million at unification, close to 2 million were non-Slav. Nevertheless, in the interwar period Yugoslavia was very much the country of its original name, that is the Kingdom of Serbs, Croats and Slovenes, in which members of other ethnic groups were second-class citizens. Compared with the condition of the sizeable German, Hungarian, Albanian, Macedonian and Muslim Slav communities, Croats had life easy.

Land reform was the most important legislation to be passed in the interwar period. Large estates were broken up and the land was distributed among peasants, many of whom were Serb veterans of the Balkan and First World Wars. Inevitably, these reforms came at the expense of the existing landowners who tended to be Muslim Slav, Albanian, German, Hungarian and Turkish. In Bosnia-Hercegovina land was transferred from Muslim landlords to the Serb, Croat and Muslim peasants who worked the land. In Vojvodina, Slavonia, Kosovo and Macedonia, the ethnic composition changed as Serb colonists from barren Montenegro and Hercegovina settled on land formerly owned by Germans, Hungarians, Albanians and Turks.

Relations between political parties were not the whole story in interwar Yugoslavia. Relations on the ground were equally, if not more, important. In Kosovo, Albanians waged a guerilla war against the Yugoslav state during much of the 1920s. Though the majority, they were encouraged to leave for Turkey, as were Muslims from Bosnia-Hercegovina and the Sandžak. Officious and corrupt Serb police dominated these regions, often making life miserable for non-Serb populations. While Serbs also dominated the police in Croatia, the only Croats who had to endure a similar oppression were those living in the mixed and backward areas of the old military frontier in Banija, Kordun and Lika, as well as Hercegovina. Inevitably, these were the regions from which the Ustašas drew support, as well as areas of large-scale Croat emigration.

In the final years of the first Yugoslavia the state had ceased to represent a Greater Serbia, to the dismay of Serb nationalists. The Cvetković-Maček Agreement was generous to Croat national aspirations, since the *Banovina* of Croatia contained significant chunks of what became the republic of Bosnia-Hercegovina. In addition, out of a population of 4.4 million, about 866,000 were Serbs while another 164,000 were Muslims. Already before the Second World War some Serbs living in the *banovina*, supported by nationalist factions in Belgrade and the military, were in revolt against the *sporazum*. Though this was not a full-scale uprising, it was an indication that the Cvetković-Maček Agreement was doomed and notice of how Serb nationalists were prepared to use Croatia's Serb minority to sabotage any settlement of which they did not approve.

Unstable at home despite genuine efforts to address the national question, Prince Paul found himself forced into Hitler's camp in the late 1930s. This had nothing to do with Croat influence in government for Maček and his Croat Peasant Party were vehemently hostile to Hitler and Germany. Quite simply, Paul had no alternative. Interwar alliances which had been constructed by France to keep Germany at bay were meaningless in the absence of French and British support. Franco-British appeasement gave Paul no room for manoeuvre and thrust him reluctantly into Hitler's hands.

During the 1930s Yugoslavia entered into trade agreements with Germany, which helped drag the country out of recession while also contributing to the rebuilding of Germany's military. Even during Germany's offensive against France Yugoslavia continued to supply the German war machine as a matter of self-preservation. In fact, Hitler had no immediate designs on the Balkans, but was forced to act there, when Italy botched an unannounced invasion of Greece, to prevent Britain acquiring a toe-hold on the European mainland. Given the circumstances, Paul negotiated the best deal possible with Hitler to keep the Germans out of Yugoslavia. While allowing Germany to use Yugoslav supply routes to transport goods and equipment across the country for Hitler's Greek campaign, he drew the line at military personnel. Soldiers *en route* for Greece had to travel around Yugoslavia

via Hungary, Romania and Bulgaria. However, a group of hot-headed junior officers in the Yugoslav airforce objected to the agreement, organised a *coup d'état* and seized power.

Although demonstrators took to the streets of Belgrade, Ljubljana and Split in support of the *coup* and Winston Churchill in Britain welcomed it as an act of heroism, for Yugoslavia and the vast majority of Yugoslavs it was a disaster. As soon as the conspirators won power, they realised they could not squeeze any more concessions out of Hitler than Paul had already obtained and tried to hang onto his agreement. However, by this time Hitler's patience had run out and he decided to invade Yugoslavia. Far from delaying Hitler's invasion plans for the Soviet Union, as Yugoslav propaganda used to claim (Mussolini's Greek enterprise had already achieved that), Yugoslav intervention may well have speeded up Hitler's Greek campaign. Yugoslavia crumbled within days and Germany was able to send troops as well as equipment via the most direct route to Greece.

The Second World War

In 1991, from the moment the Yugoslav People's Army (*Jugoslovenska narodna armija*) intervened in Slovenia the events of fifty years earlier in that country appeared to receive almost as much media attention as the war itself. It was as if somehow in the carnage of the Second World War there was an explanation for the atrocities of the 1990s. However, historical explanations of contemporary events often depend less on past events themselves and more on contemporary perceptions and interpretations of those events. What actually happened is often less important than what people believe, or are made to believe, happened. Though some good histories of the Second World War in Yugoslavia have been written, few people either in Yugoslavia or abroad have actually read them.

Since Yugoslavia had not been on Hitler's immediate agenda, he had made no preparations for the country's occupation. In the event, he decided to hive off whatever he could to neighbouring countries with territorial claims against Yugoslavia. Slovenia was divided between Germany, Italy and Hungary. Italy, which already possessed Istria, also grabbed much of Dalmatia and constructed a Montenegrin protectorate while parts of Croatia, including Baranja, Medjimurje and a strip of Slavonia went to Hungary, as did much of Vojvodina. German parts of Vojvodina, the Banat, became self-governing under German administration. Bulgaria acquired Macedonia as well as a corner of Serbia, and Albania, itself an Italian protectorate, swallowed Kosovo.

The problematic regions which could not be hived off—that is inner Serbia, a truncated Croatia, a piece of Vojvodina and Bosnia-Hercegovina—remained. Here Hitler looked for Quisling leaders. In Serbia he found General Milan Nedić, a senior officer in the Yugoslav Army and member of the pre-war élite, who was convinced that Germany had already won the war. In Croatia, however, Hitler's task was more difficult, since the vast majority of Croats backed Maček who refused to cooperate because he believed that Germany was going to lose the war. As a result, Hitler had little option but to turn to Pavelić and the Ustašas.

There was no precedent for the Ustašas. When they came to power, Maček broadcast a statement advising Croats to obey the new authorities, before withdrawing from political life and retiring to his home village. Maček had not anticipated, and could not anticipate, what the Ustašas were about to do. Croatia's Serb population would probably have been willing to respect Ustaša rule, had they been given the opportunity. After all, they had put up with all manner of foreign overlords in the past and had been allied politically with Croats for much of the interwar period. Indeed, even when the Ustašas began wiping out Serb villages, many survivors went to Zagreb to protest, convinced that the government could not be involved. But the government was involved.

To understand the Ustašas, it is important to bear in mind that, above all, they were terrorists who had overnight been handed total power. Moreover, they had been handed total power over lands in which only a little more than half the population were actually Croats. The Independent State of Croatia (*Nezavisna Država Hrvatske* or NDH) contained all of what became the republic of Bosnia-Hercegovina and included about 750,000 Muslim Slavs as well as 1.9 million Serbs. But the NDH did not include much of what became the republic of Croatia, since Istria and much of Dalmatia, for example, were under Italian rule. When they came to power, the Ustašas lacked popular support, since even according to their own estimates they only had about 40,000 supporters. Ustaša sympathizers came almost exclusively from Hercegovina, many of whom had been on the receiving end of Serb excesses during the interwar years and were determined to get even.

Hercegovina is situated in the middle of the Dinaric mountains which stretch from the most backward Serb-populated regions of Croatia across Hercegovina to Montenegro. It is inhospitable and barren land which has never provided anything more than subsistence living. Bitterly cold in winter and unbearably hot in summer, life there has always been brutal and all Hercegovina's peoples—whether Serb, Muslim or Croat—appear wild and backward. In addition to their backwardness, Croats from Hercegovina differ from Croats elsewhere in their religious allegiances. Though formally Catholics, the Croats of Hercegovina were effectively abandoned by the Papacy during Ottoman times and since then their spiritual needs have been looked after by the Franciscan order. Indeed, to this day the Franciscans have remained at loggerheads with Rome over control of the spiritual needs of the population.

A handful of Franciscans were prominent among the Ustašas, who—in marked contrast to the anti-clerical Croat Peasant Party—boasted of their Catholicism. The head of the notorious Jasenovac concentration camp, Miroslav Filipović, for example, was a former Franciscan. However, most Franciscans as well as the rest of the Catholic Church in Croatia were not compromised during the Second World War and the Vatican refused to recognise the Ustaša state. In addition to militant Catholicism, the Ustašas' ideology was that of Starčević's Croatian state right, taken to absurd lengths. The Ustašas viewed being a Serb as an act of political aggression against their Croatian state, and hence explains their plan to kill a third, expel a third to Serbia and convert the remainder to Catholicism.

Independence won the Ustašas some popularity among Croats, but, by manufacturing an unnecessary conflict with the Serb population, they began in June, July and August 1941 a cycle of massacres which continued throughout the Second World War and generated rebellion among Serbs. The lunacy of the Ustaša atrocities shattered Croatia's reputation, led to the deaths of thousands of innocent Croats in reprisals and did incalculable damage to the prospects of any future Croatian state. It was exactly what the Germans had wished to avoid, since Ustaša actions made the entire region unstable, but it was also the consequence of giving total power to an insane terrorist group. Indeed, so appalling was Ustaša rule that they rapidly managed to alienate the Croat population and could never trust the regular Croatian Army unless accompanied by Ustaša units, while even the mildest expression of opposition was punished by internment in a concentration camp.

Controversy surrounds several issues in the Second World War in Yugoslavia, in particular the number of dead, the scale of Yugoslavia's contribution to the overall Allied war effort and the manner in which Tito's partisans seized power.

The official number of war dead, which was supposed to exclude those who died fighting for the Axis powers, was 1.7 million. The figure was only a rough calculation arrived at immediately after the war for reparations and propaganda purposes. Tito aimed both to maximise war compensation from Germany and to demonstrate to the world that the heroism and suffering of Yugoslavs during the Second World War surpassed that of all other peoples save only the Soviets and perhaps the Poles. However, in nationalist circles on all sides, operating on the principle 'the more the better', estimates of the dead extend to absurd levels. Despite the emotions clouding the issue, serious historians have a very good idea of the actual number of war dead, which is mercifully well below the official figure.

During the 1980s independent research into the question by two men, Bogoljub Kočović, an *émigré* Serb, and Vladimir Žerjavić, a Croat, produced very similar results. Both investigations were based not on body counts or survivors' recollections but on computer analysis of census returns and demographic indices. According to Kočović, whose figures are marginally higher than those of Žerjavić, a total of about 1,014,000, or 6.4 per cent of Yugoslavia's 1941 population, died during or in the immediate aftermath of the Second World War on all sides. In absolute terms, Serbs (487,000), Croats (207,000), Muslim Slavs (86,000), Jews (60,000) and Montenegrins (50,000) were the biggest losers, while in relative terms Jews (77.9 per cent), Gypsies (31.4 per cent), Montenegrins (10.4 per cent), Serbs (6.9 per cent) and Muslim Slavs (6.7 per cent) were the greatest proportional losers. When Kočović's figures are further broken down by republic, the highest percentage losses of population were recorded in Bosnia-Hercegovina (11.8 per cent), Montenegro (10.2 per cent) and Croatia (7.3 per cent).

Among Serbs, the vast majority of casualties were from the NDH, where one in six perished. According to Kočović's estimates, 125,000 — or 17.4 per cent of the pre-war Serb population — died in Croatia and another 209,000 — or 16.9 per cent of the pre-war Serb population — died in Bosnia-Hercegovina. While shocking in themselves, the figures do not necessarily reflect the horror of the war when viewed from the perspective of those Serbs who were on the receiving end of the Ustašas' brutality, and perhaps that is why Serb nationalists are so determined to inflate them.

A high but obviously incalculable proportion of the casualties were butchered between June and August 1941 when most were not even aware of any conflict. Bands of Ustašas turned up unannounced at Serb villages and wiped out every last man, woman and child. The orgy of violence then continued at concentration camps which the Ustašas set up to eliminate their remaining opponents, both Serbs and non-Serbs. At Jasenovac, the most infamous camp, where Serb propagandists habitually claim that more than a million Serbs perished, extermination was not a regulated process along Nazi lines. There were no gas chambers, nor were the Ustašas willing to waste bullets on their victims. Instead, death was by beating, starvation or knives. The manner of death was grotesque, though the number of dead was far less than propagandists claim. According to Žerjavić's calculations, which are the most reliable figures available, about 85,000 people of all nationalities lost their lives at Jasenovac.[9]

Serb guerrilla fighters appeared in Bosnia-Hercegovina and Croatia as soon as the Ustašas began attempting to wipe out the Serb population. Initially, they were leaderless and simply concerned with staying alive. Both of Yugoslavia's celebrated wartime leaders, Josip Broz Tito,[10] the communist, and Draža Mihailović, the royalist, started their respective uprisings against German rule in Serbia in the autumn of 1941. However, the revolts were rapidly put down by the Germans and from that time until the liberation of Belgrade at the end of 1944 Serbia was more or less quiet. As a result, contrary to conventional wisdom, casualty figures from Serbia proper were modest by Yugoslav standards.

Tito and Mihailović had very different agendas. Tito was a professional revolutionary and committed communist, while Mihailović, who had been a colonel in the Yugoslav Army before the war, was loyal to the Karadjordjević royal family. Perhaps the greatest difference between the two men was that Tito aimed to win power and was prepared to do anything, including, when necessary, tactical alliances

---

[9] Of the 85,000 who lost their lives, 12,000 were Croats and Muslims, 13,000 Jews, 10,000 Gypsies and the remaining 50,000 Serbs.

[10] The name Tito is a common term of endearment in Hrvatsko Zagorje, Tito's home region, and a nickname Josip Broz picked up early in life. It is not, as many foreigners apparently believe, the combination of the words ti and to, meaning 'you [singular]' and 'that', and Broz did not acquire the nickname by giving orders.

with the Germans, to achieve that goal, while Mihailović aimed, above all, to keep Serbs, though not necessarily any of Yugoslavia's other peoples, alive. For Tito, casualties from reprisals meant more potential recruits to the partisans. To Mihailović, they were dead Serbs. In addition to being the more ruthless fighter, Tito was able to command support from all Yugoslavia's peoples while Mihailović could count only on Serbs. After the first failed uprising Tito left Serbia for Bosnia-Hercegovina. Mihailović chose to sit tight and conserve his forces in expectation of an Allied landing. Unfortunately this never materialised.

In Bosnia-Hercegovina and Croatia Tito had a massive reservoir of potential recruits among the Serb peasantry who had managed to escape the Ustašas. But here, too, Mihailović nominally had his own followers, the Četniks. Taking their name from the Serb guerilla fighters of the Turkish Wars, the Četniks were particularly strong in Italian-controlled areas especially around Knin (which again became the centre of the Serb revolt in 1990). Though these Četniks claimed to acknowledge Mihailović as their supreme commander, in reality he had little influence over them and was powerless to halt their massacres of innocent Croats and Muslims.

Inevitably, Mihailović's reputation took a battering in Tito's Yugoslavia, where he was vilified as a traitor and collaborator. As a result, there is now a revisionist school of historical thought which believes Mihailović was betrayed by the British, who abandoned him in summer 1943 for Tito. Certainly Mihailović was abandoned, but perhaps one should not overestimate the impact of one British decision on the final outcome of the war in Yugoslavia. In addition to arms and munitions from Britain, the partisans seized weapons from the Italians when Italy capitulated, manufactured them themselves, acquired them from Croatian units which increasingly came over to Tito and, in the final stages of the war, were supplied by the Soviet Union. In the absence of an Allied invasion, Mihailović was not going to liberate Yugoslavia especially since he had minimal support outside Serbia and the Serb community.

The simplified picture of the Second World War in Yugoslavia emanating from the media during the present conflict has been of Serbs—whether under Mihailović or Tito—on the Allied side and Croats on the German side. However, the actual picture was far more complex. To a large extent the Second World War in Yugoslavia was several civil wars which had little to do with the world war raging outside the country. All groups, with the exception of the Slovenes, fought against Serbs, though not in unison, while extreme nationalists on all sides were able to indulge their wildest fantasies. Apart from the initial uprising in 1941, Serbia itself remained more or less quiet until close to the end of the war. Mihailović was conserving his forces, while Nedić, in a similar manner to Marshal Pétain in France, was loyal to the Nazis. In the absence of the fighting and chaos of the NDH and under German supervision, Nedić was able to wipe out Serbia's Jewish community far more efficiently than the Ustašas could wipe out the Jews of Croatia and Bosnia-Hercegovina.[11]

From Tito's power-base in Bosnia-Hercegovina his immediate army came from the poorest and most backward Serb peasants. These were the people who after the war came to dominate Yugoslavia's rather crude security apparatus. Richer peasants sided with Mihailović or indeed any anti-communist group. Meanwhile, many of Tito's commanders were, like himself, professional revolutionaries of all nationalities, some of whom had also seen action in the Spanish Civil War. As the war dragged on, the composition of Tito's army changed, as did the enemy. The communists' principal advantage over their rivals was that they could attract support from all Yugoslavia's peoples. Given the Ustašas' insane brutality, it proved easy to recruit large numbers of Croats especially after Tito won over several prominent figures, including Croatia's greatest living writer Miroslav Krleža. However, as it became clear that the communists intended to seize power after the war, forces from all over the country, including Mihailović, who were fearful of a communist take-over, decided to concentrate their efforts against the partisans and to side by default with the Nazis as the lesser of two evils.

By Italy's capitulation in 1943 Tito had withstood all that the Axis powers were prepared to throw at him and the tide of the wider world war had turned. He had also built a multinational fighting force in which all Yugoslavia's Slav peoples, though not the non-Slavs, were well represented. Compared to other European battlefronts, the fighting in Yugoslavia was small-scale as the partisans generally tried

[11] At the start of the Second World War there were 76,654 Jews in Yugoslavia, of whom 32,000 found themselves in the NDH and 30,000 in the part of Serbia established as a German protectorate under Nedić. By the end of the war 23,000 had been killed in the NDH and 24,000 in Nedić's Serbia.

to avoid engagement while concentrating on acts of terrorism. It was a war of heroic marches and valiant retreats but few glorious victories.

Given the extent and the chaos of Yugoslavia's own civil wars, Germany never needed to commit large numbers of troops. Yugoslavia's contribution to the overall Allied effort has been greatly exaggerated, firstly by the victors themselves and more recently by statesmen wishing to justify a policy of non-intervention in the present conflict. The only time when significant numbers of German troops were in Yugoslavia was during the initial invasion in 1941 and in 1944 when units stationed in Greece retreated across the country. Otherwise, Germany relied on its allies, the Italians, Hungarians and Bulgarians, and Quisling forces to keep Yugoslavia under control, leaving German troops free for the more important battlefronts, especially those in the Soviet Union. Certainly there were never twenty-odd divisions of crack German troops pinned down by the partisans in Bosnia-Hercegovina, as various Western politicians have claimed in recent years. At the same time, given the cruelty and incompetence of Ustaša rule, it is hardly surprising that they failed to pacify the country.

As soon as the partisans liberated territory, they began constructing their communist state. Throughout the country imposition of communist rule was brutal, not least because the partisan victory was at the same time a victory for the countryside over the city. Though many of the partisans who liberated Belgrade with the support of the advancing Red Army in October 1944 were themselves Serbs, they tended to come from the most backward parts of Croatia and Bosnia-Hercegovina and had little in common with the inhabitants of the capital, who were terrified by their savagery. Members of the pre-war élite from all parts of the country who had remained in Yugoslavia during the war, including Maček, chose to flee before the communist advance. Key figures who stayed put were often executed or victimised after the war.

The war in Yugoslavia continued a full week after the end of hostilities on other European fronts as anti-communists of all nationalities attempted to fight their way out of the country. The indigenous German population had already fled with the retreating German Army, fearing reprisals. The anti-communists were determined to surrender to British or American forces rather than fall into

Tito's hands. Those who failed to make it to Austria or Italy, as well as many who made it but were then handed over by the British, were summarily executed *en masse*, including many innocents.[12] Unlike communists elsewhere in eastern Europe, Tito's partisans had liberated their country, including Croat and Slovene-populated regions of Italy, virtually on their own. Despite assurances to Britain and the United States that he would cooperate with Yugoslavia's royal government, which had spent the war in London, Tito had no intention of sharing power.

[12] According to figures compiled by Žerjavić, between 45,000 and 50,000 Croats and Muslims, between 1,500 and 2,000 Serbs and Montenegrins, and about 8,000 Slovenes whom the British handed over were executed in the aftermath of the Second World War.

4

TITO'S YUGOSLAVIA

'By reuniting the Serbs and Croats who had been set on each other by the Axis powers, and by granting the Macedonians the ethnic recognition which the monarchy had refused them, Tito's communist regime gave a more solid foundation to Yugoslavia, even if it did not actually solve her national question.' — Stevan Pavlowitch[1]

The national question

An open discussion of the Second World War in its immediate aftermath might have helped restore trust between Yugoslavia's peoples and given the country's second incarnation a more secure foundation. A better understanding of the conflict should have dispelled many of the myths which are widely believed today, and perhaps even moderated some of the hatred. But the ideological beliefs of the victorious communists ruled out such a discussion. According to Marxist-Leninist dogma, nationalism was a feature of bourgeois society which would disappear as soon as the proletariat won power and the inequalities which had bred nationalism in the first place were eradicated. While the credentials of Tito's peasant soldiers were hardly proletarian, victory was, nevertheless, in the name of the proletariat. As far as Yugoslavia's communists were concerned, their triumph was part of the march of history and the nationalisms which had torn Yugoslavia apart between 1941 and 1945 were sure to fade away.

Given the ultimate failings of communism and the brutality of Stalinism, it is perhaps difficult today to understand the commitment and passion of communists throughout the world at the time. But in the wake of the Second World War and, in particular, of the huge contribution of the Soviet Union to the defeat of Nazi Germany, Stalin and Stalinism commanded considerable respect in non-communist circles as well as complete fidelity within the communist movement.

[1] Stevan Pavlowitch teaches Balkan history at the University of Southampton, England. Among his books is *The Improbable Survivor: Yugoslavia and its Problems, 1918–1988*, London, C. Hurst, 1989.

51

It was a creed which appealed not only to impoverished peasants of Bosnia-Hercegovina but also to intellectuals from the top stratum of British society. Even many non-communists feared that the communist model might prove more efficient than capitalism. Yugoslavia's communists were sure of it. They were committed to the Marxist-Leninist blueprint for society and aimed to emulate the example of the Soviet Union, where—to communist minds—the national question had already been solved.

Despite wartime assurances that he would work with the government-in-exile, Tito moved quickly to silence all opposition as soon as his forces controlled the country. In a series of show trials in Belgrade, Zagreb and Ljubljana, he set out to discredit the remaining domestic opponents. The most infamous were those of Draža Mihailović, who had been captured in March 1946, and Alojzije Stepinac, Archbishop of Zagreb and head of the Catholic Church in Yugoslavia. Both were tried alongside notorious collaborators and found guilty of collaboration. Mihailović was executed and Stepinac, whose real offence was refusing to kowtow to Tito, was sentenced to sixteen years' hard labour. Ironically, the trials failed to achieve their objectives. Instead of discrediting Mihailović in Serb eyes and Stepinac in Croat eyes, as intended, they merely confirmed mistrust of Serbia and Mihailović among Croats and the collusion of the Catholic Church in Ustaša atrocities among Serbs.

In the partisans' folklore, anti-communists were demonised and labelled collaborators, irrespective of who they had been fighting for or whether they had been fighting at all. The Second World War was interpreted as an epic anti-fascist struggle and proletarian revolution, but not a civil war. This simplistic and heavily doctored version of the events of 1941-5, which conflicted with personal recollections, became the official communist history of the war. However, an alternative history was passed on by word of mouth to succeeding generations, ensuring that open wounds continued to fester long after the war was over.

Despite the obvious shortcomings of Marxist-Leninist analysis of the national question, Tito's national policy was nevertheless a key element in the partisans' military victory. By trading national loyalties for allegiances based on a universalist ideology, the communists were able to draw recruits from all Yugoslavia's Slav peoples, though it should be pointed out that they failed to attract many non-Slavs into their ranks. The Communist Party was a club anyone could join, irrespective of national origins, with a mission to mould history. In Bosnia-Hercegovina, the main theatre of war, partisan units contained all three major national groups, Serbs, Croats and Muslim Slavs, fighting together under the slogan 'brotherhood and unity' (*bratstvo i jedinstvo*).

The foundations of the post-war state were laid during the war at the second meeting of the Anti-Fascist Council at Jajce, a recently liberated town in Bosnia, on 29 November 1943. In the event of a communist victory Yugoslavia would become a federation consisting of Serbia, Croatia, Macedonia, Slovenia, Montenegro and Bosnia-Hercegovina. Exactly two years after the Jajce meeting a communist-dominated constituent assembly abolished the monarchy and proclaimed the Federal People's Republic of Yugoslavia. And just over two months later on 31 January 1946 the country's first communist constitution was unanimously approved. It was Yugoslavia's third constitution in twenty-five years and confirmed the country's new structure as a federation of the six republics as agreed at Jajce, as well as the autonomous province of Vojvodina and the autonomous region of Kosovo[2] within Serbia.

The division into federal units was not meant to divide the country but to create as equitable a balance as possible between Yugoslavia's peoples and to prevent conflict over disputed territories. Borders between republics were drawn up on a mixture of ethnic and historic principles. In this way, Macedonians won recognition of their separate national identity and their own republic. Montenegro, too, became a republic in its own right in respect of its independent history, while Bosnia-Hercegovina maintained its former Ottoman contours including a segment of the Adriatic coast. The border between Croatia and Vojvodina meandered between villages depending on whether they had a Croat or a Serb majority. Kosovo became an autonomous region and Vojvodina an autonomous province within Serbia because of the large non-Serb populations living there.

The 1946 constitution was modelled on that of the Soviet Union of 1936 drawn up by Stalin. According to article 12, inter-republican borders could only be altered after negotiations between the republics themselves with the agreement of all sides. In addition, each republic, though not Vojvodina and Kosovo, had the right to secession and

---

[2] At the time Kosovo was called Kosmet, a short form for Kosovo and Metohija. When the region's status was upgraded to that of a province in 1968 the allegedly provocative Orthodox name Metohija was dropped.

self-determination, although clearly these were rights which they were not meant to exercise. The communist revolution was supposed to be the culmination of a historical process and there was certainly no provision for a possible break-up of Yugoslavia. Officially, Yugoslavia's peoples had exercised their right to self-determination 'once and for all' during the national liberation struggle, when they chose to live together in a multinational federation.

The issue of autonomy for predominantly Serb regions of Croatia was considered but eventually set aside. Presumably, had autonomy been granted to these regions, then the same status would have had to be accorded to the predominantly Muslim Sandžak in Serbia and, in time, to predominantly Albanian regions of Macedonia. But autonomy, even limited cultural autonomy, was deemed unnecessary because, as far as Yugoslavia's communists were concerned, the end of capitalism meant the end of national oppression. In reality, though, it was not mentioned anywhere in the constitution. All power lay with the Communist Party just as in the Soviet Union. The highest authority in the land was Tito and his trusted lieutenants, Alexander Ranković, Milovan Djilas and Edvard Kardelj. For, despite its federal structure, Yugoslavia was if anything more unitary and centralist than it had been under King Alexander. What had changed was the concept of Yugoslavism.

No nation would be allowed to dominate the Federal People's Republic of Yugoslavia the way that Serbs had dominated the first Yugoslav incarnation. Communist Yugoslavism was hostile to all the parochial nationalisms of the peoples of Yugoslavia, while attempting to cultivate a multinational and thoroughly Yugoslav patriotism emanating from the wartime struggle for national liberation. It was revolutionary, idealistic and supposedly part of a wider, ongoing revolution aspiring to universal, socialist goals which could only be achieved through the unity of working people throughout the world. National equality was fundamental and extended as far as the participation in the National Liberation War. For, according to the official interpretation of the Second World War, all Yugoslavia's peoples had contributed equally to the defeat of fascism. While, strictly speaking, this may not have been the case, it was an attempt to wipe the national slate clean and allow all peoples to join the new state free from any historical mortgage.

Though all Yugoslavia's Slav peoples were well represented in Tito's army by 1945, few non-Slavs joined the partisans. Yugoslavia's

German, Albanian and Hungarian populations remained for the most part allied to the Axis powers until the end of the war and played a minimal role in the national liberation struggle. As a result, in the immediate aftermath of the war the commitment to national equality did not extend to include them. The fate of the German minority in Yugoslavia was the same as that of German minorities throughout eastern Europe. It disappeared. Those who could escape Yugoslavia with the retreating German Army did. Those who failed to make it out of the country were rounded up and bore the brunt of anti-German sentiments. Some were summarily executed, most were expelled and the few who remained faced a lifetime of persecution devoid of all rights.

Yugoslavia's Hungarians and Albanians were hostile to the new state and suspicious of its intentions towards them. In December 1944, soon after the partisans had 'liberated' Kosovo, the region's Albanians rebelled against the reimposition of Yugoslav rule. The uprising lasted several months and 30,000 Yugoslav troops were required to put it down. The Yugoslav communists had hoped to deal with the non-Slav minorities within the wider context of a union of communist states of eastern Europe or at least a Balkan federation and did not address the question immediately. However, the break with Stalin in 1948 ruled out this option and forced them to evolve a more comprehensive national policy.

The eventual solution was typically Yugoslav. It was supposed to be scientific but was in reality complex and arbitrary. Yugoslavia's peoples were split into nations and national minorities. Initially, nations corresponded to those peoples who had a home republic, that is Slovenes, Croats, Serbs, Macedonians and Montenegrins. But in 1971 the status of Muslim Slavs was elevated to that of a constituent nation. Meanwhile, the Hungarians and Albanians, as well as all other peoples living in Yugoslavia, were classified as national minorities. Each republican and provincial constitution listed the nations and national minorities living there and officially both nations and national minorities had the same rights and duties. For example, in Bosnia-Hercegovina Serbs, Croats and Muslims were listed as the republic's constituent nations. In Croatia and Vojvodina Croats and Serbs were listed as the constituent nations. Hungarians who lived in both Croatia and Vojvodina were listed as national minorities in both even though they outnumbered Croats in Vojvodina. Albanians were classified as a national minority in Kosovo, even though they formed the majority there and despite the fact that by the 1980s there were more Albanians in Yugoslavia than Montenegrins, Muslim Slavs, Macedonians and Slovenes.

Whatever the precise constitutional arrangement, relations between Yugoslavia's peoples were bound to remain stable in Tito's lifetime. He was Yugoslavia's ultimate arbiter who, on account of his unassailable power base, was able to step in and resolve any conflict which he feared might be getting out of hand. During thirty-five years at Yugoslavia's helm Tito was able to mould the country in his own image, so that when he died on 4 May 1980 he was genuinely mourned throughout the country. Tito's funeral was televised live at home and across much of the world and attended by many of the world's most distinguished statesmen. To outsiders the very words Tito and Yugoslavia were indelibly linked, and inevitably foreign commentators began to speculate on Yugoslavia's future. In the event, Yugoslavia outlived Tito by less than a third of the time he had ruled the country.

Titoism

During his life Tito was the subject of many sycophantic studies both at home and abroad. Domestic eulogies were understandable, since Tito was careful to keep a tight rein over the home media, through which he cultivated his chosen image of father to all Yugoslavs. But foreign commentators were also prone to optimistic assessments both of the man and of his state. Tito's undeniable charisma certainly contributed to his favourable image abroad but the main reason was quite simply that Yugoslavia was not part of the Soviet camp.

It is perhaps ironic that Tito's popularity and reputation abroad stemmed from the 1948 break with Stalin, for, at the time, Tito considered himself the most loyal of Stalinists. Certainly Tito had much to be grateful to Stalin for and there is much evidence to suggest that, despite the break, Tito remained at heart a Stalinist to the end of his life. The reputations of even the greatest dictators suffer after their death and, in this respect, Tito was no exception. The cracks were already apparent in the final years of his life as the Yugoslav economy stalled and spluttered, bankrupting his experiment. Popular attitudes towards Tito and his achievements changed quickest in those parts of Yugoslavia where in the same manner as the media was once manipulated to worship him it was in turn manipulated to demolish his reputation. But in the light of Yugoslavia's disintegration Tito's entire record must be reconsidered.

Tito was born in the tiny village of Kumrovec on the Croatian border with Slovenia in 1892 while it was part of the Habsburg Empire. His father was Croat, his mother Slovene. At 19 he left his home village and eventually made his way to Vienna where he became a non-commissioned officer in the Habsburg Army. During the First World War Tito took part in the invasion of Serbia, before being transferred to the Russian front where he was taken prisoner. Following the Bolshevik Revolution Tito converted to Marxism-Leninism, so that by the time he eventually came home to Yugoslavia in 1920 he returned a committed communist.

In 1928 Tito was sentenced to five years in prison. It was a term he put to use to improve his education and to study Marxism-Leninism. On his release he entered the Central Committee of the Communist Party of Yugoslavia (CPY) and began making frequent trips to the Soviet Union at exactly the time when Stalin's purges were at their height. Foreign communists were far from immune to the purges and most of the leading Yugoslav communists perished in these years. However, the purges gave Tito his break and catapulted him to the top of the CPY in 1937. Only the most committed Stalinist could have survived and prospered in the 1930s in the way that Tito did. Indeed, he was handpicked by Stalin to purge the CPY and it is likely that he sacrificed many of his colleagues on his way to the top.

The Second World War gave the CPY the opportunity to seize power. Though Tito was not a great military commander, he was politically astute and able to weld what had been spontaneous and uncoordinated insurrections to the communist cause. Tito had great expectations of the communist movement and in terms of personal ambition he aimed to be up there alongside Stalin in its hall of fame. He sincerely believed that the victory of the proletariat was imminent throughout the world and was determined to do his utmost to spur it along. While Stalin cautiously constructed a buffer zone of satellite states around his Soviet Empire, Tito was actively spreading revolution by financing and supplying the Greek communists in that country's civil war. Cominform, the new international wing of the communist movement which replaced Comintern, was founded by Yugoslavia and headquartered in Belgrade. Tito also had ambitious plans to link all eastern European states together in a communist federation modelled on that of the Soviet Union. But he had reckoned without Stalin.

It is no exaggeration to say that Titoism did not exist until Stalin invented it. Indeed, the break which shattered the myth of the communist monolith was as great a surprise to Tito and Yugoslavia's communists as it was to the Western world. The same paranoia which led Stalin to destroy the lives of millions of innocent people in brutal and irrational purges also caused him to pick a quarrel with someone who had, hitherto, taken pride in his loyalty. Tito did not take Yugoslavia out of the international communist movement of his own volition, instead, it was Stalin, via Cominform, who expelled Yugoslavia. Tito's crime was his willingness to use his own initiative and the fact he was not entirely under Stalin's thumb. At the same time, Titoism was merely an excuse to begin yet another purge of the latest generation of communist leaders. But so great was the propaganda in Yugoslavia surrounding Stalin that even at the end of the emergency meeting of the CPY called to discuss the country's expulsion from Cominform delegates were still required to shout 'Tito, Stalin, Tito, Stalin'.

In time, the break with Stalin forced Yugoslavia and Tito to change course and led to the evolution of the Yugoslav way. But in the immediate aftermath of Yugoslavia's expulsion from Cominform Tito and his lieutenants actually renewed their efforts to build socialism on the Stalinist model by completing the nationalisation of industry and speeding up the collectivisation of agriculture. Since Yugoslavia was being accused of doctrinal revisionism, Tito hoped to demonstrate his Stalinist credentials to win his way back into Stalin's favours. But because the dispute was in Stalin's mind and had nothing to do with doctrine, there was no way back into the movement. The economic consequences of such policies were predictable and Yugoslavia rapidly found itself on the verge of starvation.

Economic collapse and the very real threat of invasion forced Tito to chart a new course. Even then Titoism did not exist as an ideology. The volte-face was part pragmatism, part desperation, for Tito was a conspirator and guerrilla fighter with a heightened sense for survival, but never an ideologue. When eventually the Yugoslav communists evolved their own ideology, distinct from that of the Soviet Union, which became known as Titoism, it was the work of Milovan Djilas and Edvard Kardelj, not Tito.

In 1948 there was no time for ideology; it was simply a matter of survival. In the best Stalinist traditions survival meant a thoroughgoing purge of the administration, the CPY and the military, to weed out potential dissenters or 'Cominformists' as they were called. According to official figures, more than 11,000 Cominformists were arrested and expelled from the Party, while another 2,500 were sentenced to imprisonment on Goli Otok (the barren island), Yugoslavia's miniature gulag. In addition, strategic industries were shifted to more secure parts of the country and, in particular, many key defence installations were moved to Bosnia-Hercegovina. The Yugoslav propaganda machine turned against Cominform, the Soviet Union and eventually Stalin himself. At the same time, it mobilised the country against the possible threat of outside intervention with repeated calls to a Yugoslav patriotism. The threat was real and in this case the potential enemy was genuinely foreign unlike the 'fascist' enemy of the Second World War.

Having stamped out all possibility of domestic opposition, Tito took advantage of the hand extended to him by the West. Whatever the reasons for the split in communist ranks, the Western powers were determined to exploit it and drive a wedge between Yugoslavia and the rest of the Soviet bloc. While Stalin hoped to oust. Tito and reassert his authority over Yugoslavia, he was, nevertheless, cautious and reluctant to risk any conflict which might jeopardise the rest of his Empire. As soon as the United States intervened against communism in Korea and made it clear that the Truman doctrine 'to protect the free world' extended to include Yugoslavia, Stalin had to content himself with yet another purge of imagined Titoists in eastern Europe. After Stalin's death in 1953, the Soviet threat to Yugoslav independence effectively disappeared in Soviet, though not in Yugoslav or Western, minds.

Without Western economic support Yugoslavia would probably have crumbled in the face of a concerted economic blockade by the Soviet bloc. In September 1949 the Truman administration granted Yugoslavia a $20 million aid package and by 1960 Yugoslavia had consumed more than $2 billion worth of non-repayable Western aid. As far as the Western powers were concerned, aid was an insurance policy against Yugoslavia slipping back into the Soviet camp, with the spin-off that it enabled them to slash defence spending in Italy. For Tito, who made sure that the aid came without any strings, it enabled him to remain a communist, albeit independent of Moscow. Aid became fundamental to Yugoslavia's development and allowed Yugoslavs to live way beyond their means, while Tito and his successors became expert at raising the spectre of the Soviet bogey to procure yet more economic assistance. The result was communist extravagance paid for by a seemingly endless supply of Western credit. Yugoslavia's communists were able to indulge in a ludicrous experiment with their cherished Marxist-Leninist ideology, secure in the knowledge that if and when they came unstuck the West would pick up the bill.

As the immediate Soviet threat receded, but while Stalin was still alive, Yugoslavia's communists set out to develop their own Marxist-Leninist ideology. Titoism evolved out of attempts by Djilas and Kardelj to work out where Stalinism had gone wrong and to prove that Yugoslavia and not the Soviet Union was the legitimate heir of Marxist-Leninist orthodoxy. After rereading Marx's seminal work *Das Kapital*, they decided that Stalinism had gone astray in its concentration of power within the state and the expansion of the bureaucracy. In Yugoslavia, by contrast, they decided that the state should wither away and that power should be devolved to the workers themselves. Herein lay the foundations of Socialist Worker Self-Management.

Initially, Tito was reluctant to embrace a theory which, if implemented and taken to its logical conclusion, would require the Party to give up its leading role in society. He was won over to the concept, however, because it enabled Yugoslavia to make a clean break from the Soviet Union. The Stalinist blueprint for economic development was shelved and in 1953 Yugoslavia began to decollectivise agriculture. The CPY changed its name to the League of Communists of Yugoslavia (LCY) and in the 1953 constitution Workers' Councils were set up to devolve power to the lowest level. But Worker Self-Management was a sham and the celebrated Workers' Councils were but an additional tier of bureaucracy. In 1954 a disillusioned Djilas was purged and after three trials between 1955 and 1957 sentenced to ten years' imprisonment. Despite its new title the LCY remained a Marxist-Leninist party unwilling to renounce its historical mission in society. At the same time, the leading communists, like all eastern Europe's leaders but unlike their peoples, were doing very well out of the system. On this, all attempts of the 1950s and 1960s to liberalise the economy were bound to founder.

Nobody did better out of Yugoslavia than Tito. Cushioned by Western aid, he survived Stalin and as he grew older was able to indulge his fantasies and live like the playboy he had become. At home he delighted in hunting trips, fancy cars and luxurious palaces. He even turned his home village of Kumrovec into a shrine to his own achievements, fully equipped with hotel, conference centre and museum. Abroad, he was equally extravagant. The ideological basis of Yugoslavia's foreign policy was non-alignment, independence from both East and West. When in 1961 Tito helped set up the Non-Aligned Movement, the Cold War was at its height and non-alignment appeared to fulfil a useful purpose. Increasingly, however, the Movement became little more than another vehicle to serve the dictator's vanity. He travelled further and attended more summits than any other world leader and all over the world Yugoslavia opened consulates and embassies to spread his message and enhance his prestige. Yet, for all the glory, Yugoslavia had little of substance to show for the massive expense.

Society

As Tito aged, he grew increasingly vain. He fell out with and purged former trusted lieutenants one by one and even with his wife Jovanka. Of his wartime entourage only the sycophant Kardelj, who died of cancer in 1979, managed to remain in Tito's good graces to the very end. As Tito's vanity grew, he craved love from all Yugoslavia's peoples. Hence events such as the Day of Youth, an annual celebration of his birthday in which the flower of Yugoslav youth would participate in a relay around the country. Hence also his genuine attempt to emancipate Yugoslavia's Albanians and integrate them into Yugoslav society. For, deluded as he may have become, he aimed to please everybody. His very presence ensured that there would be no conflict and his policies were designed to bring peoples together.

Whatever the shortcomings of Titoism, the years in which Tito reigned over Yugoslavia were ones of accelerating development and rapid change throughout the world and of urbanisation, industrialisation and modernisation in Yugoslavia. During these years Yugoslav society was transformed almost beyond recognition and Yugoslavs had much to be thankful for. The cycle of massacres which had characterised the Second World War was brought to an end and Yugoslavs were the beneficiaries of rising living standards as well as greater access to education and improved standards of health care.

In 1945 Yugoslavia had been a very rural and backward country whose population suffered appalling health. Only three cities, Belgrade, Zagreb and Ljubljana had more than 100,000 inhabitants while diseases such as tuberculosis and whooping cough afflicted much of the population and in parts of the south of the country even malaria was prevalent. In common with much of the communist world, Yugoslavia's health record was impressive. Improvements in public hygiene, the training of a generation of doctors and an ambitious hospital-building programme all contributed to a dramatic reduction in infant mortality and increased life expectancy. Meanwhile, the growth of industries and the move to the city radically altered the landscape of Yugoslav society as well as the ethnic composition of the country.

The ethnic map had already changed during and immediately after the Second World War. The proportion of Serbs in the total population of Croatia and Bosnia-Hercegovina declined as a result of higher wartime casualties than among Croats and Muslims, though the relative decline was not as great as recent propaganda would have one believe. Greater changes took place in Slavonia and Vojvodina, where another generation of land-hungry Serb settlers from Hercegovina and Montenegro moved into villages vacated by Germans and inherited their lands. Until 1945 Slavonian villages like Borovo Selo on the outskirts of Vukovar (which became a Serb stronghold during the war of 1991) had been populated by Germans, while Vukovar itself had also had a sizeable German population which was replaced by Serbs after 1945. Since Germans had made up about a third of Vojvodina's pre-war population, the change in ethnic composition was even more marked there. The German exodus together with a Serb influx altered the province's ethnic structure from an even balance between three communities to a Serb majority.

The move to the city, which had begun between the two wars but accelerated as Yugoslavia's communists strove to industrialise the economy, had a much greater long-term impact on the country's ethnic composition. While in 1945 most of Croatia's Serbs lived in geographically compact regions of the former military frontier, by 1991 the majority lived in Croatian cities like Zagreb, Karlovac and Zadar where they, or their parents, had found work. Some of Croatia's Serbs moved to Serbia itself in search of work, especially to Belgrade, where the population jumped from 200,000 to about 1.6 million in forty-five years, as did many Serbs from Bosnia-Hercegovina, Kosovo and Montenegro. In the same way, many Croats from Vojvodina chose to migrate to Croatian cities, while Croats from Hercegovina tended either to move to Croatia or increasingly to emigrate. Muslim Slavs remained in Bosnia-Hercegovina on the whole because there was no obvious destination for them elsewhere and with a higher birthrate than the republic's other peoples their proportion of the total population was steadily increasing.

The most obvious route to the city for Serbs from Bosnia-Hercegovina and Croatia was via the Communist Party apparatus and especially the police force, which they dominated not only in Croatia and Bosnia-Hercegovina but also in Serbia. The reason for this was that impoverished Serb peasants from the most backward regions of Bosnia-Hercegovina and Croatia had formed the backbone of Tito's army and could expect a privileged position in post-war Yugoslav society, but were not sufficiently educated to take on any function other than security. Nepotism was endemic in the police as in most areas of Yugoslav life and the 1945 intake of former partisans perpetuated itself by recruiting the next generation of officers from their home villages. While Yugoslavia's urban population tended to shun police careers in any case, the ethnic composition of the security apparatus was a perennial source of resentment among Croats, since up until 1990, even though they constituted only about 12 per cent of Croatia's total population, Serbs formed about 70 per cent of the police.

Nevertheless, the great divide within Yugoslav society was increasingly that between rural and urban communities, not that between peoples, and the disproportionate numbers of Bosnian and Croatian Serbs in the Serbian police was also resented in Belgrade. City-dwellers were more sophisticated and better educated than their rural counterparts, though even in rural areas illiteracy was steadily being eradicated. The urban population was ethnically-mixed and, since communist Yugoslavia was a secular society, intermarriage became for the first time easy and common. A generation was growing up which was more aware of its urban roots than its national origins, with the result that each major city had its own quite distinctive ambience.

The rise in living standards came, in part, from the growth of tourism. As a result of the new industry the country's economic power house shifted from the fertile agricultural plains of Slavonia and Vojvodina to the regions which attracted most foreign tourists, especially the Croatian coast as well as Slovenia and the Montenegrin coast. Remittances from workers living abroad also played a part in the country's economic growth, especially in the development of Croatia and Croat-populated regions of Hercegovina, since most so-called guest workers were originally from there. Many of the Croats, in particular those from Hercegovina, who emigrated in search of work, left Yugoslavia because they believed they had no prospects within the country on account of their ethnic origins. Yet, in the long-run, the regions they came from appeared more prosperous than neighbouring regions because the earning potential abroad was much greater.

In Yugoslavia, as in all communist countries, propaganda played a central role in society. From an early age Yugoslavs were indoctrinated, via their schooling and the media, with love for Tito, Yugoslavia and Titoism. Yugoslavs were also indoctrinated with love for one another. In school, children studied the histories and cultures of all Yugoslavia's peoples as well as their own. Croats learned of Emperor Dušan of Serbia while Serbs learned of King Tomislav of Croatia. Education was multicultural and aimed at bringing Yugoslavia's peoples together. From the day children started at school they began to learn of the National Liberation War and the contribution all Yugoslavia's peoples had made to the defeat of fascism. School trips took children on visits to neighbouring republics, and, traditionally, conscripts completed military service outside their home republic to get to know another part of the country. All peoples living in Yugoslavia, including the non-Slav Albanians and Hungarians, were taught that they could be their own nationality and Yugoslav at the same time and that they should be proud of both.

Until the very end Yugoslavia continued to produce a disproportionate number of individuals of exceptional talent and worldwide renown from all parts of the country in a wide range of fields. These included the film director Emir Kusturica, who shot two of the best European films of the 1980s, and Ivo Pogorelić, the classical pianist from Dubrovnik, who delighted audiences the world over. While Yugoslavia never attempted to be an eastern European Olympic gold medal factory, the country excelled in many sports. As the country disintegrated, Monika Seleš (a Hungarian from Vojvodina) was the queen of women's tennis, while Goran Ivanišević appeared about to take over the men's game in a similar way. Ironically, the country tended to be stronger in team sports than individual competition, and consistently produced outstanding sides in waterpolo, handball, soccer and especially basketball, where even after the country broke up Croatia won the silver medal at the 1992 Barcelona Olympics.

For so small a country Yugoslavia had an astonishing prominence in the world and Yugoslavs could be proud of their state and its achievements. While perhaps Yugoslavia's reputation, just like Tito's, was not entirely deserved, Yugoslavs could and did walk tall in the world. In Tito's later years Yugoslavia began to host a series of international sporting meetings. These included the 1976 European Soccer Championship, the 1979 Mediterranean Games and most memorably the 1984 Sarajevo Winter Olympics, whose venue was agreed while Tito was still alive. When the Slovene Boris Strel skied to a silver medal in the slalom the entire country rejoiced in his success in the same way that the entire country had mourned Tito's death. In 1980, a few months before Tito's death, a record was released written jointly by two Serbs, a Slovene and a Croat called 'Yugoslavia'. It was a song about the beauty of their common country which attempted to merge traditional styles of music from all over Yugoslavia. Nobody was forced to buy the record, yet it was a smash hit throughout the country and tourists who visited Yugoslavia in the 1980s undoubtedly heard it many times more than they might have wished.

The popular music scene was by eastern European standards remarkable. Rock bands such as Riblja Čorba from Belgrade, Bijelo Dugme from Sarajevo and Azra from Zagreb commanded enormous followings throughout the country. They all gave huge concerts, sold masses of records, earned vast amounts of money and were worshipped in every republic. As Yugoslavia's economy nosedived and living standards deteriorated, singers like Djordje Balašević, a Serb from Novi Sad whose career began when he composed a song for Tito's eightieth birthday, were able to voice the resentment of Yugoslavia's youth, who were growing up with little to look forward to. The music, the songs and the sentiments were Yugoslav and reflected the everyday frustrations and concerns of a new generation of city-dwellers throughout the country living in a consumer age but without the means to enjoy it.

Great winners in Tito's Yugoslavia were the country's smaller and more backward peoples, the Macedonians, Muslim Slavs, and to a lesser extent Hungarians and Albanians, who were shielded from the aggressive potential of Croat and, in particular, Serb nationalisms. The security provided by the Titoist system allowed Macedonians and Muslim Slavs to thrive culturally as never before and to evolve a modern and confident national identity. As a result, affection for Tito and Titoism survived longest, and nostalgia for that era is greatest, in Macedonia and Bosnia-Hercegovina. At the same time, the Titoist state bent over backwards to make sure the Serb minority in Croatia as well as the Croat minority in Vojvodina felt secure. Tito's

Yugoslavia was not some tyranny destined to collapse. Indeed, an ever increasing number of foreign tourists discovered that the country had much to recommend it and came back year after year.

From 1965 Yugoslav citizens were allowed to leave the country without any difficulty and began to travel abroad on holiday themselves. On account of Yugoslavia's wonderful geography and socialist ethics, a remarkable proportion of Yugoslavs were able to afford both skiing and beach holidays every year. To many in the West, especially those who visited the country each year, Yugoslavia was the acceptable face of communism. Its citizens appeared to have a reasonable standard of living with greater prospects and more money-making opportunities than anywhere else in eastern Europe. The potential seemed limitless, yet Yugoslavia's prosperity proved illusory.

5

TITO'S LEGACY

'The cushion of Western aid, provided to shore up Yugoslavia against Soviet influence, proved to be a disservice to Yugoslavia in the longer term because it deprived it of any incentive to reform in time.'—Christopher Cviić[1]

The Economy

The Achilles heel of all Europe's communist states was the economy. Wealthy states do not break up in civil war and prosperous regimes are not toppled by revolution. But Yugoslavia was neither wealthy nor prosperous. For an ideology which peddled visions of a better future, Marxism-Leninism was an economic catastrophe. Declining living standards, a lack of consumer goods and shortages of even the basic essentials had become the harsh reality of life in the 1980s throughout eastern Europe. Despite its independence, Yugoslavia was far from immune to the malaise afflicting the entire Eastern bloc, indeed, nowhere was the decay more evident. Tito, his cronies and successors had all failed to live up to their promises. Instead, they were bankrupt, living more and more in their distorted interpretation of the past, wedded to the empty rhetoric of Titoism and its twin pillars of Socialist Worker Self-Management and the Non-Aligned Movement.

Yugoslavia fossilised in the way that only revolutionary states, such as Tito's or that of Fidel Castro in Cuba, can do. As the revolution failed either to spread or to prosper, the early dynamism faded, the original revolutionaries burned out and their state stagnated in bureaucracy. As the economy crumbled around their ears, Yugoslavia's communists could only justify their monopoly of power by reference to their revolution. While the events of the Second World War had passed into the history books and collective subconsciousness of western Europe, the socialist revolution and anti-fascist struggle were

---

[1] Christopher Cviić is editor of *The World Today*, the monthly journal of the Royal Institute of International Affairs, and author of *Remaking the Balkans* (London, Pinter, 1991)

as fundamental to Yugoslavia's communists forty years after the end of the war as they had been in the 1940s. They remained their only source of legitimacy, with the result that the communists were locked in a time warp, trapped by their ideology and increasingly powerless to influence their own destiny.

By the late 1950s the Yugoslav economy was already coming unstuck. While the planned economy was reasonably effective at building the infrastructure for an industrial society or mobilising a country for war, it failed to adapt to changing patterns of consumption and the fickle consumer market. Attempts at reform in Yugoslavia during the 1950s and 1960s foundered as soon as the side-effects, such as unemployment, began to appear. Rather than press on with free market measures and risk worker unrest, Tito, who was never a reformer, preferred to maintain tight political control over the economy. The most ambitious reform package, begun in 1965 as a move towards what was called 'market socialism', was effectively abandoned soon after a series of student demonstrations in 1968. 'Market socialism' was replaced by a new buzz phrase 'consensus economics' and the economy limped on, unreformed, overmanned, and inefficient.

Socialist Worker Self-Management, the official Yugoslav economic theory, was always more socialist than worker self-managed since the politicians took the crucial decisions concerning investment and business priorities, not the workers. In effect, despite the rhetoric, Yugoslavia's economic system differed little from that of the rest of the Eastern bloc. The fundamental difference was political, not economic. On account of Yugoslavia's unique geopolitical position between East and West, the country could draw on lines of credit which were not open to other communist countries. Rather than reform, Tito chose to expand the number of students in higher education, to allow Yugoslavs to move abroad in search of work and, critically, to borrow. These were all short-term solutions which merely stored up problems for the future.

In the 1960s and early 1970s more than a million Yugoslavs moved abroad to live and work, principally in West Germany. Money they sent home to their families boosted the country's balance of payments, but began to decline in the wake of the First Oil Shock of 1973. As work in western Europe dried up, many were forced to return home and by the mid-1980s the number of Yugoslavs working temporarily abroad had halved. The hike in oil prices — oil more than quintupled in price between June and December 1973 — devastated Yugoslavia's balance of trade and exacerbated the inherent deficiencies in the economy. But instead of limiting domestic consumption and cutting living standards as the International Monetary Fund urged, Yugoslavia borrowed heavily from private Western banks. The country's foreign debt rocketed from under $3.5 billion in 1973 to more than $20.5 billion in 1981.

Had the mountain of debt which was amassed during the 1970s been invested wisely, Yugoslavia might have staved off the economic collapse of the 1980s. Predictably, it was not. In 1987 the then Prime Minister Branko Mikulić admitted to parliament that more than half Yugoslavia's borrowings had been used for consumption or invested in mistaken projects. Attempts to redistribute wealth within the federation — by which the wealthier units, Slovenia, Croatia, Vojvodina and Serbia contributed to and subsidised the economic development of Bosnia-Hercegovina, Montenegro, Macedonia and Kosovo — also failed. Instead of becoming narrower, the gap between rich and poor republics actually widened. *Per capita* income in Slovenia, the wealthiest republic, was about three times that of Kosovo, the poorest unit, in 1945 but six times as great by the 1980s. At the same time, Yugoslavia's universities began churning out graduates in the backward republics. While their level of education led to high expectations, these were expectations which could never be fulfilled in a shrinking jobs market. It was a long-term recipe for disaster.

The crunch came about the time of Tito's death, when the loans dried up and Yugoslavia had to begin repaying the national debt. It coincided with recession in western Europe stemming from the Second Oil Shock of 1979, while the debt burden was aggravated by high interest rates and an exceptionally strong dollar. Living standards began to slide as the government moved to cut imports and inflation took off. Between 1982 and 1989 the standard of living fell nearly 40 per cent and in December 1989 inflation peaked at more than 2,000 per cent. The final nail in the coffin of communist credibility came two years earlier when Agrokomerc, a Bosnian food processing company, disintegrated. It had been the twenty-ninth largest company in Yugoslavia and, though bankrupt for years, had survived through a series of 'political' loans. It went under with almost $900 million of unpaid promissory notes in a scandal implicating the Central Committee of Bosnia-Hercegovina's League of Communists.

The extravagant trappings of Tito's Yugoslavia disappeared as part of the 1980s austerity package. Far-flung consulates and embassies were shut and grants to the Third World dried up. Tito's yacht and private jets were put up for sale and many of his palaces were converted into hotels. However, the fundamental causes of Yugoslavia's malaise were not addressed. In Tito's absence, Yugoslavia's federal centre lacked sufficient authority to assert control over the economy of the whole country for the purpose of reforming it. The system could not reform itself, yet it was so bankrupt both materially and spiritually that it would not permit even the media to discuss the debt question.

1974 *constitution*

When Yugoslavia's federal government worked out the full extent of the country's indebtedness in 1982, the total surprised even many of the leading communists. For the figure included borrowings by all the federal units as well as the federation itself and reflected how decentralised the country had become. Of the total, only 35 per cent had been raised at the federal level. The remaining 65 per cent had been borrowed by the six republics and two autonomous provinces. Uncontrolled borrowing sprees at republican and provincial level, often unknown to the federal authorities, had become endemic. It was just one of many flaws in the arrangement Tito had bequeathed his country which were enshrined in the 1974 constitution.

Tito's fourth constitution, which was Yugoslavia's sixth and last, was drawn up to cater for life after the dictator's death. At the time, Tito was eighty-two and becoming aware that even he was mortal. Though the constitution finally made him President for Life, he had lost interest in the day-to-day affairs of state, which he was happy to delegate to his juniors, while still strutting the world stage he had grown to love. The 1974 constitution was an intricate series of checks and balances designed to prevent any individual from acquiring as much power as Tito himself had held and to prevent any of Yugoslavia's peoples from dominating the federation. It codified the arrangement which had evolved from the end of the liberal experiment of the 1960s and, in particular, out of attempts to emancipate the Albanians of Kosovo and the aftermath of the so-called Croatian Spring or *maspok*[2] of 1971.

During the first twenty years of communist rule Tito made little attempt to integrate Albanians into Yugoslav society. Order in Kosovo

[2] *Maspok* is short for *masovni pokret* meaning 'mass movement'.

was left to the security apparatus and the secret police, which were dominated by Serbs. However, with the fall of Alexander Ranković, Tito's hardline police chief, in 1966, policy towards Kosovo and Yugoslavia's Albanians changed as part of a series of measures to liberalise the regime. As repression eased Albanians were finally able to manifest their discontent and in 1968 resentment at poor living conditions exploded into street demonstrations and calls for Kosovo to be granted republican status. Instead of a return to repression, Tito decided to emancipate the Albanians and to try to win them over to Yugoslavia and Titoism.

Yugoslavia's Hungarians had already been won over in the 1950s. This task had been straight-forward since traditionally relations between the many nationalities of Vojvodina, home to most of Yugoslavia's Hungarians, were good. The Hungarians were content with their own schools and media as well as the possibility to progress within Yugoslav society. The Albanian case was more complex, however, because relations between Serbs and Albanians in Kosovo were antagonistic. Given their grim experience of life within the south Slav state since 1912, Albanians were wary of any directive emanating from Belgrade. While Tito's Yugoslavia had not encouraged Albanians to leave, as the first Yugoslavia had, Albanians were, nevertheless, systematically brutalised and deprived of rights which Yugoslavia's other peoples took for granted. Before 1966, for example, the only education that Albanians were entitled to in their mother tongue was primary schooling, while in 1956, in an especially brutal exercise searching for weapons, the Yugoslav security forces killed about 100 Albanians and manhandled some 30,000.

Reversing more than half a century of institutionalised discrimination was an exceptionally ambitious undertaking which only someone of Tito's stature could consider. In his advancing years Tito may have fallen victim to his own propaganda for one factor motivating him was undoubtedly his desire to keep all Yugoslavia's peoples happy. Police rule in Kosovo was a stain on Yugoslavia's record and ran counter to the benevolent image Tito liked to project both at home and abroad. Whatever his motives, Tito attempted to win over Kosovo's Albanians through a combination of increased autonomy, cultural freedoms and an injection of much-needed economic aid.

Kosovo's status was raised to that of autonomous province alongside Vojvodina, but not republic. To make Kosovo a republic was not an option because it was unacceptable to both Serb and Macedonian opinion. Instead, both Kosovo and Vojvodina acquired almost all the trappings including the autonomy, though not the title, of a republic. Albanian became an official language in addition to Serbo-Croat, and, in practice, given the relative size of the Albanian population, it became Kosovo's main language. Priština, the provincial capital, acquired its own university as well as an Albanalogical Institute and, as Albania opened up in the 1970s, cultural exchanges began between the two countries.

Federal funds began to flow into Kosovo to finance a crash programme of economic expansion and Albanians were encouraged to join the League of Communists, the state administration and even the police force. Between 1971 and 1975, 70 per cent of Kosovo's budget and investments were paid for out of federal sources. Kosovo's allocation of the Fund for the Development of Underdeveloped Regions, set up to aid Bosnia-Hercegovina, Macedonia and Montenegro as well as Kosovo, rose from 28.8 per cent between 1961 and 1965 to 37 per cent between 1976 and 1980. At the same time, the proportion of Albanians in Kosovo's League of Communists, the provincial administration and the security apparatus was steadily rising as a result of a policy of positive discrimination.

In Croatia, Tito intervened to preempt what he considered a potentially dangerous upsurge in nationalism and purge that republic's League of Communists in 1971. The purge finally ended Yugoslavia's experiment with economic liberalism as Tito took the opportunity to move against the meritocrats who had risen to power during the 1960s throughout the federation. Leading communists in Slovenia and Serbia including Stane Kavčič, the President of Slovenia, and Marko Nikezić, the President of Serbia, were also purged and replaced by a generation of mediocrities whose credentials for government were fidelity to Tito and Titoism. At the same time, Tito decided to give way to many of the devolutionary demands of the Croatian communists whom he had just purged.

The purged Croatian communists had embarked on the path of economic reform with a similar agenda to their counterparts in Slovenia and Serbia, aiming to devolve decision-making away from the federal centre in the interests of economic efficiency. But as the balance of power within the country shifted towards the republics and as Tito reined in his security forces, it also became possible for opposition to manifest itself. In the liberal climate of the 1960s frustrated nationalists were able to vent their fury for the first time since Tito had come to power. Predictably, it was in Croatia, with its separatist traditions and inherent suspicion of Yugoslavism, where a nationalist alternative first appeared.

The upsurge of Croat nationalism in the late 1960s and early 1970s began as a cultural movement. It was led by many of the republic's most distinguished intellectuals who were motivated by the perennial fear among Croats that they risked losing their separate national identity within a unitary Yugoslav state. This worry was compounded, at the time, by a massive exodus of Croats from Yugoslavia as soon as Yugoslav citizens were permitted to leave the country. Both in percentage and in absolute terms, Croats—some emigrating for good others moving abroad temporarily to find work—far outnumbered Yugoslavia's other peoples in the migration. In 1967, 140 intellectuals, including the seventy-five-year-old Miroslav Krleža, put their names to a *Language Declaration* demanding that Croat be officially recognised as a separate language from Serb.

Instead of stamping out the early and seemingly innocuous manifestations of Croat nationalism as Tito would have expected, Croatia's ruling triumvirate, Savka Dabčević-Kučar, Nikola Tripalo and Pero Pirker, attempted to harness it to their own cause. At the federal level Yugoslavia was divided between economic reformers in the wealthier republics and economic conservatives in the more backward regions, and the result was deadlock. Croatia's leaders were prepared to use the threat of the nationalist card to back up the demands of their economic programme. However, their gamble failed as the national movement rapidly gained a momentum of its own, feeding off the rise in unemployment which accompanied and resulted from the earlier economic reforms of the 1960s.

As the movement became more militant, it also began to take on an anti-Serb character. Riots at football matches, the destruction of signs in Cyrillic and inflammatory articles in the Croatian press were making Croatia's Serb population nervous, especially since the Croatian leadership appeared reluctant to clamp down on the nationalist upsurge. When student leaders Dražen Budiša and Ante Paradžik called a student strike over Croatia's right to retain the foreign currency generated within the republic, Tito decided to intervene. On 1 December 1971 he met with Croatia's leaders at his Karadjordjevo retreat in Vojvodina and persuaded them to resign. The Croatian Spring petered out in a series of arrests, the banning of certain nationalist publications and a thorough purge of Croatian society. A group of *émigré* Croat Ustašas, who had infiltrated the country in the hope of organising an insurrection, failed to attract any support and was rounded up and liquidated in Hercegovina.

While Tito purged Croatia's League of Communists as well as reformers and technocrats throughout the country, he also attempted to defuse the nationalists' appeal by devolving yet more authority from the federal to the republican level. The eventual outcome of these reforms was the 1974 constitution. With 405 clauses it was the world's longest constitution, and, probably on account of its absurd length, was virtually untranslatable and largely nonsensical.

The devolution process which began in the early 1950s following the break with Stalin had by the 1970s turned Yugoslavia into a federa-tion with some of the trappings of a confederation. According to the constitution, all Yugoslavia's republics were sovereign and indepen-dent. Foreign affairs, defence and essential economic matters remained the prerogative of the federal centre, but still required a consensus among the federal units. Otherwise the republics and provinces were able to pursue their own, often conflicting, policies. The unifying bonds which tied the country together were Tito himself, the armed forces, which Tito had created and still dominated, and the LCY, which Tito had just purged. At a time when he was already in his eighties and could not expect to live much longer, he had made himself more indispensable to Yugoslavia than he had ever been before.

Federal institutions, from the Presidency and National Bank to cultural and sporting bodies, contained representatives from all federal units. Offices were strictly rotational so that every republic and autonomous province had equal access to positions of power. While the system was designed to be manifestly fair, it exacerbated the post-Tito malaise. Federal Presidents and office-holders in general had neither the time nor the authority to attempt to iron out the failings of the Titoist system to improve it. At the same time, republican leaderships were wary of moves to expand the prerogative of the federal centre at their expense and were prepared to use their represen-tatives in the federal institutions to maintain the status quo.

Devolution had turned the LCY from a highly centralised body into little more than a talking shop for the eight republican and provincial Leagues of Communists. While all eight Leagues were committed to Tito, they were also chronically short of talent in the aftermath of his thorough-going purge of meritocrats and reformers. Personal loyalty to Tito and ideological orthodoxy had replaced ability as the key to self-advancement within communist ranks. In the absence of liberal thinkers, each unit began to pursue its own development strategy—with predictable results.

During the liberal experiment the more successful Yugoslav enterprises had begun to expand out of their home republics across the entire country. This was especially the case in Slovenia, the most economically advanced republic. Slovene companies and products made major inroads into the markets of the rest of the country during the 1960s to such an extent that in Vojvodina local communists began to complain of Slovene economic domination. But as the liberal experiment came to an end, local communists were able to reassert control over their own republican and provincial economies. Instead of a single economy, Yugoslavia was fragmenting into eight mini-states. Worse still, at a time when the European Community appeared to be coming together and the many European economies were converging, Yugoslavia's mini-economies were actually fragmenting.

All republics and provinces were guilty of pursuing their own 'national', rather than Yugoslav, economic goals, often at the expense of the rest of the federation. Double capacity and even protectionism between republics were features of Yugoslavia's economic landscape. Each federal unit appeared to require its own strategic industries, oil refineries, steel works and, for those republics with a coast, commercial harbours. Both Slovenia and Montenegro, for example, developed their own ports at Koper and Bar, respectively, even though the port of Rijeka in Croatia already existed and could easily handle all Yugoslavia's sea trade. Duplication and the often high costs of these prestige projects were apparently prices worth paying for republican self-sufficiency.

After Tito's death, Yugoslavia's only remaining institution which was both unitary and centralist was the armed forces. During his lifetime the Yugoslav People's Army had been Tito's personal toy which he chose to indulge in every way possible. Officers were among the most privileged members of Yugoslav society and the defence budget was sacred. Perhaps it is ironic, given today's huge UN operations in the former Yugoslavia, that in an earlier era Tito delighted in sending Yugoslav troops overseas as peace-keepers. For Tito, the Commander-in-Chief, viewed Yugoslavia's military as a source of great national pride. He believed it had distinguished itself in the Second World War and its might and prestige were sufficient to deter Soviet aggression. In turn, the JNA was fiercely loyal to

Tito and, in common with the Soviet military, a bastion of conservative communism.

Tito's armed forces were not excessively Serb-dominated even though Serbs and Montenegrins formed a far greater proportion of the officer corps than of the Yugoslav population in general. The JNA was forged during the Second World War and, as a result, most officers came from the main theatres of the war, from Bosnia-Hercegovina, Croatia and Montenegro. In the immediate aftermath of war, Croats were well represented in the officer corps and it was not until the 1960s that the number of officers from Serbia outnumbered those from Croatia, though obviously many of the officers from Croatia were themselves Serbs. Serbs and Montenegrins were attracted to the military partly for traditional reasons and partly because they tended to come from poorer regions with few alternative careers open to them. Slovenes and Croats aspired to professional careers or careers in industry and tourism rather than in the military. Meanwhile, since the language of the armed forces was Serbo-Croat, Slovenes, Hungarians, Macedonians and especially Albanians often felt ill at ease serving in the military. Whatever the reasons, by the late 1980s Serbs dominated the infantry, though not the air force or the navy.

The JNA was at the same time Yugoslavia's armed forces and the military wing of the LCY with its own seat on Yugoslavia's collective Presidency. Its role was not only to defend Yugoslavia from external attack but also to protect and maintain the country's social and political order from internal disintegration. In the 1980s, as the civilian government failed to resolve the country's crisis, the military began to play a greater political role and generals even dared to criticise politicians. It was a state within a state which was determined to preserve its own privileged position in society as much as anything else.

By the end of the 1980s, Yugoslavia was split into five military districts for defensive purposes. The division corresponded only very roughly to republican borders but, since 1969, following the Soviet invasion of Czechoslovakia a year earlier, each republic had its own territorial defence force. Yugoslavia's military planners had evolved a strategy called General People's Defence based on the concept of the nation in arms. The JNA was a small professional fighting force but it could also call on a huge reservoir of recruits who had all received a basic military training during national service. The republics had to pay for and equip their territorial defence forces, which were organised and commanded by retired generals. Theoretically, in the event of war every citizen knew where he or she was supposed to go and, in the case of the territorial defence forces, where to collect weapons.

Yugoslavia was one of the world's top ten arms manufacturers and largely self-sufficient in weaponry. Arms sales, which were principally directed towards non-aligned countries and included unsavoury destinations such as Iraq and Ethiopia, made a substantial contribution to the country's balance of trade. For historical reasons the industry was concentrated in Serbia and Bosnia-Hercegovina. Serbia had developed a large military with its own arms industry during the 19th century and many key defence installations were shifted to Bosnia-Hercegovina in 1948, when Yugoslavia feared Soviet invasion, on account of the republic's inhospitable terrain. Since the Habsburgs had concentrated their arms industry in Bohemia and this was inherited by Czechoslovakia when the Empire disintegrated, neither Slovenia nor Croatia had an independent arms-manufacturing capacity. Like most eastern European armies the JNA refused to discard any of its arms and ammunition even when obsolete. It had stockpiled a massive arsenal stored throughout the country with which it hoped to be able to fight almost indefinitely.

The Serb question

In the months leading up to and immediately after Tito's death the JNA was on a state of alert in case the Warsaw Pact decided to invade the country at this critical juncture. In reality, Yugoslavia's new leaders exaggerated the Soviet threat in an effort to bring the country together. The Soviet Union had shelved its invasion plans for Yugoslavia nearly 30 years earlier when Stalin died. Even had Leonid Brezhnev, the Soviet leader who was among the foreign dignitaries attending Tito's funeral, wished to invade Yugoslavia, he could hardly have spared the manpower since Soviet forces had just become embroiled in Afghanistan. The threat to Yugoslavia's security came in the absence of external danger. For the real threat came not from without, but from within.

In the first Yugoslavia, Serbs had been privileged and Croats had formed the principal opposition to the state. Other peoples and other parts of the country had also resented the new state and may have had greater grievances than the Croats, but had been too down-trodden to be able to express their opposition. In the second Yugoslavia, Tito set out to please everybody and, in the process, risked satisfying nobody. No nation was privileged and Serb and Croat nationalists were equally frustrated. After Tito's death the most vociferous opposition to the Yugoslavia he had built came from Serbs.

Contrary to nationalist propaganda, Serb opposition to Tito's state was not the result of any unique oppression Serbs had to endure in Yugoslavia; indeed, if anything it may have been the comparative lack of oppression which allowed them to manifest their opposition to the state. For where oppression is genuine and deep, people are too downtrodden to express their resentment. Though barometers of oppression are at best imprecise, in Yugoslavia comparative figures for the proportion of political prisoners from a particular nationality, for example, or the numbers of a particular nationality which had emigrated, may be vaguely indicative of relative levels of national persecution. According to these criteria, Albanians and Croats were easily the most persecuted peoples in Yugoslavia, certainly not Serbs. Nevertheless, all nationalists from the former Yugoslavia continue to insist that their nation was the most oppressed, as if this justifies their present claims to anything and everything.

As Yugoslavia's six republics and two autonomous provinces evolved into mini-states, great differences became apparent between the constituent federal units. Tito's purge cut deepest in Croatia with the result that, despite its relative wealth, Croatia became economically and politically one of the most conservative parts of the country and was dubbed the 'silent republic'. Nothing controversial seemed to take place there: the press was tightly controlled, potential dissent was stamped out immediately and communist functionaries from Croatia were perhaps the most colourless in all Yugoslavia. However, resentment was brewing under the surface. By purging Croatia's League of Communists to eradicate Croat nationalism, Tito had promoted a large number of Croatia's Serbs to positions of authority, giving them a disproportionate share of political power within Croatia to the resentment of most Croats.

The federation's poorer units—Bosnia-Hercegovina, Macedonia, Montenegro and Kosovo—also tended towards political and economic conservatism, though for different reasons. Party bosses could rely on a continuous flow of funds from Yugoslavia's wealthier units, but these funds were rarely invested wisely. Instead, they served to build mini-empires and maintain lines of patronage. In these republics the media tended to be dull and any expression of opposition, even the mildest criticism of Tito, was viciously put down.

The beacons of liberalism in Yugoslavia were Slovenia and Serbia, and to a lesser extent Vojvodina, where Tito's purge had not been so keenly felt. In both Slovenia and Serbia, the local leaderships were prepared to tolerate a much broader range of opinions than anywhere else in the federation, and especially in Slovenia a private sector was allowed to thrive within prescribed limits. The media in both Slovenia and Serbia were unparalleled in quality in the communist world and prepared to publish a wide range of views. While the language barrier limited the reach of the Slovene media to Slovenes, the Serbian daily *Politika* and its sister title the weekly *NIN* were read widely throughout Yugoslavia and were often the reason that Croats and even Slovenes learned Cyrillic. Given the comparative openness of both Slovene and Serbian society in the late 1970s and early 1980s, it was hardly surprising that opposition to Titoism first emerged in these two republics.

Even in Slovenia and Serbia potential opponents of the regime had to remain cautious and to couch their criticisms of society in reformist and socialist terms, while maintaining at all times complete deference to Tito. Opposition tended to form around specific issues, especially questions of human rights and the economy, and reformers in each republic attempted to work together whenever possible with like-minded colleagues elsewhere in the federation, to improve Yugoslav society in the interests of all Yugoslavs. However, among the many critics of the Tito experiment who had begun to acquire a following in Serbia was one group whose platform was incompatible with that of non-Serb reformers, namely the Serb nationalists.

As in Croatia in the late 1960s and early 1970s, the upsurge in Serb nationalism began as a movement of intellectuals. But, in contrast to the Croatian Spring, there was no Tito to step in to prevent the movement escalating out of control. The decisive event which alienated Serb nationalists from Tito's Yugoslavia was his decision to emancipate Kosovo's Albanians. Before then they had been reasonably satisfied if not totally enamoured with communist Yugoslavia. However, as far as Serb nationalists were concerned, Kosovo was sacred land and Tito could not be forgiven for allowing an alien culture to take root and blossom there.

The deadly Greater Serbian agenda for the late 20th century grew out of the thinking and writing of Dobrica Ćosić, one of Serbia's most distinguished novelists. Ćosić was renowned as a writer of popular, historical epics, mostly set during wars and overflowing with

references to Serb mythology. He had been a partisan during the
Second World War and a friend of Tito's for more than twenty years,
yet he could not come to terms with Albanian emancipation and was
purged from the LCY for nationalism in 1968. In his frustration after
his fall from grace Ćosić dreamed up a complex and paradoxical theory
of Serb national persecution under communism which over two
decades evolved into the Greater Serbian programme.[3] Increasingly,
Ćosić's ideas permeated the Serbian Association of Writers and fuelled
an acrimonious dialogue between Serb and Slovene intellectuals within
the Yugoslav Association of Writers. As early as 1986, five years
before Yugoslavia's shooting war began, this Association became the
first all-Yugoslav institution to break up, as its non-Serb members
feared that the popularity of Ćosić's ideas heralded a return to Serb
hegemony in Yugoslavia.

According to the 1981 census, carried out a year after Tito's death,
Serbs made up about 36 per cent of Yugoslavia's population. Of these,
close to 2 million lived outside the republic of Serbia while another
1.3 million lived in Serbia's autonomous provinces, in addition to the
4.9 million Serbs of inner Serbia. Given the choice, most Serbs would
probably have opted to live within a centralised state, just as most non-
Serbs would have chosen a federation. Nevertheless, the form of
federalism which Tito had created in 1945 at first suited Serbs because,
in essence, the state remained centralist. Moreover, since, at the time,
Serbs dominated both Vojvodina and Kosovo and wielded considerable
power in Bosnia-Hercegovina and Croatia as well as in Serbia and
Montenegro, the federal arrangement actually strengthened the Serb
hand within the country. However, the Yugoslavia of the 1970s and
1980s was a very different country from that of 1945. Yugoslavia had
evolved into a genuine federation of eight units and had even acquired
some of the trappings of a confederation. Both devolution and, in
particular, the emancipation of Yugoslavia's non-Slav populations went
against the grain of the previous 150 years of Serbian state tradition.

During the 19th century the *raison d'être* of the Serbian state had
been to unite all Serbs living in the Balkans. In pursuing this aim Serbia
had been remarkably successful. By 1918, through wars and great
power alliances, the goal of national unity had been achieved, though
Serb unity had come largely at the expense of many of the other

---

[3] In 1983 Ćosić's reinterpretation of Yugoslav national policy since 1968 was
published in the book *Stvarno i moguće* (Reality and Possibility).

peoples living in the Kingdom of Serbs, Croats and Slovenes. Royal Yugoslavia satisfied Serb nationalists in a way that Tito's Yugoslavia, which aimed to keep all Yugoslavia's citizens happy, never could. The second Yugoslavia was no Serb tyranny. Indeed, that was precisely what Serb nationalists found most objectionable about Tito's state. For, to twisted nationalist minds, Tito had robbed Serbs of their Yugoslav Empire and now devolution appeared to be threatening their very national existence.

The Serb case against Tito's Yugoslavia was set out in a now notorious Memorandum drafted in 1985 by a working group of the Serbian Academy of Arts and Sciences. The document, which was a reinterpretation of Yugoslavia's recent past viewed through a Serb nationalist prism, slated Tito's Yugoslavia for being inherently and systematically anti-Serb. The Memorandum would have been derided had it not been prepared by a highly respected body and supported by many of the most celebrated intellectuals in Serbia, including such renowned dissidents as Mihailo Marković and Ljubomir Tadić as well as Dobrica Ćosić.

Essentially, the Memorandum was an elaborate, if crude, conspiracy theory. It alleged that Tito's communists had imposed an alien, that is federal, model of Yugoslavia onto a reluctant Serb nation and had since then systematically discriminated against Serbs. These discriminatory policies dated back to the 1930s and stemmed from an alleged anti-Serb bias in the Comintern, based on the mistaken conviction that Serbs had oppressed other nations in the first Yugoslavia. By 1941 this anti-Serb bias had supposedly become engrained in the CPY which had accordingly pursued a policy of 'strong Yugoslavia, weak Serbia'. According to the authors of the Memorandum, Croats, in the person of Josip Broz Tito, and Slovenes, in the person of Edvard Kardelj, had deliberately constructed federal Yugoslavia in such a way as to exploit Serbia economically. Moreover, Tito had ensured that Serbs would remain weak and exploited by dividing them between several federal units and, in particular, by carving the autonomous provinces of Vojvodina and Kosovo out of Serbia in the 1974 constitution. Serbs faced discrimination throughout Yugoslavia, the Memorandum alleged, while in Kosovo they were being subjected to 'genocide' at the hands of irredentist and separatist Albanians!

Despite the obvious absurdity of most of the Memorandum's allegations, it was not an isolated analysis of Yugoslavia's predicament and recent past. It was but the most influential of several blatantly propagandist and nationalist polemics published in Serbia in the mid-1980s. Fringe groups with extreme and often racist views exist in all societies but thankfully rarely have any chance of winning power. Had the opinions expressed in the Memorandum remained those of a tiny faction of largely frustrated, though celebrated, intellectuals, they would have done nobody any harm. But in the hands of an unscrupulous politician they posed a serious threat to the Yugoslav federation, since the Memorandum's xenophobia and simplistic analysis struck a chord among many Serbs at a time of declining living standards and severely diminished expectations.

In Tito's absence it was up to the Serbian leadership to take on the nationalists in their own republic, but the leadership was split. When the contents of the Memorandum were leaked in 1986 both Ivan Stambolić, President of Serbia, and Dragiša Pavlović, head of the Belgrade League of Communists, denounced it in public. However, although the Central Committee of the Serbian League of Communists also formally condemned the document, this fact was suppressed at the insistence of its President, Slobodan Milošević.

6

DISINTEGRATION

'If a nation adopts the right to be angry, how can it deny the same right to another? A confrontation of two nations leads to a war.' — Dragiša Pavlović[1]

Slobodan Milošević

When Tito died in 1980 Slobodan Milošević was a thirty-eight-year-old Party *apparatchik* whose political career was only just beginning. At the time, few could have predicted the monumental impact he was going to have on Yugoslavia, since, both before and after he came to power, Milošević was careful to keep as low a profile as possible. He only granted media interviews when absolutely necessary and always stuck to a carefully rehearsed script. Considering the worldwide notoriety he has since acquired, relatively little is known about the man himself. Nevertheless, Serbian analysts who have followed Milošević's career closely insist he was not a nationalist, but that he was ruthlessly ambitious and prepared to use and abuse anybody and any ideology to fuel that ambition. His driving force was an overwhelming lust for power, not visions of a Greater Serbia, and for that reason he was far more dangerous than a nationalist.

The key to Milošević's early career was his close friendship with Ivan Stambolić, the rising star of Serbian politics who became Prime Minister the year Tito died. Milošević had got to know Stambolić, who was five years his senior, while at university and had used this friendship and Stambolić's connections[2] to rise within the Party. For twenty years, wherever Stambolić went Milošević followed, first in business and then in politics. During the 1970s Milošević succeeded Stambolić twice in key business positions, first as head of Serbia's gas conglomerate Tehnogas and then as a director of Beobanka, one of

---

[1] Dragiša Pavlović was President of the League of Communists of Belgrade between 1986 and 1987 and Slobodan Milošević's chief adversary within the Serbian League of Communists. In 1988 he published the book *Olako obećana brzina*, which remains probably the best critique of Milošević's brand of communist nationalism.

[2] Ivan Stambolić was the nephew of Petar Stambolić, a former partisan and one of the most powerful communists in Serbia.

Yugoslavia's largest banks, with which he spent two years in the United States, before following him into politics. In 1984 Milošević succeeded Stambolić as head of the Belgrade League of Communists, when Stambolić was promoted to head the League of Communists of Serbia; and when Stambolić became President of Serbia in 1986, Milošević again moved into his mentor's old job. High political office was a long way from his humble origins in provincial Serbia.

Milošević was born in the town of Požarevac, about 40 miles south east of Belgrade, on 20 August 1941, soon after the Germans occupied Serbia in the Second World War. His father, Svetozar, was a seminary-trained teacher of religion from Montenegro and through him the young Slobodan must have acquired a basic grounding in Serb mythology. His mother, Stanislava, was a primary school teacher and communist activist. His parents quarrelled incessantly over ideology and split up soon after the war. Both mother and father (as well as one of Milošević's uncles, an army officer) committed suicide, Svetozar in 1962 and Stanislava in 1974.

At secondary school in Požarevac Milošević met Mirjana Marković, his wife-to-be and lifelong confidante, and they married while both were students at Belgrade University, Slobodan of law and Mirjana of sociology. Mirjana was as well connected in communist circles as Stambolić. Her mother had been secretary of the Belgrade Communist Party at the beginning of the Second World War but was executed in 1942 when Mirjana was only a year old. Since she had been born out of wedlock, Mirjana was brought up by her aunt, who had been Tito's personal secretary and reputedly one of his many mistresses. When she was fifteen, Mirjana's father, Draža Marković, another of Serbia's leading communists, finally recognised her as his daughter. Mirjana became a communist hardliner and went on to teach Marxism at Belgrade University, where, from within its own League of Communists, she helped to weed out liberals and reimpose a strict ideological orthodoxy on the faculty.

By nature Milošević was a bureaucrat, not a warlord. He was the product of Yugoslav socialism, a communist careerist through and through who was content to live in a reasonably modest Belgrade flat and drive a Yugoslav-manufactured Zastava instead of enjoying the luxury villas and foreign cars which many of his colleagues opted for. His stints at Tehnogas and Beobanka as well as his early forays into politics were unexceptional and offered few pointers to his later rise. However, during these years he came to understand the power of the communist state apparatus as well as the potential power of Serb nationalism, and worked to harness both to his own cause.

The parallels between Milošević's rise and the way in which Stalin seized power in the Soviet Union in the 1920s were immediately commented upon by contemporaries. Stalin had also been a rather unexceptional Party functionary who rose to a position of absolute power by being the inside man within the communist apparatus and using the system for his own ends. All communist societies were hierarchical and thus prone to produce tyrants from within the system. The Communist Party, or in Yugoslavia's case the League of Communists, existed alongside the regular organs of government to keep them in line, since he who appointed the piper, or rather the office-holders, also played the tune. While Yugoslavia, and Serbia in particular, were reasonably relaxed societies by communist standards, the potential for a dictatorship to assert itself was always present. Indeed, as a young *apparatchik* Milošević had witnessed this twice at first hand; in 1966 when Tito purged the conservatives and again in 1972 when he purged the liberals.

When Stambolić became President of Serbia in 1986 he viewed the new post as a promotion and was happy to see his friend Milošević replace him as President of the republican League of Communists. Another Stambolić *protégé*, Dragiša Pavlović, succeeded Milošević as head of the Belgrade League of Communists and Stambolić was confident his position was unassailable. Yet it was now Milošević who was the most powerful politician in Serbia, not Stambolić, since it was Milošević who controlled patronage in the League of Communists and hence it was Milošević who made new appointments. From an identical power base to that of Stalin, Milošević worked to stamp his authority over Serbian society, moving *apparatchiks*, whose only qualifications were personal loyalty, into key posts and edging out liberals, until he was strong enough to move against his mentor. Meanwhile, Stambolić trusted him implicitly and even helped him on the way, despatching him as his personal envoy to Kosovo to try to resolve the escalating conflict between Serbs and Albanians.

Kosovo

It was in Kosovo, Yugoslavia's poorest region and the part of the country which virtually nobody, not even other Yugoslavs, visited, that Tito's state came unstuck. Conditions in Kosovo went unreported in the West, while in Slovenia and Croatia the province was simply viewed as an unavoidable drain on the budget and the worst possible posting for conscripts during national service. Yet it was over policy towards Kosovo, or rather the change in that policy during the 1960s, that Serb nationalists fell out with Tito, and this was the major reason they came to reject his vision of Yugoslavia. And it was a result of the rift which developed over Kosovo that Serb nationalists began to evolve a new set of long-term political goals.

Tito's change of policy towards Kosovo in the mid-1960s had radically altered relations between the province's Albanians and the hitherto privileged Serbs. In certain ways, the situation resembled that in Zimbabwe immediately after independence, for in 1980 whites formed about the same percentage of Zimbabwe's total population as Serbs did in Kosovo. While Zimbabwean whites remained vastly more affluent than blacks, and the Kosovan Serbs, though generally poorer than Yugoslavs outside Kosovo, were still economically better off than their Albanian neighbours, both peoples had lost the privileges associated with political domination. In addition, because of population explosions among Zimbabwe's blacks and Kosovo's Albanians, the demographic balance was shifting against the formerly privileged minorities. As a result, both Zimbabwe's whites and Kosovo's Serbs were worried about their future under majority rule and highly critical (often with reason) of the new administrations. There was, however, one fundamental difference between the two situations. For, although many whites did not wish to come to terms with black rule in Zimbabwe, they had no way of turning the clock back to the colonial era. In Kosovo, by contrast, Serbs knew that as soon as Tito had died, majority rule was potentially reversible. Indeed, in the minds of Serb nationalists there was a moral imperative to reverse it.

The Serb obsession with Kosovo may never cease to perplex foreigners. Serbs have not formed the majority there since the end of the 17th century and few Serbs, apart from those who actually live in the province, have ever visited it. Nevertheless, as far as many Serbs, not all of them extreme nationalists, are concerned, Kosovo is sacred land which is destined to remain Serbian forever. This emotional attachment to Kosovo, the so-called 'cradle of the Serb nation', can be explained only as part of a collective sense of disappointment among Serbs at what might have been, had the medieval Serbian Empire not been destroyed by the Turkish assault on Europe. It is rooted within the Serbian Orthodox Church, which cultivated and preserved national consciousness under Ottoman rule, and in stories from Serb folklore which have been passed from generation to generation through the ages.

Kosovo was both the scene of the decisive battle between the Serbian Army and advancing Turks in 1389 and the spiritual home of the Serbian Orthodox Church. The Serbian Orthodox Patriarchate was founded there in the town of Peć in 1346 and Peć remained the centre of the Church for the first three centuries of Ottoman rule. Today, the oldest and most celebrated Serbian Orthodox monasteries still stand across Kosovo as a powerful historical reminder of this bygone age. Legends of the infamous battle of Kosovo pervade Serb folklore and have inspired generations of artists. In fact, all the Balkans' Christian peoples, including the Albanians, probably fought against the Turks at Kosovo, though the event is commemorated only among Serbs because it signified the end of their Empire and the beginning of Ottoman rule. Though a defeat, tales of the heroic bravery and self-sacrifice of Serb warriors at the battle served as a source of comfort and inspiration during centuries of alien government.

Serb claims to Kosovo were, and still are, irreconcilable with the fact that Albanians make up the majority of the province's population, hence the brutality of Yugoslav rule in Kosovo between the two world wars and even right up until the 1960s. When Tito decided to emancipate Kosovo's Albanians, the new policy inevitably came at the expense of the province's Serbs and Serb national dreams. As a result, although he strove to be impartial in his dealings with the two peoples, and thus refused to turn Kosovo into a republic as Albanians desired, Tito failed to reconcile Serbs to the new order. Perhaps, in retrospect, the undertaking may simply have been too ambitious.

Whether in Yugoslavia, which is home to 40 per cent of Europe's Albanians, or in Albania proper, Albanians were, and still are, one of Europe's most backward peoples. Most are Muslim, and on account of a higher birthrate among Muslim Albanians their proportion of the total population has been increasing throughout the 20th century. There is also, however, a significant Catholic minority, including the world's most famous Albanian, Mother Teresa of Calcutta, who was born in a village near Skopje in Macedonia when it was still part of the Ottoman Empire. Despite converting to Islam, Albanians remained backward even by Ottoman standards and, until the Empire finally disintegrated, lacked even the most basic schooling in their own language. Ottoman rule, or rather misrule, eventually spawned an Albanian national movement, which organised itself into the League for the Defence of the Rights of the Albanian Nation in the town of Prizren, Kosovo, in 1878. While Albanian nationalists aimed to unite all Albanians in one country, the Albanian state which became independent in 1912 was militarily weak and failed retain its hold on Kosovo and predominantly Albanian regions of Macedonia, which were annexed by Serbia.

Although only a little less than a third of Kosovo's Serbs actually moved into the province in the 20th century to settle land seized from Albanians, relations between Serbs and Albanians in Yugoslavia were essentially colonial. Two cultures existed side by side in Kosovo, but the Yugoslav state apparatus was only concerned with the interests of the Serb population. The ideal solution as far as many Serbs were concerned was expulsion to Turkey and Albanians were certainly encouraged to emigrate. Ironically, many who did leave for Turkey themselves became a privileged settler class in Turkish Kurdistan.

With the switch to majority rule in the 1960s, Albanians began to rise in Yugoslav society and were able for the first time to take pride in their national origins. While still socially backward in comparison with Yugoslavia's other peoples, they made great cultural gains. Primary schooling became universal and Albanian secondary schools opened up throughout the province offering a thoroughly Albanian curriculum with access to books and, occasionally, teachers from Albania proper. Economically, however, the province was not better off even though Albanians were now guiding its destiny, since the growth in population outstripped any increase in GDP. As was frequently the case in recently independent former colonies, power in Kosovo was concentrated in the hands of a tiny oligarchy which was good at affirming Albanian national identity, but which lacked the experience and expertise to manage an economy. The stream of aid which the federal authorities ploughed into the province was poorly invested and largely frittered away on prestige projects or wasted on privileged lifestyles for the new élite.

Although the proportion of Albanians in Kosovo's administration never reached the actual percentage of Albanians in the wider population, the tables had been turned on the province's Serbs. Deprived of their former privileges and concerned by sharp increases in the Albanian population, Kosovo's Serbs were dissatisfied and some began to move out of the province. Between 1961 and 1981 the number of Serbs living in Kosovo declined both in percentage and in absolute terms from 227,016 or 18.4 per cent of the total population to 209,498 or 13.2 per cent. At the same time, the Albanian population jumped from 646,605 to 1,226,736. Before 1981 this Serb exodus from Kosovo was not an issue in the Yugoslav media. However, after an outbreak of unrest there in 1981, parts of the Serbian press began publishing articles alleging that Albanians were harassing and intimidating Kosovo's Serbs and forcing them to move out.

On 11 March 1981 students at Priština University in Kosovo organised a demonstration against poor living conditions on campus. In subsequent negotiations with the academic authorities they complained of their poverty and the level of unemployment in Kosovo, before marching to the headquarters of the provincial League of Communists, where police broke up the demonstration. Once the students had dispersed, the police moved to round up the ringleaders on instructions from local communist leaders, who feared further demonstrations. However, the arrests had the opposite effect as more students came out onto the streets calling for the release of their colleagues, complaining about their lack of prospects and demanding that Kosovo be granted republican status. When the police used excessive force against the demonstrators, unrest spread throughout Kosovo, the local communists appealed to Belgrade for help and on 3 April martial law was imposed.

The student demonstrators had been motivated by Kosovo's extreme poverty, which was being exacerbated at the time by the downturn in the Yugoslav economy. As living standards began to slide throughout the country, the impact was most marked in the poorest regions. During the late 1960s and 1970s Kosovo's Albanians had frequently manifested their grievances in street protests, so the demonstrations were not in themselves a new departure. What was new was the extent of the repression since troops and armed police were rushed into Kosovo from other republics to seal off the province. Priština University was closed and martial law remained in force for two months. According to official figures, twelve people died in the unrest and more than 150 were wounded, though the province was closed to foreign journalists and actual casualty figures may have been considerably higher.

The consequences of the unrest and subsequent repression in 1981 were not immediately obvious, although the use of force was deeply significant. Tito's Yugoslavia had been designed in such a way that, theoretically, all Yugoslavia's peoples could feel that they belonged and that they would be treated in the same manner as the rest of the country. Tito himself endeavoured to remain impartial at all times and never to favour one people over another, so that he could step in and resolve whatever conflict might arise. However, as soon as the JNA turned its guns against the country's Albanians, the Titoist vision of Yugoslavia had come unstuck. Within a year of his death and more than a decade before the country disintegrated in war, Tito's Yugoslavia had already died in spirit, if not yet in form.

In the aftermath of the unrest exceptionally heavy jail sentences were handed out to more than 1,600 Albanians, many of whom were university or even secondary school students whose offences were often no greater than scrawling graffiti on walls to the effect that Kosovo should be a republic. The federal authorities had for the first time taken sides in a dispute between two of Yugoslavia's peoples. Moreover, by labelling the unrest counter-revolution they enabled Serb nationalists to intervene in Kosovo with the backing of the LCY and, in Tito's absence, to reestablish Serbian control over a province in which, according to the 1981 census, Serbs made up 13.2 per cent and Albanians 77.4 per cent of the population.

Milošević's irresistible rise

When Milošević travelled to Kosovo in April 1987 he was still a relatively minor figure and it was actually Stambolić who was widely feared outside Serbia for being a nationalist. At the time, non-Serbian politicians considered Milošević to be one of Stambolić's henchmen and not a terribly bright one at that. Stambolić appeared to be the danger because he had made it clear that he intended to recentralise authority both within Serbia and within Yugoslavia and that to achieve this he was prepared to play the Serb national card.

During the 1970s disgruntled Serbian communists had already attempted to modify the 1974 constitution to reintegrate the autonomous provinces of Vojvodina and Kosovo into Serbia. A document known as the *Blue Book* was compiled by a working commission of the Serbian League of Communists, setting out the case for Belgrade to control the provinces' judiciary, police and economy. But to achieve this required the consent of both provincial assemblies as well as that of the republic, and the provinces were reluctant to give up their recently-acquired autonomy. Moreover, the rest of the federation was equally wary of Serbian attempts to recentralise authority and the project was shelved. As a result, Stambolić was keenly aware of potential opposition to constitutional reform and sought to build the largest possible coalition around himself, including both liberals and nationalists, before attempting once again to reintegrate Vojvodina and Kosovo into Serbia.

Stambolić was, in certain respects, to Serbia what Savka Dabčević-Kučar, the President of Croatia during the Croatian Spring of 1971, had been to Croatia. Like Dabčević-Kučar he had a clear programme which was being obstructed by other federal units and again like Dabčević-Kučar he hoped to use the nationalist threat as a bargaining counter in negotiations with the rest of the federation. The obvious difference between the situation in Croatia in the late 1960s and early 1970s and Serbia in the mid-1980s was that Tito had left the scene. When Dabčević-Kučar appeared to condone certain manifestations of Croat nationalism, Tito had her removed from office in case the movement evolved into something which could threaten Yugoslav society. But when Stambolić attempted to harness Serb nationalism to his cause, there was no Tito to prevent the movement getting out of control.

Increasingly, Stambolić turned to the Serbian media to articulate his programme. Commentaries by Serb nationalists and liberal economists, both of whom advocated a recentralisation of Yugoslav society though for different reasons, became a feature of the Serbian press. While Stambolić did not necessarily agree with these opinions, especially those of the more extreme nationalists, he hoped to use them to put pressure on the rest of the federation. But by giving Serb nationalists a free hand in the Serbian media, he was creating a dangerous precedent.

Articles written by nationalists which would never have been published during Tito's lifetime began to appear in Serbian newspapers in the aftermath of the unrest in Kosovo in 1981. To an extent this was a reflection of the liberal climate prevailing in Serbia at the time, since the authorities were prepared to tolerate a wide range of dissenting views, not merely those of nationalists. However, many of the nationalist analyses of the situation in Kosovo were but thinly-disguised attempts to criminalise Yugoslavia's Albanian population in Serb minds. Indeed, they were the sort of opinions which may not be expressed in Western countries since they would be considered an incitement to racial hatred. The result was that by the mid-1980s

Stambolić had given Serb nationalism a respectability it did not deserve
and one which would ultimately be his downfall.

The frustrated intellectuals who had conceived the Greater Serbian
vision of Yugoslavia during the 1960s and 1970s could, by this time,
count on an increasingly broad base of support for their simplistic and
xenophobic ideology. This included former members of the security
apparatus, whose status in Yugoslav society had plummeted since
Ranković's fall in 1966, and many Serbs from Kosovo, who also
yearned for a return to the Ranković era, as well as influential circles
within the Serbian Orthodox Church and a motley assortment of
political opportunists disillusioned with Yugoslav society. By the end
of 1986 Serb nationalists were confident enough to begin organising
protest rallies, and the Kosovo Committee of Serbs and Montenegrins,
a pressure group aimed at turning the clock back to the Ranković era,
was founded. In April 1987 more than 60,000 Serbs from Kosovo
signed a petition warning they could no longer endure the 'genocide'
being inflicted on their community by Albanian irredentists and
demanding the purge of Kosovo's Albanian leadership and the reimposition of martial law. The allegations were hysterical and patently
false, yet Stambolić had unleashed forces which he could no longer
control.

What was actually happening in Kosovo during the 1970s and early
1980s depends on whom one asked. The only in-depth and non-
partisan study was published by Branko Horvat, a respected Zagreb
academic and committed Yugoslav, at the beginning of 1988. Horvat
had hoped to stimulate a rational discussion throughout Yugoslavia
of the most appropriate policy towards the province which, at the
time, appeared to be tearing the federation apart. But, in the face of
a concerted smear campaign in the Serbian media, the discussion
Horvat hoped for failed to materialise. The result was that the received
wisdom among Serbs came to be that expressed in the Memorandum
of the Serbian Academy of Arts and Sciences, namely that Serbs were
being terrorised into leaving Kosovo by Albanian irredentists bent on
creating an ethnically pure Kosovo. As part of this terror campaign
Albanians were allegedly systematically raping and murdering Serbs
and desecrating Serb graves to erase all trace of Serb heritage from
Kosovo, while simultaneously waging demographic warfare through
their high birthrate.

To anyone who cared to question the allegations, the picture of
Kosovo painted in the Memorandum was a gross distortion of reality.

According to official figures, the incidence of both murder and rape in Kosovo was extremely low, much lower in fact than in the rest of Serbia, while the incidence of Albanians murdering or raping Serbs was negligible. A more appropriate explanation for the Serb exodus is that it was an economic migration and the result of the high unemployment and lack of prospects for all people in Kosovo. Certainly there was a similar migration elsewhere in Yugoslavia out of the poorer regions towards wealthier parts. Meanwhile, the high Albanian birthrate could be attributed not to demographic warfare but the relative lack of education and development among Kosovo's Albanians. Where Kosovo lagged behind was in the number of educated women for, as Horvat pointed out, women with a university education had a similar number of children, irrespective of nationality. Sadly, in the case of Kosovo and then the rest of the country, reality became less important than perceptions of reality, with tragic consequences.

What is abundantly clear is that relations between Serbs and Albanians in Kosovo were tense, while standards of living were abysmally low and declining. Kosovo's Albanians were determined to hang on to their recent gains in autonomy and had decided they could best achieve this if Kosovo became a republic in its own right. Meanwhile, Kosovo's Serbs, who felt increasingly apprehensive as their proportion of the total population continued to decline, would not countenance such a move and were determined to reverse Kosovo's quasi-republican status. The issues were increasingly clouded in the nationalist emotions which Tito had successfully contained but which could be exploited by an unscrupulous politician.

Despite his willingness to threaten the nationalist card, Stambolić, nevertheless, attempted to reconcile the interests of Serbs and non-Serbs within some sort of Titoist formula. In Kosovo he aimed to avert a return to repression by supporting a more pliant Albanian leadership under Azem Vllasi which he helped come to power in 1986 and by persuading them to accept a minimum number of constitutional amendments to placate Serb opinion. While Vllasi appeared willing to give up some of Kosovo's autonomy, Stambolić's plans were scuppered by Serb nationalists who continuously upped their demands. In desperation, Stambolić turned to his old friend Milošević.

On 27 April in the village of Kosovo Polje, scene of the infamous battle and headquarters of the Kosovo Committee of Serbs and Montenegrins, Milošević launched his assault on Stambolić and effectively on Tito's Yugoslavia. He had ostensibly gone there to hear at first hand the grievances of Kosovo's Serbs, but, instead of restraining their anger and attempting to reconcile their differences with their Albanian neighbours, as Stambolić wished, Milošević hijacked the nationalist movement. In a televised speech Milošević endorsed the allegations of genocide against the Serb nation and appealed to Serbs' warrior traditions, promising them: 'Nobody will ever beat you again.' News of the speech reverberated across Serbia and the shock waves spread fear throughout the federation.

Before Milošević's speech at Kosovo Polje no communist politician, not even Stambolić or Dabčević-Kučar, had overtly appealed to the parochial nationalism of one of Yugoslavia's peoples. In the best Titoist traditions political speeches were usually mind-numbingly boring and couched in a complex jargon which served to obscure any potential controversy while reinforcing faith in Titoism. Milošević became the first politician to drop the Titoist jargon and with it all commitment to national equality. Over a series of speeches his message became plain: that Serbs had to fight for their rights as a nation and that he, as head of Serbia's League of Communists, could best prosecute that struggle on behalf of all Serbs. It was a blow from which Tito's Yugoslavia would never recover.

The decisive battle in Yugoslavia's disintegration was fought not in 1991 but in 1987. The struggle was not between Serbs and non-Serbs but between two wings of the Serbian League of Communists, between adherents of a Serb nationalist ideology which was incompatible with a multinational country and those who clung to the concept of a multinational state. The principal protagonists were Slobodan Milošević on behalf of a Greater Serbia and Dragiša Pavlović, who became chief defender of the Stambolić wing of the League of Communists, and the battleground was the League of Communists of Serbia itself and the Serbian media. However, the odds were stacked against Pavlović and Stambolić because Milošević had prepared his offensive well in advance and had already placed his supporters in the key posts.

Hitherto, liberal reformers had been a more powerful and influential force in Serbian society than the nationalists. Yet once Milošević added the weight of the League of Communists to the nationalist cause the liberals were rapidly silenced. To support him, Milošević promoted a generation of careerists, most of whom came from the provinces, to positions their ability and level of education would never have justified. Few came from Belgrade itself. The purge of Serbian life was thorough, nowhere more so than in the media.

The media, more specifically the Serbian media and Serbian journalists, bear huge responsibility for the resurgence of national hatred in Yugoslavia in the 1980s, as well as the scale and nature of the fighting when the country finally disintegrated in war. In Yugoslavia the media had always been a political tool, though before the rise of Slobodan Milošević its role had been to bring Yugoslavia's peoples together with the Titoist message of 'brotherhood and unity'. Since there were few alternative sources of information, the media had an enormous impact on public opinion to the extent that what average Yugoslavs believed depended almost entirely on what their media were telling them.

The potential for control of minds through the media was probably greater in Serbia than anywhere else in Yugoslavia. Paradoxically, the reason for this was that the Serbian media had traditionally had a high reputation, with the result that people implicitly believed what they were told. Hitherto, Serbian newspapers had prospered or failed largely according to the ability of their journalists, most of whom were professionals and themselves critical of the early manifestations of Serb nationalism. Had the Serbian media been less professional, Serbs might have been more sceptical towards their news. By contrast, the Croatian media were so notoriously poor during the 1970s that Croats grew naturally suspicious about their news and, as a result, tuned into the BBC World Service's Serbo-Croat broadcasts in greater numbers than any of Yugoslavia's other peoples.

During 1987 Milošević and Pavlović slugged it out within the media organs that each man controlled. The evening tabloid *Politika Ekspres* and even the quality daily *Politika* became rabid in their denunciation of Pavlović while *NIN*, the quality weekly, attempted to stand by Pavlović and was at first highly critical of the upsurge in Serb nationalism. At the same time, Milošević increased the pressure on Pavlović and Stambolić with mass protest rallies. The rallies, or meetings as they were called, were carefully stage-managed and reinforced the message which was coming from the Milošević-controlled media. On occasions, more than 100,000 people came to hear Milošević tell them how they had been exploited in Tito's Yugoslavia, how they were facing genocide, and how now they had to fight for their rights as a nation. Those who attended the meetings were bussed in at no expense, had the day off work and were fed to boot.

The power struggle within the Serbian League of Communists came to a head at the eighth Plenum in September 1987 when Milošević called for Pavlović's expulsion. Again Milošević had prepared the ground well and came to the Plenum having already won the backing of senior communists for a return to strict Party discipline before launching his final offensive. Like his meetings, the Plenum was stage-managed: during it Milošević was inundated with telegrams and messages of support from Serb communists the length and breadth of Serbia, Kosovo and Vojvodina, all of which had of course been carefully arranged in advance. On 23 September the battle was won and Pavlović expelled. Three months later, a powerless and broken Stambolić resigned as President of Serbia and Milošević replaced him with another of his stooges. Triumphant in Serbia, Milošević set his sights on Vojvodina, Kosovo and Montenegro.

The new Serb nationalism

With Pavlović out of the way, Milošević further purged the League of Communists and media to silence all remaining dissenting voices. The hitherto liberal weekly *NIN* as well as Radio and Television Belgrade were brought firmly under Milošević's control. Journalists who were not loyal to him were sacked or shifted to inferior jobs. Control of television was especially significant since it was the principal source of news for most of Serbia's population. The purges were all part of the so-called 'anti-bureaucratic revolution', an ongoing quest reminiscent of the Chinese Cultural Revolution. The campaign was supposed to weed out corruption in the League of Communists but, in practice, served to purge those elements which were prepared to think for themselves. Meanwhile, the hate campaign against every-thing which was not Serb went into overdrive in the media and at Milošević's now notorious rallies. Ironically, the Serbian media were more extreme in their denunciations of Yugoslavia's other people's in 1988, 1989 and 1990 than in 1991 after the shooting war had actually broken out, by which time their xenophobic message had inevitably become somewhat jaded.

The Serb national psyche which has so revolted the world since 1991 is not the product of centuries of historical evolution but has been deliberately manufactured and intensively cultivated by the Serbian media since 1987. The reason that the vast majority of Serbs are ada-mant that they are threatened by genocide on all fronts and that they were mercilessly exploited in Yugoslavia is quite simply because their media have been telling them so day in and day out for years. Myth, fantasy, half-truths and brazen lies were packaged each night into television news. The conspiracy theory dreamed up by frustrated nationalists in the late 1960s, 1970s and early 1980s became the literal truth, and anyone who challenged it was labelled an 'enemy of the Serb nation'. Every conceivable event from Serb history was dredged up and distorted to feed the persecution complex of ordinary people, who were gradually taken in by the barrage of xenophobia. The atmosphere was so heated and the campaign so all-encompassing that people lost touch with reality and, with no alternative source of information, became ready to believe anything they were told.

The media offensive of Milošević's Serbia in the 1980s resembled very closely the propaganda campaign of Nazi Germany in the 1930s. Indeed, the central theme—that all Serbs should be united in a single Serbian state—was identical. The great difference was that by the 1980s the media were infinitely more powerful than in the 1930s and consequently the capacity for disinformation was that much greater. While Hitler had the press, an infant film industry and the radio waves to disseminate his political philosophy, Milošević was able to beam his new Serb nationalism into every home in Serbia and beyond via saturation television. Virtually the entire press was located within the *Politika* publishing house, with the result that for almost three years, until in 1990 a handful of exceptionally brave journalists founded the independent weekly *Vreme*, there was hardly a dissenting voice in the Serbian media.[3] Access was restricted to the most fanatical nationalists, while respected and serious historians (for whom Serbia had traditionally been noted) were unable to put the record straight.

The unhealthy obsession among Serbs with twisted interpretations of the past dates from the 1980s. What had or had not actually taken place ceased to matter. Between 1987 and 1989 the media offensive was focused against Albanians, an alleged Islamic conspiracy and Tito's vision of Yugoslavia. As soon as Milošević was triumphant in Kosovo, Vojvodina and Montenegro, as well as in Serbia, the Serbian media moved against the rest of the country and, in the process, dredged up absurd and exaggerated interpretations of past relations between Serbs and non-Serbs and, in particular, of the Second World War.

---

[3] The one dissenting voice easily available in Serbia was Yugoslavia's only national daily newspaper, *Borba*.

These again became the literal truth. So great was the hysteria that ordinary Serbs genuinely came to believe that all sorts of crimes were continuously being perpetrated against them.

The allegations against anyone who dared to question Milošević on any matter were equally preposterous. The hate campaign against Milošević's two most outspoken critics, Pavlović and Bogdan Bogdanović (Mayor of Belgrade between 1984 and 1986), was ludicrous, yet by this time reality had gone out the window. Both were accused of being enemies of the Serb nation, though to outsiders they both represented all that was traditionally finest and most appealing in Serbia. Bogdanović, who was an architect by profession, had even designed the monument of the eternal flame to the dead from the notorious Ustaša concentration camp at Jasenovac! In 1988 both men published books warning prophetically of the impending catastrophe for both Serbia and Yugoslavia resulting from the return to strict Party discipline within the Serbian League of Communists and from the upsurge of state-led Serb nationalism, but to no avail.[4]

The same tactics which had started the ball rolling in Kosovo were extended throughout Serbia and into the Serb communities across Yugoslavia. Agitators, either from the Kosovo Committee of Serbs and Montenegrins or, increasingly, from the Serbian secret police, ensured that vast numbers of Serbs attended Milošević's meetings. The obvious attraction for demonstrators was a day's paid holiday and a free feed. The momentum was sustained by paying unemployed young men to go around the country from meeting to meeting while Serbs from all over Yugoslavia, including Bosnia-Hercegovina and Croatia, were also encouraged to come. Demonstrators, or *mitingaši* as those who attended the rallies became known, carried pictures of Milošević, waved nationalist flags, sang nationalist songs and habitually called for the execution of Kosovo's Albanian leadership. There was nothing spontaneous about the meetings, which were all carefully stage-managed but which the Serbian media dubbed the 'third Serb uprising' (the first two had been at the beginning of the 19th century against Ottoman rule). Moreover, there was no precedent in Serbia's past either for the scale or the nature of these truly grotesque displays, which inevitably filled non-Serbs, especially the Albanians at whom most of the hatred was aimed, as well as many Serbs with terror.

---

[4] Both books, *Mrtvouzice* by Bogdanović and *Olako obećana brzina* by Pavlović were published in Zagreb because no Serbian publisher was prepared to touch them.

In the course of 1988 the rallies spread first to Vojvodina and then to Montenegro, where Milošević was able to capitalise on an upsurge of labour unrest after the republic declared itself bankrupt. Steadily Milošević increased the pressure on the leaderships of both Vojvodina and Montenegro, which were already unpopular and generally considered corrupt and out of touch, until towards the end of the year tens and even hundreds of thousands of demonstrators regularly surrounded the parliaments demanding the resignations of the governments. In the absence of any support from the federal authorities both governments were paralysed by the explosion of rabble nationalism and caved in, Vojvodina in October 1988 and Montenegro in January 1989. As soon as the governments resigned, they were replaced with Milošević supporters who proceeded to carry out a thorough purge of society, the Party and the media. Since the demonstrators threw yoghurt which was left over from their free meals at the parliament buildings, the overthrow of Vojvodina and Montenegro's governments became known outside Serbia as the 'yoghurt revolutions'. Though free of violence, they were, nevertheless, real revolutions which altered the balance of power within federal Yugoslavia in Milošević's favour.

While Milošević was dismantling Tito's Yugoslavia piecemeal, the federal authorities were at a loss how to react. At the height of the assault on Vojvodina the federal President, Raif Dizdarević, warned that he might have to impose a state of emergency, but backed down rather than risk civil war as more than 350,000 people rallied in Belgrade to denounce the interference of the federal government. Quite simply, Yugoslavia's federal government was not equipped to deal with so determined an assault on its authority. This was partly the fault of the Titoist system itself, since the centre lacked sufficient power to bring Serbia back into line, but it was also the result of a malaise in the rest of the country. Montenegro, Macedonia and Kosovo had gone bankrupt, the leadership of Bosnia-Hercegovina was compromised by the Agrokomerc scandal and Croatia was still governed by the generation of mediocrities whom Tito had installed after the Croatian Spring. In addition, the Macedonian leadership generally sympathised with Serbia in its conflict with Kosovo's Albanians, since relations with Macedonia's own Albanian minority, whose living conditions were arguably worse than those in Kosovo, were increasingly strained.

As Milošević moved against Kosovo, an increasingly forlorn federal LCY decided that its best tactic was to sacrifice the recalcitrant province. Non-Serbian communists were terrified by the upsurge of nationalism in Serbia and convinced themselves that by sacrificing Kosovo they might satisfy Milošević's ambitions, while, simultaneously, hoping that Kosovo might yet prove his undoing. As a result, Vllasi and Kaqusha Jashari, Kosovo's Albanian leadership, were dismissed in November 1988 and replaced with Milošević appointees. The dismissals provoked widespread demonstrations among the province's Albanians which by February 1989 had escalated into a general strike as well as an underground hunger strike by 1,300 miners from the Trepča lead and zinc mines. When Kosovo's new, pro-Milošević leadership resigned on 28 February, it appeared that the strikers had won the day; victory, however, was short-lived.

In Belgrade Milošević organised fresh rallies, which were attended by close to one million people, at which he promised demonstrators that the organisers of Kosovo's general strike would be punished. Once again the federal authorities acquiesced. The resignations were withdrawn, Vllasi was arrested on charges of 'counter-revolution', a partial state of emergency imposed and the military moved in. On 23 March Kosovo's beleaguered assembly, ringed by tanks and with Migs flying low overhead, was coerced into accepting a new constitution returning authority to Serbia.[5] Five days later, amid great rejoicing, the Serbian parliament also formally proclaimed the constitutional changes which finally destroyed all vestiges of Tito's Yugoslavia. Meanwhile, Albanians took to the streets to defend the old constitution and demonstrators clashed with armed police throughout the province. According to official figures, twenty-four people were killed, though eye-witness accounts spoke of between 120 and 140 dead.

The balance of power within Yugoslavia had shifted decisively towards Milošević following his victory in Kosovo. By this time he controlled four of Yugoslavia's eight federal units and was strong enough to ignore federal opposition. Indeed, he was now able to use his own newly-acquired federal muscle to extend his power base further, for, far from satisfying him, victory in Kosovo had merely whetted his appetite. In Kosovo itself the new authorities set about changing the ethnic balance by encouraging another wave of Serb colonists with promises of jobs and houses. While Kosovo's Albanians

---

[5] Kosovo MPs supposedly voted for the new constitution. However, so fraudulent was the ballot that many of those who cast votes did not belong to the parliament.

were prepared to fight to hang on to a minimum of human rights, the prospect of full-scale war was remote because they did not have the weapons to retaliate with. Instead, they suffered what was effectively a system of apartheid in silence, while a new generation of non-communist leaders attempted to organise peaceful protests. Thus far, the LCY had remained united and had acquiesced in the face of Milošević's onslaught, but that changed in the aftermath of the Kosovo clamp-down when, under pressure from its domestic public, the Slovene communists broke ranks.

The Slovene challenge

Perhaps the most depressing feature of Milošević's rise was the ease with which he managed to take control of half of the country. The failure first of the Serbian communists and then the federal authorities to stand up to his ambition was the most damning indictment possible of the system Tito had bequeathed Yugoslavia. In his absence, Titoism proved incapable of organising effective resistance to a political philosophy which would ultimately destroy the Yugoslav state as well as the lives of many millions of its citizens. When finally some form of credible opposition materialised it came from outside the official channels, from Slovenia, where a rainbow alliance of opposition groups pressurised a reluctant Slovene leadership to challenge Milošević. And it was this rift which developed between Slovene and Serbian communists which went on to destroy Yugoslavia in form. The country had already died in spirit.

The 1980s in Slovenia were something of a golden age as far as cultural creativity and artistic innovation are concerned. The same disillusionment with Yugoslavia's bankrupt Marxist-Leninist ideology which evolved into extreme nationalism in Serbia spawned a confident, albeit cynical, modern Slovene national identity, prepared, if necessary, to go it alone and turn its back on the rest of the country. By comparison with modern Serb nationalism and its unhealthy obsession with the past, Slovene nationalism was a level-headed affair free of historical hang-ups and focused on the future. Yet it, too, contained a xenophobic dimension which emanated from Slovene fears that as a small people their separate cultural and linguistic identity was threatened by Yugoslavia's Serbo-Croat-speaking majority.

Traditionally, Slovenes were perhaps the most contented people in

Yugoslavia. Certainly they were very committed both to the Yugoslav ideal and the state which had shielded them from German and Italian nationalisms and enabled them to evolve a thriving and independent culture. Apart from the first decade of the royal Yugoslav state when Serbia effectively squeezed war reparations out of all the former Habsburg lands, Slovenia had always done reasonably well in Yugoslavia. Since Slovenia had no borders with Serbia, contained no Serb minority and was further insulated from Serb nationalism by a separate language, there was no possible reason to fall out with Serbia and, as a result, relations between the two were almost invariably excellent. As far as most Yugoslavs were concerned, the Belgrade-Ljubljana axis was as close as inter-republican alliances came. In marked contrast to Croatia's political leaders, Slovene politicians had always adopted a pragmatic approach to Yugoslavia and were prepared from the very beginning to fight hard for Slovene rights.

Slovene discontent within Yugoslavia can be traced back to the economic recession in western Europe following the First Oil Shock in 1973. When jobs in western Europe dried up and Yugoslav workers were forced to return home, Slovenia became the favoured destination for the next generation of Yugoslav migrant workers. Slovenia's relative wealth—*per capita* income was roughly double the Yugoslav average—and zero unemployment became a magnet for impoverished Serbs and Muslims from Bosnia-Hercegovina and Albanians from Kosovo. The result of this internal migration was the appearance of a Serbo-Croat-speaking minority of guest workers within Slovenia. As Slovenes shunned work in factories or heavy industry, ghettos of Serbo-Croat-speaking workers sprang up in a handful of industrial towns across Slovenia to the disgust of many Slovenes, who perceived the arrival of non-Slovenes as a threat to their cultural independence.

The desire to maintain a distinct Slovene cultural identity was also at the heart of the increasingly acrimonious dialogue between Slovene and Serb members of the Yugoslav Association of Writers. The dispute began as a seemingly innocuous attempt by Serb educationalists to reform the curriculum taught in Yugoslavia's schools soon after Tito's death, but rapidly spiralled out of control until the Association itself disintegrated. Serb educationalists were motivated by a fear that Yugoslavia was evolving into eight mini-states, in which Serbs were divided between seven federal units, and hoped to replace the country's eight existing curricula with a single 'Yugoslav' curriculum. Meanwhile, their Slovene counterparts viewed any move towards a

'Yugoslav' curriculum as an attempt to dilute their separate national identity, and rejected it outright.

Slovenia's communist leadership was well aware of the cultural fears of a significant section of Slovene society and pandered to them. At the federal level they worked to retain as much autonomy as possible, while at home they attempted to promote a sense of Slovene national pride. In the mid-1980s this included a publicity drive around the theme 'Slovenia My Homeland', which consisted primarily of a series of television commercials portraying the beauty and diversity of the Slovene countryside. The campaign proved hugely successful, to the extent that over-priced tee-shirts with '*Slovenija Moja Dežela*' (Slovenia My Homeland) emblazoned across them became almost as prominent a feature of Slovene life as pictures of Slobodan Milošević in Serbia. In addition to promoting pride in Slovenia, the Slovene communists used the media to articulate their own vision of Yugoslavia's future. But as the Yugoslav economy nosedived in the 1980s, they became increasingly prepared to use the media to blame other republics and especially the federal government in Belgrade for the country's economic ills, making it clear that they were tired of subsidising the poorer federal units when living standards were also declining at home.

Despite obvious attempts by Slovenia's communists to court popularity at home, in the long run the growth of opposition to the communist state was a more significant factor in the evolution of Slovene nationalism. Traditionally, Slovenia's communists had tolerated a far broader spectrum of views with many more dissenting voices than any other part of Yugoslavia, which nevertheless remained within the framework of communist society. But in the 1980s, as the failings of the communist system became too great to conceal, a new generation of dissenters began to mould a political opposition around specific issues and via alternative art forms. Pressure groups were founded which lobbied for a whole host of causes including the environment,[6] conscientious objection to military service and even gay rights. And as the communist regime lost credibility this rainbow alliance gained confidence and its programme became increasingly political.

Meanwhile, the generation of Slovene artists which came to maturity during the 1980s set out to parody contemporary Yugoslav

[6] The environment became a matter of special concern to Slovenes after the 1986 Chernobyl disaster in the Soviet Union since Yugoslavia's only nuclear reactor was at Krško on Slovenia's border with Croatia.

society and, in the process, developed a self-consciously nationalist Slovene school of art. They drew inspiration from everything which was taboo in Yugoslavia, yet which, ironically, appeared to have so much in common with Yugoslav society. Inevitably, this meant Nazi Germany, since the more discredited communist rule became in Yugoslavia, the more the communists harped on about their epic defeat of fascism and the more the totalitarian aspects of their society appeared in mischievous minds to mirror that of the Third Reich. Collectively the movement became known under the deliberately provocative German title *Neue Slovenische Kunst* (New Slovene Art).

Abroad, the most successful exponents of the *Neue Slovenische Kunst* were the rock band *Laibach* (the German name for Ljubljana), whose records sold remarkably well throughout western Europe. *Laibach* dressed in bizarre military uniforms and communicated their philosophy via pretentious pamphlets which they issued at irregular intervals and spectacular videos laced with allusions to totalitarianism. Much of the symbolism was pure hype designed at selling records and the band added to their mysterious image by refusing media interviews. However, it was also deeply offensive to the communist authorities, who were further incensed when Slovenia's Youth Organisation designed a poster for the 1986 Day of Youth, part of the annual ritual for Tito's birthday, which, after it was officially endorsed, turned out to be a replica of a Nazi youth poster from the 1930s.

Traditionally, the communist youth movement had served as a sort of safety valve within Yugoslav society. It was a forum for the discussion of new and often unorthodox ideas, in which prospective politicians cut their teeth. However, by the 1980s Slovenia's Youth Organisation had clearly exceeded its mandate and had become the focal point for opposition to communist rule. The muck-raking journalism of its weekly magazine *Mladina* was a permanent thorn in the side of the political establishment and especially the military. While Slovenia's Youth Organisation campaigned for an alternative to military service for conscientious objectors, a series of articles in *Mladina* at the beginning of 1988 embarrassed the then federal Defence Minister, Branko Mamula, into an early resignation. After a visit to Ethiopia to sell that country arms *Mladina* described Mamula as a 'salesman of death', while also revealing how he was using conscript soldiers to build himself a villa at Opatija on the Croatian coast. The JNA was not amused and decided to strike back.

On 31 May 1988 Janez Janša, a senior *Mladina* writer on military affairs and candidate for President of Slovenia's Youth Organisation, was arrested on suspicion of betraying military secrets. Soon after, two other *Mladina* journalists and a non-commissioned officer were also charged with offences relating to the disclosure of military secrets after classified documents were found at *Mladina*'s offices. The documents in question were widely believed to be plans for a military take-over of Slovenia, though this was never officially confirmed. But in the eyes of the Slovene leadership and the population at large, the trial was nothing short of an attack on Slovenes and Slovenia. Almost immediately *Mladina* journalists founded a Committee for the Protection of Human Rights to monitor the trial and Slovenes took to wearing *Janez Janša* badges in solidarity with the accused.

Whether or not the four defendants had actually committed an offence had ceased to matter as far as most Slovenes were concerned. The four were widely viewed as martyrs who had been framed by the military which *Mladina*'s investigative reporting had already discredited. Meanwhile, the JNA further incensed Slovene public opinion by insisting that the trial be held in Serbo-Croat. The result was a remarkable homogenisation of Slovene society and national mobilisation behind the accused. When all four were found guilty and sentenced to terms of between five months and four years, more than 50,000 people surrounded the courthouse in the centre of Ljubljana, a staggering number for a city of just 300,000 with no tradition of public protest, and prevented the military authorities from taking them immediately to prison. In the event, they all served reduced sentences under what were, by Yugoslav standards and given the gravity of the alleged crimes, exceptionally lenient conditions.

In the aftermath of the Janša trial, relations between the JNA and Slovenia continued to deteriorate amid persistent rumours of a military *coup d'état*. An already tense situation was aggravated by the resurgence of Serb nationalism and Milošević's assault on Vojvodina, Montenegro and Kosovo. Since the JNA's officer corps was roughly 70 per cent Serb or Montenegrin and the language of command was Serbo-Croat, Slovenes increasingly viewed it as a purely Serbian institution concerned solely with Serbian interests, a conviction which events in Kosovo served merely to confirm. While Slovenia's communist leadership still hoped to appease Milošević, the republic's increasingly vociferous opposition made it clear that its sympathies lay with Kosovo's Albanians.

In fact, Slovenia's communists must share some responsibility for the bloodshed in Kosovo. Without their acquiescence Milošević would not have been able to dismiss Vllasi and Jashari nor would the federal Presidency have been able to impose a state of emergency in Kosovo. To be fair, they found themselves in an extremely difficult position and opted for the path of least resistance. However, to ordinary Slovenes the parallels between what was happening in Kosovo and what might happen in Slovenia appeared so great it was time to take a stand. Albanians formed a similar proportion of the total Yugoslav population to Slovenes, and if the JNA was going to intervene in Kosovo it might just as easily move against Slovenia.

When the Albanian miners began their underground hunger strike the Committee for the Protection of Human Rights threw its weight behind the strikers and began collecting money for them and their families. Despite the severity of Yugoslavia's economic recession, ordinary people in both Slovenia and Croatia dug deep into their pockets to pledge money in support of the strikers. When the federal Presidency sent the military into Kosovo more than 1 million Slovenes, that is half the total population, signed a petition against the state of emergency, 450,000 in one day. On 27 February Slovenia's opposition organised a rally at Cankarjev Dom, Ljubljana's cultural centre, to demonstrate solidarity with Kosovo's Albanians and, in the face of intense public pressure, the republic's communist leadership decided belatedly to join the protest. Leading communists, including the President Milan Kučan, shared the platform with the non-communist opposition. The rally was broadcast live on television and radio and for the first time Slovenia's communists openly defied the federal LCY. Soon after the Cankarjev Dom meeting Slovenia withdrew its police contingent from Kosovo.

Collapse of communism

The decision to break ranks was not taken lightly. At the time, Milošević's star was clearly in the ascendant. He controlled Serbia, Vojvodina, Montenegro and Kosovo and was extending the same rabble rousing tactics to the Serb communities of Bosnia-Hercegovina and Croatia. But Kučan was a shrewd politician and was well aware of the risk involved in standing up to Milošević, but viewed it as the least of many evils. The bloodshed in Kosovo, which was on a par with that in Tiananmen Square, Beijing in the same year (though significantly out of range of television cameras), had visibly shocked him and made him fear for his own security. At the same time, like communists throughout eastern Europe, the Slovene communists were exceptionally unpopular despite attempts to democratise society during the 1980s, and the opposition was growing increasingly confident. For Kučan, Kosovo was as much an opportunity as a threat. By taking a firm stance he calculated that he would be able to rejuvenate the Slovene League of Communists and boost his own popularity at home even if that meant a head-on collision with Milošević.

The Serbian media reacted swiftly and predictably. The hate campaign which had, hitherto, been directed primarily against Albanians was switched to Slovenes. Though it was difficult to dredge up a history of animosity between Serbs and Slovenes, enterprising Serbian propagandists rose to the task and within days everybody in Serbia knew how Slovenia had systematically exploited Serbia ever since the creation of Yugoslavia, how Slovenes had invented Worker Self-Management to weaken Serbia economically and even how Slovenia's relative wealth was derived from Serbian factories which were transplanted to Slovenia in 1948! The allegations were endless and the propaganda campaign was so overwhelming that it became dangerous to speak with a Slovene accent or even to carry a Slovene newspaper in Serbia.

At the same time, Milošević attempted to pressurise the republic into submission via an economic boycott and further nationalist rallies, this time in Ljubljana. The markets of Serbia, Vojvodina and Kosovo were shut to Slovene companies and a meeting to 'bring the truth' about Kosovo to the Slovene public was scheduled for 1 December 1989. Faced with the prospect of several hundred thousand Serbs descending on the Slovene capital for the 'Meeting of Truth', as it was dubbed in Serbia, Kučan took fright and banned the rally. The 'truth' about Kosovo had already been displayed for all the world to see on 28 June 1989, the 600th anniversary of the battle of Kosovo Polje, when more than a million Serbs descended on Kosovo to commemorate the event.

Nationalist hysteria in Serbia was at its height during the summer of 1989 with an avalanche of books, films and plays commemorating the battle to mark the celebration. The bones of Prince Lazar, the Serb leader on that fateful day, were exhumed and paraded around the republic. Serbia was reborn and victory over Kosovo's Albanian majority had avenged the defeat on that day six centuries earlier! Milošević addressed the assembled faithful with a clear message for Yugoslavia's non-Serbs. He told them: 'Six centuries [after the battle of Kosovo Polje], we are again engaged in battles and quarrels. These are not armed battles, but the latter cannot be ruled out yet.'

However, even at his moment of triumph Milošević's promises, which had brought Serbia to fever pitch, were beginning to ring hollow. He had promised Serbs the resurrection of their economy as well as a swift solution in Kosovo. Instead, he was bankrupting Serbia and had alienated the province's Albanians beyond any conceivable compromise. The economic programme was farcical. In the absence of foreign credits Milošević decided to organise a loan from Serbs throughout the world who wished to make Serbia great again. Anticipating $1 billion, he raised a paltry $25 million, and Serbian industry remained over-manned, unproductive and loss-making. With no other course open to them, Kosovo's Albanians began a veritable *intifada* against Serbian rule. The police bill alone was equivalent to half of Yugoslavia's defence budget and, though the entire country was footing the bill, Milošević would not allow any other republic to 'interfere' in what he deemed to be Serbia's internal affairs.

The total cost to Yugoslavia of suppressing Kosovo was potentially greater still. International human rights organisations monitoring the situation had begun to campaign against the flagrant abuses in Kosovo, and the country's reputation, which had been relatively good during Tito's lifetime, was by now in tatters. US Senator Robert Dole, whom George Bush narrowly defeated as Republican nominee for President, was the most prominent of a number of Western politicians who had taken up the Albanian cause and were pushing for some form of sanctions against Yugoslavia unless there was an end to human rights violations in Kosovo. But since sanctions could not be limited to Serbia, they threatened the entire country including Slovenia and Croatia, even though the two northern republics were equally hostile to the state of emergency in Kosovo. As a result, by the middle of 1989 most Slovenes had come to the conclusion that Yugoslavia had precious little left to offer them, whereas they had a lot to lose by remaining part of the country.

The recentralisation of Serbia's League of Communists and Milošević's assault on federal Yugoslavia was preventing the country from following the rest of eastern Europe in abandoning or at least reforming communism. As soon as Mikhail Gorbachov began questioning the basis of Soviet rule at home, all eastern European communist regimes which had been installed in power by the Red Army effectively had their legitimacy pulled out from under them. In the absence of Soviet support, the failings of Marxism-Leninism proved too great and communist rule disintegrated. Yugoslavia differed from the rest of eastern Europe since the Yugoslav communists had come to power without Soviet support. Yugoslav communism was an indigenous creation and therefore more difficult to discard, since Yugoslavs could not blame Moscow nor anybody else (except perhaps each other) for their ills. Nevertheless, the crisis of legitimacy and the economic and political failings of communist rule in Yugoslavia were just as great.

Developments in Slovenia were broadly in line with the rest of eastern Europe. The leadership decided that they could not stem the tide of democracy and opted for a multiparty system. However, any move towards Western-style democracy in Slovenia would be scuppered if Milošević succeeded in recentralising Yugoslavia. As a result, Kučan began to espouse a confederal arrangement in which each republic could choose its own form of government. According to Kučan's vision of Yugoslavia, republics which desired to remain communist could do so, while those wishing to evolve into a multiparty democracy would also be free to abandon communism. On 27 September 1989 Slovenia's parliament passed fifty-four amendments to its constitution formally renouncing the League of Communists' monopoly of political power and including the explicit right to self-determination, that is secession from Yugoslavia.[7] At the time, the threat to secede was meant merely as a precautionary last resort. It was not a statement of intent, and whether Slovenia exercised this right or not would depend on developments elsewhere in the country, especially in Serbia.

Serbia's apparent commitment to hardline communism did not stem from any innate Serbian affinity for Marxism-Leninism, nor had Serbia done unduly well out of the communist system. Quite simply, the League of Communists had been the key to Milošević's rise and, to date, the most powerful weapon in his assault on the rest of the federation. Ordinary Serbs were as disillusioned with communist rule as any of eastern Europe's peoples but Milošević had managed to breathe new life into the Serbian League of Communists by revamping it with nationalism. Despite the disintegration of communist rule elsewhere,

---

[7] While Yugoslavia's first communist constitution of 1946 had included the explicit right to self-determination, that right was merely implied in the 1974 constitution; hence the need to modify it.

Milošević still intended to use the League of Communists, in the same way that he used rabble nationalism, to exert maximum pressure on his opponents and extend his political control throughout the country. To this end, he called an extraordinary 14th Congress of the LCY for January 1990.

The Congress was billed as the clash of alternative conceptions of Yugoslavia's future development. Milošević intended to use it to impose his model of a Serbian League of Communists, regenerated through unity, discipline and the exclusion of dissenting voices, on the federal Party, whereas Kučan hoped to expand local autonomy within Yugoslavia by turning the LCY into a loose association of separate Communist Parties. But in the event, Kučan was shouted down by Milošević's supporters and was unable even to present his proposals adequately, let alone discuss the future shape of Yugoslavia. Since Kučan had already committed himself to elections in April of that year, he knew he had to win concessions from Belgrade to have any chance of remaining in power. As it became clear there could be no negotiations, the Slovene delegation walked out of the Congress on 20 January never to return.

When the Slovene delegation left Belgrade, they had no idea what was going to happen next. Neither did anyone else. Indeed, the wider implications for Yugoslavia of both the break-up of the federal Party and the demise of communism throughout eastern Europe were not immediately clear. Nevertheless, as the Slovene delegates left the extraordinary Congress, they were keenly aware that after more than four decades the second Yugoslav experiment had come to an end, and that the country's future was now fraught with danger. For one of them, Sonja Lokar, the emotional strain and the overwhelming sense of foreboding were simply too great and as she left the hall she broke down in tears.

Lokar's fears for her country's future were well-founded. While, in itself, the break-up of the LCY did not automatically make the demise of Yugoslavia inevitable, the manner in which it disintegrated was ominous. For, at the extraordinary Congress, there was no effort to create a framework in which all Yugoslavia's peoples could live together. Instead, the Milošević bloc had attempted to use its numerical superiority to impose a blueprint for Yugoslavia on the rest of the country, irrespective of non-Serbian opinion. It was a rerun of the eighth Plenum of the League of Communists of Serbia when Milošević destroyed Pavlović and took full control over the Serbian

Party. But this time the stakes were even higher, for non-Serbs could not accept Milošević's terms without effectively resigning themselves to second-class citizenship. Instead of capitulating, the Slovene communists chose to turn their backs on the institution which had united all Yugoslavia's peoples during the Second World War but which had come to serve as an instrument for Greater Serbian nationalism.

In the absence of the Slovene delegation, Milošević attempted to resume the Congress but when the Croatian delegation, too, walked out, the Bosnian and Macedonian communists were no longer prepared to continue and the meeting was suspended. The tide of democracy which had just swept eastern Europe, leading to the reunification of Germany, was unstoppable and would thwart any further attempts by Milošević to recentralise Yugoslavia via the LCY. In the short term, the disintegration of communist authority in eastern Europe had checked his ambitions and appeared to give the rest of the country some breathing space. But in the longer term, it was actually Yugoslavia's undoing.

Until this time Yugoslavia had occupied a position of geopolitical significance between East and West, which Yugoslav politicians had relied upon as insurance against economic disaster. They had calculated correctly that the West would not stand by and watch Yugoslavia founder. But Yugoslavia's status changed when the Soviet Union chose not to intervene to restore communist rule in eastern Europe. Without the Soviet bogey, Yugoslavia lost its claim to international importance and Yugoslavs could no longer rely on Western support to bail them out. Meanwhile, the focus of Western attention and financial aid switched to the emerging democracies which had just thrown off the Soviet yoke.

7

COUNTDOWN TO WAR

'With Nikezić[1] I'd enter into a federation. With Stambolić I'd enter into a confederation. But with Milošević I wouldn't even enter a bus.' — Abdulah Sidran[2]

A third Yugoslavia

For almost forty-five years communism had been the gel which, with considerable success, had held Yugoslav society together. In its absence Yugoslavia remained intact, though the country which Tito had built was no more. In a climate of goodwill it would certainly have been possible to erect a third Yugoslavia out of the ruins of the Titoist state, since, in practice, it is remarkably difficult for any country, no matter how oppressive or corrupt, actually to fall apart. The disintegration of a country is rarely in the interest of its people and is invariably opposed by the international community, which has to deal with the consequences. In effect, the demise of communism had merely reopened the debate which had preoccupied Yugoslav politicians during the 1920s as to the best form of government for their common state.

While the experience of the 1920s was not a good omen for the prospects of a third Yugoslav incarnation, the country had come a long way in the intervening sixty-odd years. Having learned about each other and each other's cultures in school for the past forty-five years, Yugoslavs had grown more aware of the ethnic complexity of their country and should have been more tolerant of one another. The number of people who chose to declare themselves 'Yugoslav', either out of conviction or because they were indeed the progeny of mixed marriages, rather than Serb, Croat or any other Yugoslav nationality, leapt with each census and augured well. At the same time, the logic which had made the Yugoslav ideal so powerful a political philosophy during the 19th century was as compelling as ever. The country was

---

[1] Marko Nikezić was President of Serbia in the early 1970s.

[2] Abdulah Sidran is a Muslim Slav who wrote the screenplay for the Oscar-nominated *When Father was Away on Business (Otac na Službenom Putu)* which won the *Palme d'Or* at Cannes in 1985.

still a mosaic of nationalities whose destinies could not be separated. A single Yugoslav state enabled the vast majority of south Slavs to live within the same country and ensured that rival national claims to ethnically-mixed territories would not spill over into conflict.

Urbanisation, inter marriage and universal schooling had moved the national question on since the 1920s, yet many aspects remained the same. All of Yugoslavia's eight federal units were, to some extent, ethnically mixed and no single nationality formed a majority of the total population. The most homogeneous regions were Slovenia and Kosovo where in both cases more than 90 per cent of the population was of the same nationality.[3] In Croatia, according to the 1981 census,[4] 75.1 per cent of the population were Croats, while 11.6 per cent were Serbs. In inner Serbia and Vojvodina, Serbs formed an absolute majority of 85.4 per cent and 56.8 per cent of the population, respectively. And in Bosnia-Hercegovina, Muslim Slavs accounted for 39.5 per cent, Serbs 32 per cent and Croats 18.4 per cent of the population. Serbs were indigenous to seven of the eight federal units and formed 36.3 per cent of Yugoslavia's total population.

Countries come into existence for a variety of reasons, both internal and external, and communism had not been the only unifying force that held Yugoslavia together. The first two Yugoslav incarnations had evolved out of wars and in both cases the external threat was one of the most important factors holding the country together. In Royal Yugoslavia, a common south Slav state provided Serbs, Croats and Slovenes with a secure sanctuary from the designs of Italy, Hungary and Austria on lands inhabited mainly by Slavs, while in Tito's Yugoslavia the external threat came from the Soviet Union. But as the menace of the Warsaw Pact's armies receded in the 1980s, Yugoslavia had never been as secure. In the absence of external danger Yugoslavs would only come together to form a third Yugoslavia for internal reasons, either if

[3] While Albanians only formed 77.4 per cent of the total population of Kosovo at the time of the 1981 census their numbers rose rapidly during the 1980s as a result of an exceptionally high birthrate. Since Albanians boycotted the 1991 census, there are no exact figures for Kosovo's current population, though estimates based on demographic indices suggest that Albanians make up more than 90 per cent.

[4] A census was carried out in the months before the outbreak of war in 1991 which may not be entirely reliable. However, nobody can dispute the figures from the 1981 census, which was carried out in a more temperate climate. In addition to the various national categories, 5.4 per cent of Yugoslavia's population declared themselves 'Yugoslav'. These were mainly the progeny of mixed marriages, though a certain number of Serbs also chose to register as Yugoslavs.

they decided it was in their best interests, or if they were coerced into the state.

At the beginning of 1990 the Yugoslav scene was extremely fluid. The existing state apparatus remained intact by default since nothing had emerged to replace it, yet clearly it had become anachronistic given the demise of the LCY. The country was in a sort of limbo-land and Yugoslavs were conscious this state of affairs could not be permanent. The form a third Yugoslavia might take was the subject of debate and speculation in every republic. However, the spectre of repression in Kosovo hung over the debate and most of Yugoslavia's greatest minds were keenly aware of the threat resurgent nationalism posed to the country's future.

In February 1989 Branko Horvat, the Zagreb academic whose attempts to stimulate a rational discussion of Kosovo had been stymied by a smear campaign in the Milošević-controlled media, founded the Association for a Yugoslav Democratic Initiative (*Udruženje za Jugoslovensku demokratsku inicijativu* or UJDI). UJDI was a forum for many of the country's best minds to analyze a blueprint for the future as Yugoslavia evolved out of communism. It included members of all nationalities from every republic and generated an impressive amount of research. In an effort to stave off the slide towards ethnically-based political parties, UJDI even came up with a form of democracy tailored to Yugoslavia's needs. According to this proposal, Yugoslavia's future parliamentary system would be restricted to two parties, one communist and the other anti-communist, but neither ethnically-based. While it is easy to understand why such a contrived structure never got off the ground, it was infinitely preferable to the set-up which was to materialise. UJDI members watched with horror as in one republic after another the Yugoslav ideal was rejected and the nation became the overriding factor in Yugoslav politics.

Had there been a genuine discussion of the best living arrangement for all the peoples of Yugoslavia during 1990, the Yugoslav idea would almost certainly have come out on top. When considered rationally it was the only settlement which could hope to satisfy everybody. If proof of that were needed it came in the carnage of 1991, 1992 and 1993, but, by then, it was too late to turn the clock back. Sadly, during the seventeen months between the break-up of the LCY and the outbreak of a full-scale war, the Yugoslav ideal was not tried, tested and found wanting, it was not tried at all. The problem in Yugoslavia was not that different peoples could not live together but that they were not given the chance.

During 1990 three blueprints for Yugoslavia's future were on the table: Serbia was insisting upon a recentralised federation; Slovenia was proposing that Yugoslavia become a loose confederation; and the federal Prime Minister, Ante Marković, hoped that by getting the economy moving again he might be able to maintain a Yugoslav entity in which the precise structure, whether federal or confederal, ceased to matter. However, the hysterical climate of ethnic hatred which was being whipped up in Serbia, coupled with Milošević's total intransigence at the negotiating table, ruled out any serious discussion of the country's future. According to the Serbian media, Serbs had been so mercilessly exploited and persecuted in Tito's Yugoslavia that now, quite reasonably, they were merely demanding 'equality' with the country's other peoples! It was a rerun of Kosovo. But this time, in addition to the Albanians, all Yugoslavia's peoples were labelled racial enemies. The allegations were patently ridiculous but once again reality had ceased to matter.

The political stalemate suited Milošević, whose designs on the rest of the country were undimmed, since his offensive had always been two-pronged. On the one hand, he used official channels, be they the League of Communists or Yugoslavia's residual federal institutions, when they served his purposes and enabled him to dictate terms. On the other hand, he maximised pressure on his opponents through unofficial means such as the use of rabble nationalism. When his attempt to recentralise Yugoslavia via the LCY foundered in January 1990, Milošević merely renewed efforts to destabilise the four federal units outside his control by stirring up the Serb communities there.

Hitherto, each Yugoslav republic had been sovereign, and republican leaders had represented all people living in their republic irrespective of nationality. In Serbia's amended constitution of March 1989, this was altered and the concept of sovereignty within the republic was replaced by that of sovereignty within the nation. In future, in addition to his own republic, Milošević claimed the right to represent all Serbs throughout Yugoslavia. Since large Serb communities lived in six of Yugoslavia's eight federal units,[5] this direct appeal to them above the heads of their republican leaderships was an exceptionally

---

[5] The six units are Serbia, Vojvodina, Kosovo, Montenegro, Bosnia-Hercegovina and Croatia. While Macedonia also contained an indigenous Serb minority, it was much smaller than in either Bosnia-Hercegovina or Croatia. According to the 1981 census, there were about 44,500 Serbs in Macedonia, or 2.3 per cent of the total population.

powerful weapon in the Milošević arsenal which he used to undermine authority in the governments of Croatia and Bosnia-Hercegovina.

Contemporary Yugoslav commentators were immediately struck by the similarities between the way in which Milošević sought to manipulate Serb communities outside Serbia and the tactics Adolf Hitler had employed towards German minorities living outside Germany during the 1930s. Hitler's remilitarisation of the Rhineland and the failure of the international community to react in 1936 corresponded to Milošević's assault against Serbia's autonomous provinces and the inertia of Yugoslavia's federal authorities in 1988 and 1989. *Anschluss* with Austria in 1937 was akin to the Milošević *coup d'état* in Montenegro. Similarly, the Serb communities of Croatia and Bosnia-Hercegovina served the same purposes as the German minorities in Czechoslovakia and Poland.

During the summer of 1989 the rabble-rousing tactics which had borne fruit in Serbia, Vojvodina, Montenegro and Kosovo were extended to Croatia and Bosnia-Hercegovina. Again the Serbian media had prepared the ground in advance. At the beginning of 1989 radio transmitters in Vojvodina, which had, hitherto, been used to broadcast to the province's many national minorities, were redirected to beam Serbian propaganda at Bosnia-Hercegovina and Serb-populated regions of Croatia. Serbian secret police began moving into Serb villages to "investigate" Serb emigration, and fresh nationalist rallies were staged, this time in Croatia. Notwithstanding the scale of Milošević's offensive and the impunity with which he had ridden roughshod over the federal authorities between 1988 and 1990, the bravest attempt to preserve Yugoslavia nevertheless came from the federal centre in the shape of Ante Marković, the country's last Prime Minister.

Ante Marković's attempt to save Yugoslavia

Marković was the eternal optimist. As Prime Minister of Yugoslavia in the 1990s he presumably had to be. Right up until the JNA moved against Slovenia in June 1991, he remained publicly confident that somehow he would manage to hold his country together. Marković was certainly Yugoslavia's best hope and, despite an increasingly acrimonious propaganda war between Serbia and the rest of the country, he managed to attract an impressive degree of support in every republic. Even after war broke out he worked incessantly to patch together a compromise which might keep Slovenia and Croatia in the federation. But by then, if not much earlier, it was far too late for compromises and Markovic's endeavour was doomed.

In fairness, the odds were stacked against him from the start. Marković became Prime Minister in March 1989 just over two months after his predecessor, Branko Mikulić resigned in the face of impending economic catastrophe at the height of Milosević's assault on Montenegro and Kosovo. As strikes paralysed the Yugoslav economy, as unemployment neared 20 per cent and inflation spiralled out of control, Mikulić had belatedly found himself compelled to adopt the stiff economic medicine the International Monetary Fund had been recommending for close to a decade. But Mikulić was deeply unpopular and the austerity measures he introduced entailed a further deterioration in living standards and provoked widespread resentment. He lacked the courage of the IMF's convictions and rather than soldier on passed the poisoned chalice to Marković.

Poisoned chalice or not, it was the chance Marković had been waiting for ever since he entered politics. By profession and inclination Marković was an industrialist, not a politician. Spiritually he was of the generation of meritocrats which rose to power during the 1960s and had been purged by Tito in the early 1970s. As managing director of one of Yugoslavia's largest enterprises, Marković found the political constraints on business too great to run an efficient company and went into politics to reform the country's economic structure. Ante Marković was ethnically Croat,[6] but temperamentally he was a committed Yugoslav, in the sense that he understood how essential the Yugoslav state was to the well-being of all its citizens. He was acutely aware of the potential carnage in the event of civil war and hence his tireless struggle to keep Yugoslavia together.

When the LCY broke up at the beginning of 1990, Yugoslavia's state apparatus replaced the Party structure as the device holding the republics together and Marković emerged by default as the country's leading federal politician. His immediate task was to bring about some form of rapprochement between Slovenia and Serbia, already at loggerheads for nearly a year. As mediation proved fruitless, he attempted to reconcile both republics within his own, alternative vision of Yugoslavia's future. Marković reasoned that since the political crisis which had brought the country to the brink of disintegration was rooted in the economic downturn of the 1980s, the solution, too,

---

[6] The surname Marković is one common to both Croats and Serbs.

would be found in the economy. He convinced himself that as long as he managed to turn the economy round he would also be able to halt the slide towards civil war. The deadlock in inter-republican negotiations gave Marković the opportunity to put his own strategy into action, again by default.

As soon as Marković became Prime Minister, he began to assemble a team of technocrats to put together a radical reform package to reverse Yugoslavia's economic decline. For this he had the support of most of the best minds in the country, including Horvat's UJDI. But merely to steer the necessary legislation through the federal assembly against a host of vested interests was a major battle and many of the new laws passed at the end of 1989 were only accepted as temporary measures.

To fight inflation, which had spiralled above 2,000 per cent, the dinar was devalued, made convertible and pegged to the German mark. Wages were frozen for six months and prices liberalised. The results were better than even Marković had dared hope. By the end of February inflation dipped beneath 10 per cent and the country's foreign currency reserves jumped to $7.1 billion — twice the level of May 1989. In recognition, Marković's popularity soared at home, and abroad he came to command more respect than any Yugoslav politician since Tito. However, Marković's early economic achievements were not accompanied by any corresponding progress on the political front and there was no reconciliation between Slovenia and Serbia. The Serbian boycott of Slovene goods remained in place and there was no relaxation of police oppression in Kosovo. Though it was the economic crisis which had brought Yugoslavia to the brink of civil war, Marković became aware that holding the country together required more than merely economic remedies.

Marković aimed to capitalise on his economic successes by founding his own non-communist political party, with which he hoped to contest as yet unscheduled federal elections. He reasoned that if he could organise nationwide elections he might just be able to give the federal government a democratic mandate and legitimacy which the republics, all still governed by communists, lacked. For the initiative to have had any chance of succeeding, Marković needed to hold federal elections before any of the republics went to the polls. But since Slovenia's communist leadership had already committed themselves to multiparty elections in April 1990, he had to persuade them to delay their poll. This time, however, Kučan refused to back down, thereby scuppering the initiative even before it could be launched.

As far as Slovenia's communists were concerned, any move aimed at increasing the authority of Yugoslavia's federal centre was a potential threat, and they were certainly not prepared to commit Slovenia's future to the outcome of elections which had not yet been organised and which might easily evolve into another vehicle for Greater Serbian nationalism. Centralisation, whether by Marković or by Milošević, had become synonymous with Serb domination and was unacceptable. The Slovene communists began their election campaign as soon as they walked out of the 14th Congress of the LCY. They ceased contributing the portion of the Fund for Underdeveloped Regions earmarked for Serbia, changed their name to the Party of Democratic Reform and even discarded the word 'socialist' from Slovenia's official title.

As scheduled, Slovenia went to the polls on 8 April before Marković had had the time to found his own party. Two weeks later Croatia followed. In Slovenia, despite their belated attempts to court popularity, the communists were defeated in the parliamentary elections by *Demos*,[7] a fragile coalition of five opposition parties. However, in the presidential elections Kučan managed to hang on to power. The outcome was a surprisingly comfortable cohabitation between the former communists and their former opposition. In Croatia, while the communists actually won a larger percentage of the votes than in Slovenia, a first-past-the-post electoral system worked against them and enabled a right-wing party, the Croat Democratic Union (*Hrvatska demokratska zajednica* or HDZ) to win an absolute majority in parliament on a minority poll. The elections left Yugoslavia with two democratically-elected republican governments, four communist republican governments and a communist military. In the wake of the elections and before the communists formally relinquished power in May 1990, the JNA took the opportunity to disarm the territorial defence forces of Slovenia and Croatia.

Inevitably, the elections undermined Marković's authority. The new governments in Slovenia and Croatia both now had a democratic mandate to govern, whereas Marković's authority was derived from an increasingly forlorn federal assembly. He retained the ideological support of the IMF and the psychological support of the international community, but lacked any power base where it mattered most, at

---

[7] *Demos* stood for *Demokratska opozicija Slovenije*, the Democratic Opposition of Slovenia.

home in Yugoslavia. Even had Marković had the time to organise his own political party before Slovenia and Croatia went to the polls, it is unlikely, despite his personal prestige, that it would have won many votes. He did eventually launch his own party, the Reform Alliance (*Savez reformističkih snaga*), in July, but it failed to make much headway in subsequent elections in Bosnia-Hercegovina and Macedonia, where it might have been expected to attract support, and had no impact whatsoever in Montenegro and Serbia.

Increasingly, Marković found himself simply a go-between in inter-republican disputes, desperately trying to rekindle the Yugoslav ideal and remind all Yugoslavs what they would be giving up if the country fell apart. The media in Bosnia-Hercegovina and Macedonia supported him but his message fell on deaf ears in Serbia and also in Slovenia and Croatia. To counter the propaganda war, Marković backed an ambitious and independent Bosnian television project, *Yutel*, a station which refused to pander to the national interests of any group. He also attempted to turn to his advantage several international events which Yugoslavia hosted in the course of 1990, such as the Eurovision Song Contest[8] and the European Athletics Championship. As part of the Eurovision Song Contest a ten-minute film of Yugoslavia's spectacular beauty and diversity was broadcast, aimed as much at the show's Yugoslav viewers as those abroad.

Following electoral defeats in Slovenia and Croatia, the tide had turned against communists throughout Yugoslavia. Despite a rearguard action by Serbian hardliners who tried to rule the Slovene and Croatian elections unconstitutional, the march of democracy was unstoppable and one by one each of Yugoslavia's four remaining communist republics bowed to popular pressure and called elections. In Macedonia, where voters went to the polls on 11 November, the result was a hung parliament. A coalition government was formed and, though nationalists formed the largest bloc in parliament, the former communist, Kiro Gligorov, became President. Meanwhile in Bosnia-Hercegovina, where voters went to the polls a week later, the communists lost. The Bosnian election was virtually a census. The Muslim

---

[8] The Eurovision Song Contest is an annual television jamboree in which competing countries enter a song and juries from each country vote for the best tune. The country with the dubious honour of winning the contest hosts the event the next year. The 1990 contest was staged in Zagreb and broadcast live throughout Europe because Riva, a band from Zadar, won it a year earlier with the immediately forgettable 'Rock Me Baby'.

Party for Democratic Action (*Stranka demokratske akcije* or SDA) won
41 seats, the Serb Democratic Party (*Srpska demokratska stranka* or SDS)
34, and the Croat Democratic Union (HDZ) 20, while former communists hung on to 13. A coalition government was formed in which
all three ethnically-based parties were represented and the Muslim Alija
Izetbegović became President of what was supposed to be a collective,
rotational Presidency. By contrast, in Montenegro and Serbia, where
the second round of voting was held on 23 December, the former
communists romped home with relative ease.

Victory for what were Yugoslavia's least reformist communist
parties was not entirely fortuitous. Whereas elsewhere in the country
the communists took pains to organise fair elections in which they
were defeated, in Serbia, having done his best to stave off multiparty
elections, Milošević made sure he did not make the same mistake.
While the December 1990 ballot itself was not overtly rigged,
Milošević's monopoly of the media effectively shut out all opposition
while a first-past-the-post electoral system ensured that the former
communists only required a relative majority of votes for an absolute
majority of seats. At the same time, Milošević made sure of victory
with a healthy electoral bribe, in the form of massive wage and pension
increases, on the eve of the elections.

Since the only way Milošević could raise incomes across the board
in the way he did had to be at the expense of Marković's reform programme, the Serbian election marked the end of the Marković honey-
moon. Just before Serbia went to the polls Milošević effectively stole
18 billion dinars, then about $1.7 billion, from the rest of the country.
The money came in the form of an illegal loan from Serbia's main bank
to the Serbian government. Quite simply, the bank printed whatever
money Milošević felt he needed to get himself reelected and the size
of the 'loan' became clear a few weeks later when inflation took off
again throughout the country. As the economy resumed its downward
slide, Marković knew his enterprise had failed but stayed on as Prime
Minister out of a sense of duty. He eventually resigned in December
1991 rather than endorse a war budget.

Despite its encouraging start the Marković reform programme had
been dependent on republican cooperation and unless all republics
backed him Marković had no chance of turning the Yugoslav economy
round. In practice, all republics cheated the programme at times, while
there was never any attempt to implement it in Serbia. Indeed, as soon
as Marković unveiled his reform package, the Belgrade press attacked

it as inherently anti-Serbian. To an extent this was the case, since any liberalisation of the economy certainly benefited the wealthier republics, that is Slovenia and Croatia, proportionately more than the rest of the country. But the poorest republics, Bosnia-Hercegovina, Macedonia and even Montenegro, nevertheless supported the reforms since they at least offered them the prospect of a way out of the economic crisis. The real reason for Serbian objections was quite simply that it was not in Milošević's interests to see Marković succeed. From the start he worked to sabotage the programme.

In Slovenia, where Marković's reforms were most thoroughly implemented, the result was a spate of liquidations and the appearance for the first time of unemployment. In Serbia, by contrast, Milošević ignored the wage freeze and continued to bail out bankrupt enterprises. Within months average income in Serbia equalled that of Slovenia though there had been no corresponding increase in productivity. However, bankrolling Serbia's economy was becoming increasingly difficult and Milošević had to resort to more desperate measures to keep the subsidies flowing. In October 1990 Serbia began to levy duties on Slovene and Croatian 'imports' and then, at 'spontaneous' workers' meetings, to nationalise the property of Slovene and Croatian companies. Each move was justified by the years of economic exploitation Serbia had allegedly endured. But as Slovenia and Croatia retaliated in kind, hope of an economic upturn disappeared.

When Serbs went to the polls on 23 December sufficient numbers voted for Milošević because he promised them security, both from austerity programmes such as that designed by Ante Marković, and from the many enemies who, according to the Serbian media, were forever ganging up against them. Milošević's principal opponent was Vuk Drašković, an extreme nationalist and founder of the Serb Renewal Movement (*Srpski pokret obnove*), whose electoral campaign was little short of a call to arms. Drašković was wholeheartedly committed to the creation of a Greater Serbia and promised an even more aggressive national programme than Milošević. The perceived threat to Serbia and Serbdom was virtually the only theme of the election which, on account of his monopoly of the media, Milošević could not lose. So great was the media hysteria that most Serbs genuinely believed that, in the person of Franjo Tudjman, the Ustašas had returned to power in Croatia and that Serbs everywhere were now facing genocide.

Croatia awakes

In a rational climate nobody could have claimed that Tudjman, the communist general turned nationalist historian who led the HDZ to victory in Croatia's April election, was an Ustasa. He had, after all, been a partisan officer during the Second World War and, in all likelihood, would have been executed by the Ustašas had they managed to capture him. But the climate which Milošević had cultivated in Serbia during the previous three years was anything but rational. As far as the Serbian media was concerned, whoever won the Croatian elections, it was the Ustašas returning to power. Even the leader of Croatia's former communists, Ivica Račan (whose family had been murdered by the Ustašas during the Second World War), was labelled an Ustaša. Indeed, Račan had been branded Ustaša from the moment he became President of Croatia's League of Communists nearly a year earlier.

Though Tudjman could not be described as an Ustaša he fought an unashamedly nationalistic electoral campaign and swept to power on a tide of Croat nationalism. The principal theme of the election was the perceived threat to Croatia and all Croats of the new Serb nationalism and the party which won was that which convinced the electorate it could best stand up to Milošević. The main contenders were Račan's former communists, Tudjman's HDZ and the Coalition of National Agreement (*Koalicija narodnog sporazuma* or KNS) guided by Savka Dapčević-Kučar, Croatia's disgraced leader of 1971. Croatian political commentators remarked that it was effectively a contest between the three faces of Croatian communism since the Second World War. Račan represented the traditions of the Party which evolved out of Tito's 1971 purge, Dapčević-Kučar had been the main mover in the Party during the Croatian Spring between 1968 and 1971 and Tudjman was a relic from the unreformed, pre-1966 Party. But, while both Račan and Dapčević-Kučar fought responsible electoral campaigns and attempted to appeal to the entire electorate irrespective of ethnic origins, Tudjman appealed exclusively to Croats and their bruised sense of national pride.

The HDZ was not a conventional political party but a broad coalition of disaffected elements which Tudjman and others of a similar vintage[9] managed to weave together. Disaffection was rife among

[9] Tudjman's deputy was Josip Manolić, another former partisan who had been Croatia's Interior Minister and thus head of the secret police for much of the post-war period.

Croats, more so than among any of Yugoslavia's other peoples, except perhaps Albanians, since Tito's purge of 1971 had cut so much deeper in Croatia. In the aftermath of the Croatian Spring a generation of Croats was adamant either that their lives had been permanently blighted by the clampdown or, at the very least, that they had been held back in their careers on account of their ethnic origins.[10] In addition to many of the generation of communist conservatives which Tito had removed in 1966, the HDZ attracted support from a motley assortment of political opportunists who sensed which way the wind was blowing. On a trip abroad at the end of 1989 Tudjman also won backing from significant sections of the large Croat community in the United States, Latin America, Canada, Australia and Germany, who financed his electoral campaign.

The HDZ was not the only party with financial support from abroad. Dapčević-Kučar's KNS was also bankrolled by Croat *émigrés*, though by a very different section of that community. Dapčević-Kučar's supporters tended to come from a Croat intelligentsia, while Tudjman's were largely drawn from working class communities. Many of Tudjman's backers were originally from Hercegovina, and of these some must have had links with the Ustaša state. The exact level of *émigré* contributions to the HDZ's electoral campaign is not known, though estimates extend to more than $8 million. In any case, *émigré* money alone was not the secret of Tudjman's success, since all three main parties had the means to win the election. The key to the HDZ's victory was Slobodan Milošević, the barrage of national hatred coming from Belgrade and the antics of Serb extremists in Croatia. Of the three principal party leaders Tudjman alone promised to fight fire with fire.

Milošević's assault on Croatia started not in 1990 but in 1987. As soon as he came to power, media coverage of Croatia shifted in line with the new Serb nationalism. The few column inches in Serbian newspapers which were not taken up by alleged Albanian atrocities were seemingly given over to distorted images of relations with the rest of Yugoslavia's peoples. At the end of 1988 the media offensive against Croatia went into overdrive with allegations that radioactive

[10] While undoubtedly some Croats of genuine ability were persecuted as a result of their ethnic origins in the aftermath of the Croatian Spring, for others with less to offer the clampdown was a convenient scapegoat for more personal failings. As so often in Yugoslavia, the perception of persecution was, in many ways, greater and more significant than the actual level.

waste had been deliberately dumped in Serb villages in Croatia and that Serbs were falling ill and dying as a result. The outcry was so great that Croatia's then communist authorities (at the time the head of Croatia's League of Communists Stanko Stojčević was himself a Serb) decided to dig up the alleged site to resolve the matter. While predictably no radioactive waste was ever recovered, the affair dragged on as the Serbian media demanded that further sites be examined.

In the course of 1989 various newly-founded Serb cultural institutions (political parties were still banned) began organising commemorative services to Serb dead from the Second World War at sites of Ustaša atrocities in Croatia. They also staged protest rallies of the sort which Milošević had orchestrated in Serbia, Kosovo, Montenegro and Vojvodina in an attempt to whip up nationalist emotions among Croatia's Serbs. But the turn-out at these meetings was pitiful.

Far from rushing into Milošević's arms, the vast majority of Croatia's Serbs ignored the rallies. Most now lived in cities, were well-integrated in Croatian society and embarrassed by the upsurge in Milošević's brand of nationalism. The exception was the backward Serb-populated regions around Knin, which in 1989 the Serbian media began describing as *krajina*,[11] and the Serb communities which had settled eastern Slavonia on the border with Vojvodina after the Second World War. Both communities were susceptible to the Milošević offensive, the former on account of their backwardness, the latter on account of their proximity to Serbia, and Milošević hoped to use them in the same way that he had already used nationalist protestors in Vojvodina and Montenegro to topple the government and usher in another 'anti-bureaucratic revolution'. During 1989 a group of mainly Serb hardliners did indeed attempt to seize control of the Croatian League of Communists, but, without the support of mass rallies, they failed and in a counter-*coup* by the League's liberal wing Račan came to power.

Milošević's early attempts to destabilise Croatia had a greater impact on Croat opinion than on Serb opinion within Croatia. As the LCY

[11]*Krajina* literally means the border region. The name is derived from the former military frontier of *vojna krajina* which the Habsburgs created to defend their Empire in the 16th century and remained in place until 1881. The term *krajina* is rejected by Croats since it has no geographical boundaries. The borders of the Habsburg *vojna krajina* shifted over the centuries and depended on the relative strength of their Empire *vis-à-vis* the Ottoman. The Serb *krajina*, or *krajinas* since there are several of them, essentially extend as far as Serb military victories take them.

broke up and Croatia opted to follow Slovenia on the path towards democracy, the media campaign against anything and everything Croat moved up another gear. Essentially, the Serbian media were baiting the Croat public with their constant barrage of insinuation, allegations and insults. Perhaps, given the extent and intensity of the campaign, it was inevitable that at some stage somebody would be ensnared, stand up to Milošević and answer his call to nationalism in kind. Tudjman did just that. During the election campaign his party aimed to make maximum political capital out of every conceivable Croat grievance. But his best party political broadcasts were the propaganda emanating from Serbia and the newly-formed Serb nationalist party in Croatia, the Serb Democratic Party (SDS).

The SDS was founded on 17 February 1990 by Jovan Rašković, a psychiatrist originally from Knin who lived and worked in Šibenik on the Dalmatian coast. The party evolved out of the cultural institutions which had been doing their utmost to stir up Croatia's Serbs during 1989. It was supposed to be an extension of Serbia's Democratic Party (*Demokratska stranka*) which was a liberal opposition party, but was increasingly taken over by a militant wing loyal to Milošević. Most of its founding fathers were Rašković's associates, many of them health workers, doctors, dentists and especially psychiatrists. When the SDS decided to spread into Bosnia-Hercegovina, Rašković simply contacted his professional colleagues there to get the party off the ground. The result was that another psychiatrist, Radovan Karadžić, became President of the Bosnian SDS and, in time, war leader of the Bosnian Serbs.

For Rašković, who was eleven when the Second World War spread to Yugoslavia, the years and events of 1941-5 moulded and soured his attitudes to Croatia and everything Croat. He was not a Milošević mercenary determined to stir up trouble, but instead genuinely believed there was something innately sinister in the Croat character and that Croats should never be allowed to forget, nor be forgiven, the atrocities committed by the Ustašas. It was a point of view which many of his generation shared but which succeeding generations, reared on a Titoist diet of 'brotherhood and unity', did not. Rašković did not simply play on the potential insecurity of the Serb community in Croatia, he actually lived it. Alone of the Serb nationalist leaders of the late 1980s and early 1990s he was not primarily a self-seeker. His was a moral crusade to open Serb eyes to the dangers he perceived they would inevitably face living among Croats.

While Rašković believed in the innate depravity of Croats, he also believed in the essential goodness of Serbs and this blinded him to what Milošević and his henchmen were really up to in Croatia.[12] Rašković cooperated with Belgrade at first because he assumed they had the same aims and that Belgrade was acting in the best interests of Croatia's Serbs. As he campaigned to stir up Croatia's Serbs with tales of Ustaša atrocities the two paths converged, but Rašković shied away from open confrontation with Zagreb and fell out with Belgrade. In September 1990 he went abroad to try to raise support and funds for his party among Serb *émigrés*[13] and in his absence Milošević had him ousted. Despite the appeal to Serb nationalism, Rašković failed to pick up much support in the Croatian election except around Knin. The vast majority of Croatia's Serbs voted not for the SDS but for the former communists who, since Račan took the reins, had belatedly turned themselves into a progressive party.

The former communists actually came close to winning the election and under a system of proportional representation all three principal parties might have expected a say in government. But Račan had opted for a first-past-the-post system, enabling a party to win a majority in parliament on a minority poll, in the mistaken belief that his party would be its principal beneficiary. He had calculated correctly that no party could win an outright majority, but assumed that with the support of both Serbs and Croats his party would pick up more votes than any other. However, on the day the HDZ polled 41.5 per cent of the vote while former communists picked up only 34.5 per cent[14] and Dapčević-Kučar's KNS won 15 per cent. When translated into parliamentary seats the HDZ had 69 per cent, the former communists

[12] I interviewed Rašković in February 1992, a month before he died. He was profoundly depressed and admitted he had totally misjudged Milan Babić, his successor who ousted him as SDS leader, and claimed that from the moment Babić came to power he was determined to provoke a war.

[13] Serb *émigré* communities are quite different from their Croat counterparts. While Croats have emigrated throughout the 20th century, Serbs only left Yugoslavia in large numbers in the aftermath of the Second World War. As a result, the Serb *émigré* community is much smaller than its Croat counterpart and largely made up of people who fought on the wrong side in the Second World War and their descendants.

[14] There were actually two parties of former communists, Račan's Party of Democratic Change, which won 28 per cent of votes, and the Socialists who won 6.5 per cent.

23.5 per cent and the KNS a paltry 4 per cent. On 30 May a HDZ-dominated parliament elected Tudjman Croatia's first post-communist President.

Tudjman was proud to call himself a Croat nationalist and determined to put the record straight, as he saw it, as far as Croatian history and, in particular, the events of the Second World War were concerned. He was proud because for the past twenty years he had been persecuted for his opinions[15] and nationalism was for him a badge of courage. Ironically, as a young man Tudjman had actually been a great Yugoslav patriot. His years in the partisans and then in the JNA conditioned him to love Tito and everything Yugoslav.[16] Tudjman's opinions changed when, as head of Zagreb's Institute for the History of Working Class Movements, he began to research the Second World War. For he discovered that the conventional picture of that era, which he had, hitherto, accepted implicitly, did not tally with his investigations.

Much of Tudjman's early revisionist scholarship was a serious contribution to a better understanding of the Second World War. As a general he had access to sensitive documents other historians had not been able to get their hands on and these led him to the conclusion that a great historical injustice had been done to Croatia. Controversy centres around estimates of war dead and, in particular, the number of dead from the Ustaša concentration camp at Jasenovac. Tudjman calculated that no more than 70,000 people of all nationalities could conceivably have been killed there, which was a fraction of the million plus dead that Serb historians were claiming at the time. While the broad thrust of Tudjman's early findings have since been largely corroborated by the more scientific research of Bogoljub Kočović and Vladimir Žerjavić (see chapter 3), Tudjman went on to undermine his own arguments over the next twenty-five years by dreaming up increasingly far-fetched conspiracy theories.

Tudjman's research had shattered the view of the world he had held

---

[15] In common with many Croat dissidents from the early 1970s Tudjman was jailed. However, the terms of his imprisonment and subsequent release were, as befitted a former general, considerably easier than those which most Croat dissidents had to endure. In 1972 Tudjman was sentenced to two years in prison, commuted to the ten months he had already served awaiting trial. In 1981 he was sentenced to an additional three years and banned from all public activities for five years.

[16] Tudjman's Yugoslav patriotism is reflected in his early historical writings which eulogise communist Yugoslavism as the culmination of a great historical process.

as a young man. As a result, during the many years he brooded in political disgrace, he clung to his new beliefs with the zeal of a convert. In his own mind he came to personify Croatia and Croat suffering, while the question of war dead evolved into a crusade. Anyone who disagreed with his findings or even anything which appeared to contradict them became to Tudjman part of a conspiracy to make Croatia appear 'odious in the eyes of the world'. As the years went by and Tudjman became increasingly bitter, his views became more extreme, distanced from his original research, and tainted with anti-Semitism. In time, Tudjman effectively became an apologist for the NDH and the concept of an independent Croatian state, if not for the Ustašas, while his estimates of the Jasenovac dead edged conveniently downwards.[17]

Close to two decades of artificial silence in Croatia since Tito's 1971 purge and nearly three years of taunting from Belgrade played into Tudjman's hands at the 1990 election. The tone of the campaign was set at one of the HDZ's earliest meetings in Benkovac when a deranged Serb pulled a gun on Tudjman. Though it later emerged that the gun had only been a starter's pistol, the incident and reactions to it brought nationalist emotions in Croatia to, hitherto, unprecedented levels as the HDZ traded insults with Belgrade and the SDS. National symbolism assumed a poignancy it had never held before and the HDZ cashed in by adopting traditional Croatian flags and insignia as its own and flaunting them on every possible occasion.

As the election results came through and it became clear that the HDZ had won, panic spread throughout the Serb communities in the SDS heartland around Knin. Ordinary Serbs from Knin, who were subject to the Serbian media barrage, genuinely believed that the Ustašas had returned to power and were about to descend on their villages to wipe them out. So great was the hysteria many even had their bags packed ready to flee. But as soon as Tudjman won the election he changed tack and adopted a conciliatory approach. Indeed, one of his first moves was to offer Rašković one of five vice-presidential posts in his government. The offer was genuine but, on advice from Belgrade, Rašković rejected it. Instead of trying to calm his supporters, he and other SDS leaders worked to stoke their fears and boycotted Croatia's new parliament.

[17] By 1989 Tudjman concluded in his most controversial work, *The Impasses of Historical Reality*, that the maximum number of Ustaša victims was between 180,000 and 240,000 of whom only 59,639 died in concentration camps.

The pretext for the boycott was an alleged attack on Miroslav Mlinar, a twenty-three-year-old SDS activist from Benkovac, on 19 May, at a time when the election result was known but before the formal hand-over of power. Both Rašković and the Serbian media immediately condemned the act as another 'Ustaša atrocity', though precisely what happened to Mlinar and whether or not an attack actually took place is hard to say. Doctors who examined him at Zadar hospital decided his injuries were slight but this did not satisfy the SDS leadership, who had him reexamined in Knin. After the second examination Milan Babić (Director of Knin hospital and deputy leader of the SDS) claimed that the injuries were life-threatening and that the Ustašas were trying to cover the affair up. On account of the enormous publicity the case had generated and the hysterical accusations which were again being levelled in the Serbian media at Croatia and everything Croat, the then Croatian authorities (still the former communists) established a medical commission to determine the extent of Mlinar's injuries. By the time that the commission confirmed the original diagnosis the affair had spiralled way out of control.

No culprit was ever found and, despite Babić's claims, Mlinar made a full and rapid recovery. He also became the beneficiary of a trust fund set up for his welfare in Belgrade and moved there to study drama at the prestigious Academy of Dramatic Arts. Whether or not the affair was orchestrated to discredit the new Croatian authorities and scupper Tudjman's conciliatory initiative, it poisoned the atmosphere of the new parliament even before it had convened and gave SDS MPs an excuse to suspend relations with Zagreb. Instead of taking up their seats in the Zagreb parliament, the SDS MPs formed the Union of Communes of Lika and Northern Dalmatia out of the six constituencies they had won in the election, with its own parliament, the Serb National Council, in Knin.

The Knin parliament's first move was to declare the sovereignty and independence of the Serb nation. It then permanently severed (the already suspended) relations with Zagreb and announced a Serb referendum on autonomy to be held between 19 August and 2 September. Rašković rejected any dialogue with Zagreb and Tudjman declared the referendum illegal. In the run-up to the ballot the media war between Serbia and Croatia moved up yet another gear and for the first time the Croatian media gave almost as good as it got. Knin became a no-go area for Croats and a newly-formed Serb militia cut road and rail links between Zagreb and the Dalmatian coast. On 17 August, two days before the referendum was due to begin, Tudjman despatched three helicopters filled with armed police to pacify the region, but on their way to Knin they were intercepted by two Yugoslav airforce Migs and forced back to base.

JNA forges Serbian alliance

Military intervention changed the Croatian equation. While the Croatian police should have been able to put down a rebellion by a handful of Serbs, they did not have the firepower to take on the JNA and had to abandon the entire Knin region. According to the official investigation into the events of 17 August, the decision to intervene was made at a relatively junior level, probably by the airbase commander. Nevertheless, it was clearly sanctioned higher up since no disciplinary action was taken and the JNA continued to ensure that Croatian police kept well clear of Knin. The referendum went ahead, Croatia was effectively sliced in two and Zagreb was powerless to do anything about it.

The commanding officer in Knin was Ratko Mladić. In August 1990 nobody outside Yugoslavia had heard of him, yet he was about to acquire a level of international notoriety surpassed only by his paymasters Slobodan Milošević and Radovan Karadžić. Mladić was a Serb from Bosnia whose outlook on life was shaped and twisted by his family's fortunes in the Second World War. In 1945 his father was killed in action and as a child the young Ratko was brought up on tales of Ustaša atrocities, leaving him with a pathological hatred of Croats and Muslims. During the 1991 war in Croatia Mladić proved one of the most brutal and efficient officers in the JNA. He opposed the peace accord ending that war and, between the official end of hostilities in Croatia and the outbreak of full-scale fighting in Bosnia-Hercegovina, did his best to scupper it. In May 1992 Mladić was appointed Commander-in-Chief of the Bosnian Serb Army and masterminded operations against Bosnia-Hercegovina's Muslims and Croats. Six months later the outgoing Bush administration in the United States named him a suspected war criminal.

Mladić represented an important faction within the JNA, if not the official views of the High Command. As befitted a fighting force forged under the banner 'brotherhood and unity', the very top of the armed forces retained a healthy ethnic balance[18] with a genuine commitment to Yugoslavism. Most of the highest-ranking officers were a throw-back to the Tito era when ideological orthodoxy and fidelity to Titoism had been prerequisites for a military career and nationalists languished in the middle and junior ranks of the officer corps. The half-Serb, half-Croat Defence Minister, Veljko Kadijević, for example, was above all a committed communist. He was definitely not a Serb nationalist and no friend of Milošević's. But in the decade since Tito's death a handful of avowed Serb nationalists had made it to positions of authority in the military and formed an influential coterie around him. This included General Blagoje Adžić, who became Chief-of-Staff in Autumn 1989.

Adžić, a Serb from Croatia, was probably the most fanatical of all Serb nationalists in the JNA. Like Mladić his outlook on life had been shaped by his family's experience during the Second World War, but in Adžić's case this was not merely based on other people's recollections but was what he had witnessed himself, which poisoned his mind against anything and everything Croat. Apparently, as a teenager he watched from a tree as the Ustašas slaughtered his entire family. If this was indeed the case,[19] the psychological trauma he must have gone through is difficult to imagine. It is said that on that day he vowed to get even. Almost half a century later he had risen to a position from which he was able to wreak a dreadful revenge.

The demise of communism put officers of Kadijević's ilk in an extremely awkward position. The ideological world they had grown up in and in which they fervently believed disappeared within the space of a few months. Instead of 'rolling back the frontiers of capitalism' they found themselves struggling to hang onto the remnants of their own communist society. Still more galling was the manner in which capitalism appeared to have triumphed. The entire Marxist-Leninist edifice had come crashing down, yet there had been no military defeat and the communist armed forces remained intact. Kadijević felt betrayed by Yugoslavia's civilian leaders, especially the Slovene and

[18] In the High Command 38 per cent were Croats, 33 per cent Serbs and 8.3 per cent Slovenes. Croats, not Serbs, were dominant in both the navy and the airforce.

[19] By 1991 every Serb officer seemed to be claiming that all sorts of atrocities had been committed against his family during the Second World War, which on closer examination often turned out not to be true. But in Adžić's case there can be little doubt that the Ustašas did murder his family and that he narrowly escaped a similar fate himself.

Croatian communists who had abandoned socialism without a fight: hence his decision to disarm their territorial defence forces and his refusal to recognise the new democratically-elected governments. At stake was the JNA's very existence and with it the privileged lifestyles of senior officers.

One consequence was a rapprochement with the Soviet military, the only other remaining communist army in Europe. During 1990 and 1991 senior officers from both armies met up on several occasions to work out the best way to 'preserve the gains of the revolution'. In March 1991 Kadijević himself made a secret trip to Moscow for talks with his Soviet counterpart Dimitri Yazov. During this meeting it is widely rumoured that he arranged a $2 billion arms deal, though, as a result of the failed *coup d'état* in the Soviet Union in August and the disgrace of many senior Soviet officers, few of the weapons ever found their way into the Yugoslav arsenal. In any case, cooperation with the Soviet military was never going to resolve the JNA's identity crisis nor could it resurrect a unitary, communist Yugoslavia, which was Kadijević's ultimate aim.

As far as Kadijević was concerned, a unitary state was the sole option, since that was the only arrangement which would enable the JNA and defence industry to continue in its present form. However, the military budget required disproportionate *per capita* contributions from Slovenia and Croatia, which neither republic was prepared to continue paying indefinitely. Slovenia, in particular, where the JNA's *bête noire* Janez Janša became Defence Minister after the April elections, appeared determined to reform the military, and both Slovenia and Croatia were pressing to reorganise Yugoslavia along confederal lines. Serbia alone stood unequivocally for a unitary state. As a result, much as Kadijević personally disliked Milošević, Serbia's communists emerged by default as the only party with which he and the rest of the military establishment shared any common ground.

The alliance between the JNA and Milošević's Serbia was sealed on 17 November 1990 as hardline communists and senior officers came together to form a new Communist Party, the League of Communists—Movement for Yugoslavia (*Savez komunista—pokret za Jugoslaviju* or SKPJ). In addition to Kadijević and former Defence Ministers Branko Mamula and Nikola Ljubičić, the SKPJ included Milošević's wife, Mirjana Marković, among its founding members. Immediately after the party's inaugural meeting, former Chief-of-Staff Stevan Mirković informed a Belgrade press conference that Milošević's

newly renamed Socialists were the only party to vote for in the
forthcoming Serbian elections.

Though Kadijević had been reluctant to ally himself publicly with
Milošević, a Serbian alliance entailed no appreciable change in direction. In practice, the military had already been doing Milošević's
bidding for at least two years, albeit informally. Kadijević had
countenanced the piecemeal destruction of the 1974 constitution,
which the armed forces were supposed to uphold, and in 1989 the
JNA had intervened illegally in Kosovo to strip the province of its
autonomy. Serbs and Montenegrins made up more than 70 per cent[20]
of the 60,000 officer corps and, since soldiers were as susceptible to
the Milošević media offensive as anybody else, this preponderance made
a fertile breeding ground for nationalism. By 1990 Serb nationalism
had taken root especially among younger officers, while the more formal understanding between Serbia and the military provided by the
SKPJ enabled Milošević to wage his unofficial war against Croatia with
impunity.

From Milošević's point of view the beauty of the Serb revolt in
Croatia was that Knin, the centre of the revolt, was indispensable to
Croatia, yet he could ensure the dispute between Knin and Zagreb
would never be resolved. The Knin district is a sparsely-populated
wasteland with no industry nor anything else of value, which has traditionally survived on meagre state subsidies. Knin itself lacked a cinema,
let alone a hotel, swimming pool or any other amenities which were
taken for granted elsewhere in Croatia. Nobody in their right mind
would covet the land there, yet for geographic reasons Croatia could
not afford to give it up. Knin sat on the rail and road links between
Zagreb and Split, and without them Dalmatia was effectively cut off
from the rest of Croatia. In reality, Knin was far more dependent on
Croatia than the other way round, though that did not enter the
calculations of the SDS, whose only apparent concern was the inherent
genocidal character of Croats.

In 1991 about 42,000 people lived in the Knin district, that is less
than 1 per cent of Croatia's total population, of whom about 90 per

[20] According to the Slovene defence publication *Revija Obramba*, the ethnic composition of the officer corps in April 1991 was 60 per cent Serb, 5.4 per cent 'Yugoslav'
and presumed to be Serb, 6.2 per cent Montenegrin, 12.6 per cent Croat, 6.3 per
cent Macedonian, 2.4 per cent Muslim Slav, 2.8 per cent Slovene, 0.7 per cent
Hungarian, 0.6 per cent Albanian, and 1.6 per cent other.

cent were Serbs. Even including the neighbouring districts of Donji Lapac, Obrovac, Benkovac, Gračac and Titova Korenica, where Serbs also formed a majority, the entire population was only 117,000, of whom 90,000 or 77 per cent were Serbs, that is about 2.5 per cent of Croatia's total population and 15 per cent of Croatia's Serb population. Declarations of Serb independence and sovereignty, as well as plebiscites on autonomy, were meaningless because the region was separated from Serbia proper by Bosnia-Hercegovina. Moreover, since a majority of Croatia's Serbs lived outside the SDS heartland, autonomy for *Krajina* or any other settlement between Zagreb and Knin could not provide the basis of an accord regulating relations between Serbs and Croats in Croatia. In any case, Milošević had no intention of letting Knin come to a settlement with Zagreb. The Serb question and Serb rights were simply too fundamental to his propaganda offensive.

The Serbs of Knin were among the most traditionally minded people in Yugoslavia and hence ideal material for Milošević. During 1989 they succumbed to his propaganda offensive and by the beginning of 1990 were convinced they were being subjected to genocide and that they had to fight for their very existence. A war psychosis had set in which the Zagreb authorities could not assuage, no matter what they did or did not do. Meanwhile, the SDS leadership was able to wreak havoc throughout the region, secure in the knowledge that Mladić and the JNA would ensure that no harm befell them. The SDS automatically rejected all Zagreb's conciliatory initiatives and the Serbian media continued its offensive against Croatia and, in particular, Franjo Tudjman, aware that its incessant goading would bring out the very worst in him.

Of all the politicians who came to power in eastern Europe in the wake of the demise of communism, temperamentally Tudjman was without doubt the least at home in a democracy. Though no demon, at sixty-eight he was too set in his ways to adapt to a very different world from that which he had grown up in. Tudjman was a career soldier who, from a very early age, had learned to give orders and see them carried out. He joined Tito's partisans as a teenager in 1941 and became a political commissar with the rank of major during the Second World War. In 1945 he moved to the new military headquarters in Belgrade, where he remained for the rest of his army career, rising to major-general by the age of thirty-eight. Tudjman believed that the fact that he had won multiparty elections gave him democratic credentials and that as President of Croatia he should automatically be treated with deference. Short-tempered and capricious at the best of times, he found it incredibly difficult to come to terms with even the mildest of criticism, let alone the character assassination he faced from the Serbian media.

As far as the Serbian media were concerned, Tudjman was the Ustaša and anything and everything he said or did was diabolical. Had he changed water into wine, fed the five thousand and raised Serb victims of the Ustašas from the dead, Tudjman would have remained the epitome of evil. In fact, the accusations against him were no more absurd than those levelled at any of Milošević's opponents and, perhaps, had he been a more astute politician, he might have been able to ignore them. However, despite his years, Tudjman lacked maturity and invariably reacted to the name-calling and the accusations like a spoilt child. Tudjman-baiting became a game to Serbian journalists, who knew that, given the right provocation, the old man would be unable to control himself and would inadvertently supply them with the ammunition to fuel the Serb revolt.

As Milošević replaced Rašković with Milan Babić at the head of the SDS in September 1990, the revolt acquired an unstoppable momentum. Far from being defenceless, as the Serbian media alleged, the inhabitants of Knin could effectively pick and choose weapons from the JNA's arsenal. Officially, the Knin militia, or *Martićevci* as they became known,[21] stole their weapons, though with no comparable 'thefts' elsewhere in Croatia, it would surely not have been possible to acquire so much sophisticated weaponry without military collusion. Indeed, it later emerged that throughout 1990 and 1991 the Serbian Interior Ministry had been supplying Serb communities in Croatia and Bosnia-Hercegovina with weapons via the military. Though Milošević denied any knowledge of the operation at the time, a disillusioned Prime Minister Marković provided taped evidence of Milošević's and Karadžić's scheming shortly after war broke out in Croatia.

The Serb revolt was at first confined to shooting at trains and harassing foreign holiday-makers to sabotage the end of the tourist season. But each month it intensified, the shooting incidents became more frequent and bombs started going off in towns all over Croatia. While the JNA had been quick to intervene against the Croatian police

---

[21] The *Martićevci* were named after their commander Milan Martić who had been Knin's police chief prior to the rebellion.

to prevent them crushing the revolt, it made no effort to curtail the acts of terrorism, which by autumn 1990 had become a feature of Croatian life. With the main transport links across the republic cut and tourists frightened away by the escalating violence, the Croatian economy inevitably deteriorated and this had ramifications for the rest of the country as well.

Independence

The notion of independence declarations was conceived in Slovenia in the autumn of 1990. At the time, the ruling *Demos* coalition was in crisis, the Slovene economy reeling under the side effects of Marković's austerity programme and talks on Yugoslavia's future were stalled. A plebiscite on independence appeared to offer a convenient diversion from the republic's economic ills and the government's unpopularity, as well as a bargaining counter in inter-republican negotiations. It was, however, essentially meaningless since, according to the existing Yugoslav constitution, Slovenia was already independent and sovereign. Nevertheless, on 23 December, the same day Serbia reelected Slobodan Milošević President, the plebiscite went ahead and Slovenes voted overwhelmingly for independence. As soon as the result was official on 26 December,[22] the Slovene parliament declared its intent to secede from Yugoslavia in six months' time if there was no progress towards a negotiated settlement of the country's future.

With give and take on all sides, most disputes, no matter how seemingly complex or protracted, can eventually be resolved. But negotiations will only bear fruit when all parties believe it is in their interests to compromise and in Yugoslavia this was not the case. While inevitably all sides blamed each other for the repeated break-down of talks, the fundamental obstacle to progress was that Serbia had no need to negotiate. Tactics which after June 1991 came to infuriate international mediators were but a continuation of the strategy Milošević had pursued during the seventeen months of sham talks in the run-up to the outbreak of war, and indeed throughout his political career. Serbia controlled four of the eight seats in the federal Presidency, including that of President during the critical year 15 May 1990 to 15 May 1991, and could not be voted down. Moreover, as a result of the military

---

[22] 93.2 per cent of the Slovene electorate turned out to vote at the referendum and of them 94.6 per cent, that is 88.2 per cent of the electorate, voted for independence.

alliance, alone of Yugoslavia's republics Serbia possessed the weapons to wage a war. As Serb irregulars in Croatia began carving a Greater Serbian state out of Yugoslavia, Milošević could see no reason to compromise.

On 29 May 1990, one day before Tudjman came into office, Serbia attempted to bulldoze a new Yugoslav constitution through the federal assembly. The plan was put forward by Serbia's representative on the Presidency, Borisav Jović (who had become President two weeks earlier), and envisaged strengthening the country's centre by making federal decisions binding on republics. It also set out to quash the unilateral constitutional reforms by which Slovenia and Croatia had already held multiparty elections. In essence, the plan was the same as that which Milošević had already attempted unsuccessfully to foist on the 14th Congress of the LCY. Predictably, it was favoured by the Serbian bloc and the military but, despite some initial interest in Bosnia-Hercegovina and Macedonia, the rest of the country rejected it and the federal assembly threw it out.

Jović's proposals were diametrically opposed to those put forward in the north of the country. In Slovenia, Kučan came up with a discussion document for a model of Yugoslavia inspired by the European Community which he attempted to sell to the rest of the country together with Tudjman. Under the Kučan-Tudjman proposals, Yugoslavia was to become a voluntary confederation of independent, sovereign states in which each was a separate subject of international law and each had the explicit right to secede. There was to be monetary union with a single market, harmonised infrastructure and coordinated armed forces. Ideally, the state would be a parliamentary democracy, though Kučan was prepared to accept a two-speed community in which the north (Slovenia and Croatia) was democratic, while the rest of the country remained communist-ruled, as long as the territorial integrity of the north was guaranteed.

Disagreement appeared to boil down to the structure, whether federal or confederal, of a third Yugoslav state. Yet such a simplification fails to do justice to the issues Yugoslav politicians were facing. In reality, whether Yugoslavia remained a federation or became a confederation was of secondary importance. The ultimate goal for Yugoslavia's non-Serbian leaders was security from Serbia. Given Milošević's track record, a centralised federation was not about coexistence but about stamping his own communist order on the entire country. By contrast, the linchpin of the Kučan-Tudjman proposals was the concept of 'civil society', that is, a society governed by the rule of law (as opposed to the arbitrary nature of communist authority), in which every citizen, irrespective of national origins, has equal rights and duties. While neither Kučan nor Tudjman were especially comfortably with this concept, it was only within such a community that the democratic attitudes and humanitarian values necessary to safeguard the interests of all Yugoslavia's peoples could begin to evolve. And, above all, it was the concept of civil society which Milošević rejected.

The level of devolution envisaged in the Kučan-Tudjman discussion document was little more than a codification of the state of affairs which had already emerged as a result of the demise of communism. The critical difference between what Slovenia and Croatia were proposing and the *de facto* status quo was the voluntary nature of the union and the degree of protection that this and the explicit right to secede afforded all republics from each other and specifically from Milošević's bullying. Above all the Kučan-Tudjman proposals were designed as an insurance policy against further 'anti-bureaucratic revolutions' of the sort which had already toppled the governments of Vojvodina and Montenegro.

The principal motivation for both Kučan and Tudjman during the pre-war negotiations was fear — fear, that is, of a Kosovo scenario in either Slovenia or Croatia or both. The threat was very real, as the events of 1991 were to prove. Already in 1990 the JNA began organising war games in which the enemy was Slovenia and Croatia. The manoeuvres were designed to deter Yugoslavia's northern republics from secession but had the opposite effect. As far as Slovene and Croatian politicians were concerned, the sabre-rattling was merely confirmation that the military had come exclusively to represent the interests of Serbia. After all, it tolerated a situation in Kosovo in which 90 per cent of the population was systematically deprived of even the most basic human rights, in direct breach of the constitution it was officially obliged to uphold, while in Croatia and Bosnia-Hercegovina the JNA was supplying rebel Serbs with weapons at the same time as it disarmed the legally-constituted territorial defence forces of Slovenia and Croatia.

Fear motivated all sides in Yugoslavia, not just Slovenia and Croatia, and since fear is the most powerful of human emotions, this made it extremely difficult to reach a compromise. The idealism which had enabled Tito to bring peoples together and celebrate all that was best

in each Yugoslav nation had vanished. 'Brotherhood and unity' had
given way to a very real oppression in parts of the country and a
perception of oppression or at least imminent oppression everywhere
else. Ironically, it was the nation which claimed to be the most
persecuted and shouted loudest and longest about its plight which
the rest of Yugoslavia's peoples viewed as the oppressor. Serbs were
adamant that they faced not merely persecution but 'genocide' on every
front, especially in Kosovo and Croatia.

'Genocide' must be the most abused word in the Serb language.
Literally it means the deliberate extermination of a people and it is
hard to imagine a more heinous crime. Given the gravity of Serbian
allegations, one would expect international human rights groups to
have put the plight of Serbs at the very top of their agendas. However,
in Kosovo they had actually taken up the cause of the alleged
perpetrators of genocide, the Albanians. Talk of genocide was a gross
distortion of reality, yet that did not lessen the intensity of feeling
among ordinary Serbs who, as a result of Milošević's propaganda offensive, sincerely believed and behaved as if they were facing extermination. The demonisation of Yugoslavia's non-Serbs in the Serbian media
during the 1980s was as complete as that of the Jews in Nazi Germany
during the 1930s and the perception of persecution in the minds of
ordinary Serbs was total.

The Serbian media found their most convincing ammunition in
Croatia, thanks to Tudjman's extraordinary bungling. The Croatian
President inadvertently aided Serbian propagandists and proved to be
his own worst enemy. Though he surely realised everything he said
or did was bound to be distorted and used against him, he could not
resist explaining on every possible occasion that the Ustašas were not
truly representative of Croats, that more Croats fought as partisans
than Ustašas during the Second World War, and that just because
the NDH had been a disaster that was no reason to deny Croats in
perpetuity a state of their own. It was as if he believed that by
repeating this often enough he would eventually convince Serb
nationalists that they were wrong. But it played into Milošević's hands
as, more through ineptitude than malice, Tudjman appeared to give
substance to at least some of the Serbian media's allegations.

The stupidity of many of Tudjman's off-the-cuff remarks was legen-
dary. During the 1990 election campaign, for example, he came out
with 'I am doubly happy that my wife is neither a Serb nor a Jew',
which inevitably became his best-known line. Though, according to

his advisers, Tudjman had actually been trying to make a joke at the time, which just happened to come out horribly wrong, it was hardly the kind of comment which the fifth of Croatia's population who were not Croats wanted to hear from a prospective head of state.

Electoral victory went straight to Tudjman's head, confirming in his own mind the messianic role he was destined to play in Croatian history. In retrospect, even he might accept that some of his earliest moves were tactless. The day the Zagreb parliament appointed Tudjman President it also revoked some of the finest Titoist legislation protecting the rights of minorities. The thirty-ninth amendment to the constitution, which made a two-thirds parliamentary majority mandatory for any change to laws concerning minorities, was scrapped. Moreover, it was repealed on the basis of a simple majority, which, needless to say, did nothing to inspire confidence in non-Croats. Soon afterwards the HDZ party flag, which had been based on traditional Croatian designs including the distinctive red and white chess board, became the official flag of Croatia[23] and all socialist insignia were removed from the name and emblem of the state. Meanwhile, the government set out to 'purify' the official language to remove alleged Serbisms, changing street names[24] and purging the administration, especially the media and the police force, in a manner which struck disproportionately against Croatia's Serbs.

However Tudjman's hold on power in the summer of 1990 was tenuous and insecurity accounted for much of the insensitivity of his actions. The JNA made it clear that it would not recognise the results of Croatia's election and the republic was defenceless, its territorial defence forces disarmed, the police in communist hands and largely controlled by Serbs. Like the old Communist he was, Tudjman set about making his position secure in the only way he knew how, amassing as much authority as possible within his own hands. The purges in Croatia were, in fact, no greater than anywhere else in the

---

[23] While the flag was supposed to be Croatia's traditional standard it was actually modified half a year later for another traditional design. In both cases great pains were taken to ensure the flag was different from that which the Ustašas had used during the NDH, but to no avail as Croatia's Serbs rejected it on principle.

[24] Language purification had predictably comic results as words which had died out almost half a century earlier were revived and others were invented to differentiate between Croat and Serb. Some of the new street names were also rather tactless. The most notorious example was Victims of Fascism Square (*Trg Žrtava Fašisma*) in Zagreb which became Croat Heroes Square (*Trg Hrvatskih Velikana*).

ex-communist world and Tudjman's actions, crude as they were, were not responsible for the alienation of *Krajina*'s Serbs, for the simple reason that they had already been alienated from Croatia and everything Croat at least six months if not a year earlier.

The situation in Croatia was also a cause of great anxiety to Slovenia's leaders, though they lost no sleep over the alleged plight of Croatia's Serbs. Kučan was familiar with the Serbian allegations but viewed them as merely a pretext for intervention. Indeed, even in Slovenia a Serb national party had been founded among Serb guest workers and it too was alleging 'genocide', while Serbian secret police had apparently been visiting the handful of Uniate villages[25] on the Slovene border with Croatia in an attempt to stir up the communities there. What concerned Slovenia's leaders about Croatia and the rest of Yugoslavia was how close the country was to civil war and how powerless they were to do anything about it. It appeared only a matter of months before large-scale fighting might break out either in Croatia or in Bosnia-Hercegovina or most probably in both.

Slovenia's leaders first began seriously to toy with the idea of secession when the JNA moved against Kosovo in March 1989. While Slovenes could not claim that they, too, were victims of Serbian oppression, they felt an affinity for Yugoslavia's Albanians since the two peoples formed a similar proportion of the country's total population and neither spoke Serbo-Croat. In the course of the next year and a half the situation in Kosovo as well as the broader Yugoslav picture, continued to deteriorate so that by the end of 1990, when Marković's economic programme came unstuck, even the most Yugophile Slovenes could not see any future within Yugoslavia. Many feared that the most they could realistically look forward to was being milked to pay for the bloated security apparatus necessary to hold down any people Milošević decided to move against. The time had come to cut losses and get out.

Slovenia was unique among Yugoslavia's republics in that it was in a position to extricate itself from the rest of the country with relative ease. It was by Yugoslav standards ethnically homogeneous and,

[25] The Uniate Church is essentially a mixture of the Catholic and Orthodox Churches. Uniate rites are largely in keeping with Orthodox traditions, though the Church acknowledges the Pope as its spiritual head. There are half a dozen or so Uniate villages in Slovenia, whose ancestors were presumably Orthodox settlers who fled northwards in the wake of the Ottoman advance.

critically, had no indigenous Serb minority. Though in recession, Slovenia's leaders were confident the economy would not suffer unduly from a divorce. Despite seven decades as one country, the Slovene economy remained relatively detached from the Yugoslav market, which, in 1989, accounted only for about 15 per cent of purchases and 21 per cent of sales. Moreover, since October 1990, when Serbia imposed taxes on Slovene 'exports', the proportion of trade with the rest of the country had in any case been declining. Whether or not Slovenia would thrive as an independent state, Slovenia's leaders preferred their chances outside rather than inside Yugoslavia and, as soon as the results of the plebiscite were official, began preparing for independence in earnest.

Unstoppable slide to war

The year 1991 was a year of independence declarations both in Yugoslavia and in the Soviet Union. Behind the rhetoric of national self-determination, however, nobody, not even those making the declarations, were clear precisely what independence entailed. In Yugoslavia the picture was especially confused, since Yugoslav republics were already supposed to be independent and therefore a declaration of independence could be interpreted as merely a reaffirmation of the existing state of affairs. Indeed, Slovene politicians would have been delighted with the safeguards stipulated in the 1974 constitution, had they been enforceable. But the flaw in the Yugoslav constitution, as in almost all communist constitutions, was that while exemplary on paper — few constitutions, for example, have ever guaranteed human rights as comprehensively as that which Stalin devised in 1936 — it failed to deliver in practice, and existing constitutional guarantees had proved worthless in the face of Milošević's assault.

Slovenia's leaders knew that they could not simply declare independence and leave Yugoslavia forthwith since, unless the international community sanctioned it, any declaration was meaningless. In fact, the June declaration was designed as no more than the beginning of a process of 'dissociation' which would largely depend on developments elsewhere in the country. Since Milošević made dialogue futile, Slovenia drew up a unilateral schedule for separation, including proposals for the country's debt and the future of the armed forces. However, Kučan stressed that if Yugoslavia could offer Slovenia a secure future — if, say, Serbia ended its economic boycott, ceased threatening Croatia and Bosnia-Hercegovina and granted Albanians a reasonable degree of autonomy—then Slovenia would be glad to forge closer ties with the rest of the country. Essentially, as long as Serbia behaved itself, Slovenia was prepared to remain part of Yugoslavia. But since nobody expected Milošević to change his ways, Slovenia's leaders were aware that they were playing with fire and planned for every possible scenario, including war.

Much of Slovenia's military planning was in conjunction with Croatia, though there was never any alliance between the two republics. Slovenia's leaders knew that they were in a stronger position and feared that a formal alliance might embroil them in the very conflict they were trying to avoid. Since Janša had been tipped off before the JNA disarmed Slovenia's territorial defence forces, Slovenia managed to hang on to about 40 per cent of its weapons. This gave Janša a base from which to build an army, which his Croatian counterpart, former partisan and JNA general Martin Špegelj, did not have. Given the threat of war and the actions of Serb militants in Croatia, both republics did all they could to procure arms on the international market. Most of the weapons they succeeded in buying came via Hungary, including a cache of 10,000 Kalashnikovs which came to Croatia in January 1991 in an operation filmed by Yugoslav military intelligence (*Kontra obaveštajna služba* or KOS) and turned into a television documentary.

While Ljubljana pressed ahead with independence preparations, Zagreb followed cautiously behind, aware that Croatia would be in a better position if it could work together with Slovenia but anxious not to give Belgrade a pretext for intervention. Tudjman was terrified of losing power and, as the Serb revolt escalated, attempted belatedly to woo Croatia's Serbs. He helped set up a party of 'loyal' Serbs called the Serb People's Party (*Srpska narodna stranka*) and even gave in to the SDS's demands for autonomy in *Krajina*. However, as soon as Tudjman conceded autonomy, the SDS upped its demands. The tactics were identical to those Milošević himself pursued in inter-republican negotiations and disturbed Croatia's Serb intellectuals who feared that the greatest losers from SDS intransigence would be the majority of Croatia's Serbs living outside *Krajina*. In an attempt to modify SDS policies many of Croatia's most distinguished Serbs came together in the Serb Democratic Forum (*Srpski demokratski forum*). However, their calls for restraint fell on deaf ears in both Knin and Belgrade.

As far as members of the Forum were concerned, the Serb revolt was detrimental to long-term Serb interests since it appeared to be fuelled not by the condition of Serbs in Croatia but by Milošević's position in Belgrade. As pressure intensified at home, the number of 'incidents' in Croatia rose proportionately. In the run-up to Serbia's December election and in its aftermath, as the opposition alleged fraud, the media worked overtime to direct Serbian frustration against Croatia and away from the deficiencies of Milošević's rule. But as the promises Milošević had made to win the elections proved hollow and inflation wiped out the value of higher pensions and salaries, the opposition organised a petition demanding Milošević's resignation and staged a demonstration on 9 March involving half a million people.

For two days Milošević appeared on the verge of losing power and was forced to call on the JNA to restore order in Belgrade. In street fighting two people, a student and a policeman, were killed and hundreds more injured. The demonstrators produced a list of demands including the resignation of Milošević's police chief and media barons but failed to go for the jugular when Milošević was at his most vulnerable. Unrest was confined to Belgrade and Milošević retained control of the security apparatus. In counter-rallies the leader of *Krajina*'s Serbs, Milan Babić, appealed for Serb unity behind Milošević and accused Drašković, the opposition leader, of collusion with Tudjman. As Milošević succeeded in diverting anger back at Croatia, the opposition lost its momentum and the demonstrations petered out.

Together with Jović, the federal President and head of the country's armed forces, Milošević had been working to impose a state of emergency on Yugoslavia for many months. They came closest on 25 January after the federal Presidency ordered all illegally-armed units to disband, though without specifying whether this meant republican militia or Serb insurgents. That evening Belgrade television screened the KOS documentary implicating Špegelj in illegal arms purchases and the JNA was placed on full alert. The documentary contained damning evidence against Špegelj, almost as if KOS had set up the entire arms deal,[26] though the Croatian authorities denied its authenticity and refused to hand him or Croatia's Interior Minister over for court-martial as the military demanded. In the event, the JNA returned to

[26] KOS may indeed have arranged the entire affair, though clearly Špegelj was desperate to get his hands on every last Kalashnikov. Details remain unclear since one of the principal characters committed suicide soon after the documentary was screened.

barracks, the militia was not disarmed and the Presidency took no further action.

Following the 9 March demonstrations Milošević and Jović renewed efforts to impose a state of emergency throughout Yugoslavia. On his own, however, Jović was unable to declare martial law since he required the support of the rest of the Presidency and representatives from Slovenia, Croatia, Bosnia-Hercegovina and Macedonia refused to back the move. On 15 March he resigned and took the representatives of Vojvodina, Montenegro and Kosovo with him[27] claiming that the balance of power within the Presidency was leading to the break-up of the country, but inducing the constitutional crisis himself. The same night Milošević went on Belgrade television to state that Serbia would no longer obey the federal Presidency and was mobilising police reservists to avert rebellion in Kosovo and the Sandžak. He also urged Serbs to unite behind him to defend themselves. The next day the Serb National Council in Knin proclaimed the secession of *Krajina* from Croatia and Serbia's Prime Minister informed his assembly that Bosnian and Croatian forces were preparing an offensive against Serb-populated towns.

When Jović resigned nobody could work out what this meant for Yugoslavia since, officially, two months of his term in office remained. If his aim was to tip the country over into civil war he failed because, despite the Serbian Prime Minister's claims, neither Croatia nor Bosnia-Hercegovina gave Serbia the slightest pretext. Six days later Jović returned to the Presidency without any explanation, followed by the representatives of Montenegro, Kosovo and Vojvodina and it was business as usual again. But now Tudjman saw an opportunity to take advantage of Milošević's domestic crisis and the failure of Jović's scheming, and arranged to meet the Serbian President for bilateral talks to try to resolve their differences.

The two leaders met at Karadjordjevo, the retreat where Tito had ended the Croatian Spring in 1971, on 25 March. The precise content of these talks has not been published, though it is clear that Tudjman proposed the division of Bosnia-Hercegovina as a way of avoiding conflict between Serbs and Croats. Tudjman's ideal solution was the *sporazum*, or Cvetković-Maček Agreement, reached in 1939, though he was aware that on account of Croatia's military weakness he could

[27] The representative of Kosovo did not resign of his own accord but was unconstitutionally dismissed by the Serbian parliament for not resigning.

not expect as much territory. Indeed, it appears that Tudjman was even willing to offer parts of Croatia, including regions where Croats formed a majority, such as Vukovar, in exchange for a peaceful settlement. Though this proposition was largely at the expense of Bosnia-Hercegovina's Muslim community, it seemed to Tudjman the logical answer and infinitely preferable to war.

Had the issue in Yugoslavia in 1991 been the condition of Serbs in Croatia, Tudjman certainly gave Milošević the opportunity to resolve it at Karadjordjevo. For Tudjman had become so terrified by the prospect of war and, in particular, the threat war brought to his own position that he was willing to agree anything which offered him security, even a diminished Croatia. He was also prepared to recognise any settlement with Croatia's Serbs which was not personally humiliating, including autonomy for *Krajina*, and believed that since Milošević was on the rack at home, he could be persuaded to come to an agreement. But he could not. Indeed, Milošević had many opportunities to reach agreement regulating the condition of Serbs in Croatia, had he so desired. But scapegoats and imaginary enemies were the essence of his rule and, at that time, Milošević had no desire to end the conflict with Croatia.

For all the insensitivity of the early days of HDZ rule, Tudjman had never been in a position to harm Croatia's Serbs in the way that the Serbian media alleged. Croatia lacked the arms to pose a physical threat to the Serb community while the JNA was present throughout the republic and, given the preponderance of Serbs within its ranks, could easily have stepped in if Croatia's Serbs were in real danger. Sadly, oppression is a very common state of affairs in the world, though one which rarely leads to war. If it did, the war in Yugoslavia would have broken out in Vojvodina, the Sandžak or Kosovo, not in Slovenia. However, by its very nature oppression takes place in silence. The oppressed do not generally have access to sophisticated weaponry, neither can they afford to reject conciliatory initiatives from their alleged oppressors, nor do they benefit from slick propaganda campaigns highlighting their plight. They have no choice but to put up with the daily persecution which is their lot.

More important than what was actually happening in Yugoslavia during 1990 and the first half of 1991 were perceptions of what was taking place. This depended not on real events but on the atmosphere created by the rival media, since a climate for war existed months, and even years, before any shooting started. In Serbia the media had been at war since 1987. At the end of the 1980s the Slovene media joined battle, albeit in a comparatively sober manner, while from about the time Tudjman came to power the Croatian media, too, was on a war footing. It was this media war and the manner in which the flames of ethnic hatred were continuously and deliberately fanned over many years which led to war in Yugoslavia, not inherent animosity between the country's peoples.

The republican media mirrored the outlook of their leaderships. In Serbia the media showed no restraint or willingness to compromise whatsoever. In Slovenia, too, though open on most issues, they spoke with one voice as far as relations with the rest of the country were concerned and refused to consider any other course. In Croatia the media were determined to stand up to the Serbian onslaught, yet insecure and unsure of the best way to respond. The purge of Croatian radio and television when the HDZ came to power was on a similar scale to that in Serbia in the mid-1980s and left a dearth of journalistic talent. While, to begin with, the Croatian media attempted to differentiate between militant Serbs, labelled Serbo-Četniks, and moderates, as the conflict escalated, distinctions became blurred. Increasingly, the media became slavishly obedient to the ruling party and prone to crude ethnic stereotyping which, while never anywhere near as primitive or extreme as in Serbia, contributed to the alienation of moderate Serb opinion in Croatia.

Despite the propaganda war, most of Croatia's Serbs were, at this stage, embarrassed by Milošević's nationalism and unaffected by the HDZ's purges. Similarly, the SDS's early intransigence under Rašković was often not as extreme or unreasonable as the Croatian media's reaction to it. However, a sequence of 'incidents', such as the Mlinar affair, and subsequent over-reactions to them played into the hands of extremists who had been doing their utmost to create conflict from the very beginning. The escalating media war also placed the majority of Croatia's Serbs, who wished merely to keep their heads down and steer clear of trouble, in an increasingly awkward position.

From the moment Babić took charge of the SDS Serbs in *Krajina* went on the offensive, aware that, with Mladić's protection, they, though not Serbs outside the enclave, were secure from Croat reprisals. As Babić imposed his very personal rule across the region, there were daily 'incidents' with every conceivable gory implication reported by both the Croatian and Serbian media, each raising the temperature of the already heated Yugoslav political debate. Life in *Krajina* became unbearable for Croats, who began leaving, as well as for Serbs who did not share Babić's opinions. At the same time, elsewhere in Croatia angry Croats began taking their frustrations out on Serbs who had nothing to do with Babić, Milošević or Knin. Nevertheless, the actual level of conflict bore no resemblance to the media picture and, despite hysterical reporting, bonds between peoples proved remarkably resilient. Indeed, the climate of fear was far greater than the intensity of the conflict merited.

That said, by autumn 1990 Croatia was locked in a spiral of violence which, though manageable, was pushing the republic steadily towards bloodshed. While this prospect terrified Croatia's leaders and persuaded them to try to come to terms with the Serb rebels, Babić rejected all conciliatory gestures and continued his campaign of terror across *Krajina*. Each month the conflict escalated and relations between communities deteriorated accordingly. Once trust between the peoples was shattered the condition of Serbs in Croatia deteriorated until they came to be the last hired and first fired. Even so, Belgrade's early attempts to precipitate war failed because Croatia's Serbs who lived outside Babić's dominions were not prepared to tip the republic over the edge.

The first showdown took place in Pakrac, a town in western Slavonia. Although the heaviest fighting of the war later that year came in eastern Slavonia, Serbs formed a greater proportion of the population in western Slavonia, and in Pakrac were in the majority.[28] On 2 March armed Croats and Serbs faced each other across the town while the JNA waited in the wings. It was the culmination of several weeks' struggle over control of the police station and neither side was prepared to give way—the Serbs were determined to add Pakrac to *Krajina*, the Croats to remain within Croatia. The media were also there in force and, though shots were fired, both militias backed down and the day passed off without casualties. Nevertheless, Radio Belgrade reported that six Serbs had been killed.[29] This deliberate misinformation was presumably designed to generate a pretext for intervention but failed because local Serbs were fearful of the consequences and exercised restraint.

[28] According to the 1991 census, Serbs formed 48.4 and Croats 36.0 per cent of Pakrac's 27,000 population.

[29] The report was sent by a journalist sent to Pakrac especially to cover the showdown. Hitherto, Radio Belgrade had generally been a cut above the rest of the Serbian media and Croatian affairs were covered by the station's Zagreb correspondent, Vesna Knežević, who had been appointed in 1984 before Milošević's purges. She was specifically ordered not to go to Pakrac that day.

In Pakrac both the Serb and Croat militias were largely made up of people from the town itself. Many had lived their entire lives there and knew their adversaries personally. A sense of community persisted and neither side could demonise the other to a level necessary for fighting to break out. Indeed, had territorial disputes been left to the locals, they could have been worked out easily since all sides had too much to lose in the event of war. But outsiders, who did not have the same sense of community or of the potential losses involved in a conflict in their own back yard, increasingly took the lead. Pakrac was the last showdown in which local Serbs called the shots and the last occasion when Serb forces exercised any restraint. In future clashes fanatical Serb irregulars, some of whom had been in training since 1989, made sure that by their actions they dashed all hopes of a peaceful settlement.

The most notorious of the many Serb militias which set about acquiring a name for themselves in 1991 were the Četniks, loyal to the former dissident Vojislav Šešelj, and the *Arkanovci*, loyal to the former secret service hitman and Belgrade ice cream parlour owner, Željko Ražnjatović, otherwise known as Arkan. Though ostensibly beyond Milošević's control, both armies were trained in Serbia and armed by the Serbian state. Moreover, Šešelj had special reason to be grateful to the Serbian President, since Milošević effectively gave him a seat in parliament by not fielding a socialist candidate in the constituency he fought at the December 1990 election. The Četniks and *Arkanovci* became two of the most destructive weapons in Milošević's arsenal and increasingly made their presence felt wherever there was any trouble.

The first people to die in ethnic violence in Croatia were a Croatian policeman and a Serb rebel who were both killed on 31 March as the *Krajina* militia clashed with Croatian police over control of the Plitvice national park. The park, a series of spectacular lakes and waterfalls attracting thousands of tourists every year, was a worthy prize on the edge of the territory Babić controlled. After a day's fighting the Croatian police had the upper hand and had captured twenty-nine Serb rebels. But that night the federal Presidency met in emergency session and, at Jović's insistence, ordered the JNA to occupy the park to prevent further bloodshed.[30] It was the beginning of a pattern which

---

[30] The JNA units which moved in were commanded by a Croat colonel who, like many Croats in the military, was unsure how to behave. At the time, he believed he was doing the right thing by intervening and thus avoiding further bloodshed. But that summer he resigned his commission and joined the Croatian Army.

was to last until the autumn, when the military finally gave up all pretence of neutrality. Serb rebels attacked Croatian positions and as soon as the Croatian police appeared about to reassert control the JNA arrived to restore peace and separate warring factions.

Three days before the Plitvice clashes Yugoslavia's six republican Presidents began a series of weekly summits aimed at resolving the crisis. Though Bosnia-Hercegovina and Macedonia were eager to agree anything which might hold Yugoslavia together, the gulf between the Serbian position and that of Slovenia and Croatia was too great to be bridged. Meanwhile, as Jović's term as President neared its end, Milošević increased his efforts to stir up conflict in Croatia and Bosnia-Hercegovina. Rebel Serbs established three new *krajinas* in Bosnia-Hercegovina refusing to recognise Sarajevo's authority, and on 2 May twelve Croatian policemen were killed, several of them brutally mutilated. This first atrocity was carried out in Borovo Selo, a Serb village just outside Vukovar, by Šešelj's Četniks. The police had been ambushed on their way into the village to rescue two of their colleagues who had been taken prisoner there a day earlier. That night, after another emergency session of the Presidency, JNA units were again deployed to separate warring factions.

Borovo Selo was the last occasion when Jović could use his position as President to direct federal policy. His mandate ran out on 15 May when he was due to hand over to Croatia's representative on the Presidency, Stipe Mesić. The hand-over should have been a formality as every year on that date a new President was appointed and the office went to each federal unit on a rotational basis. However, though it was Croatia's turn to head the Presidency, the Serbian bloc rejected Mesić's appointment. The Presidency was divided, Mesić was not elected and Yugoslavia was left without a head of state. When desperate mediation by Ante Marković[31] failed to break the deadlock, the representatives of Slovenia, Croatia and Macedonia left Belgrade and returned home.

---

[31] Marković persuaded the Serbian bloc to recognise Mesić as President in return for the federal assembly accepting the new Kosovo representative on the Presidency. Since Kosovo's former representative had not backed Jović's March resignation, he had been replaced with a Milošević appointee with no support whatsoever in Kosovo. Slovenia would not agree to the compromise since it came at the expense of Kosovo's Albanians, but a desperate Croatia went along with it. However, even after the federal assembly accepted Kosovo's new representative, the Serbian bloc refused to endorse Mesić as President.

Meanwhile, the situation on the ground in Bosnia-Hercegovina and especially Croatia deteriorated further as the pattern of Serb provocation and Croat reprisal acquired a self-sustaining momentum. When the *Krajina* militia blockaded the Croat village of Kijevo, 10 miles from Knin, Croats demanding an end to the blockade clashed with soldiers in Split and a Macedonian conscript was killed in the scuffles. Days later, after a Croat was killed by *Krajina* forces, Croat youths in Zadar and Šibenik went on an anti-Serb rampage which was immediately followed by anti-Croat riots in *Krajina*. Every escalation of the conflict added to the resolve of Slovenia's leaders to distance themselves from the rest of the country and spurred their preparations for independence. Terrified by the prospect of being left behind, Croatia's leaders decided to follow Slovenia and, in a hastily arranged referendum on 19 May, the vast majority of Croatia's population voted for independence.[32]

Ironically, despite his obsession with Croatian statehood, Tudjman was reluctant to rush ahead with an independence declaration. For the previous six months he had been careful to avoid giving Milošević any pretext for intervention and, though he feared war was inevitable, Tudjman believed every month it could be averted enabled Croatia to grow stronger. Since the Serbs of *Krajina* had organised their own plebiscite a week before the Croatian referendum, in which they voted unanimously to remain part of Yugoslavia, Tudjman was aware that an independence declaration appeared to play into Milošević's hands. However, he viewed it as the least of many evils. Since Slovenia was pressing ahead with its declaration, he decided that the risk of remaining part of a Yugoslavia without Slovenia was greater than that of declaring independence. The date set for the formal declaration was 29 June, three days after Slovenia's proposed date to give Tudjman time to see how Serbia and the JNA reacted to it, and, in the intervening month, Croatia joined Slovenia in intensive lobbying of international opinion.

Hitherto, the international community had played no direct role in the Yugoslav drama and had no intention of becoming involved.

---

[32] 84 per cent of the Croatian electorate voted at the referendum of whom 93 per cent, that is 78.1 per cent of those eligible, supported the creation of a 'sovereign and independent' country guaranteeing cultural autonomy and 'rights of citizens to the Serbs and members of other nationalities in Croatia' which would enter into an alliance of sovereign states with other republics. 92 per cent rejected remaining within a federal Yugoslavia.

While the major powers were aware that the country was disintegrating, they could see no easy solutions and felt no obligation to try and resolve the internal problems of another country. When the Cold War ended, Yugoslavia lost its strategic importance as a buffer state between East and West. Instead, it had become a nuisance and diplomats lost patience with the country's seemingly irrational obsessions and intractable problems. Moreover, other regions of the world had superseded Yugoslavia in the pecking order of international importance. Eastern Europe's emerging democracies became the focus of diplomatic activity and foreign investment in the region, while events in the Middle East, Iraq's invasion of Kuwait and the Gulf War, eclipsed all others.

Nevertheless, international opinion mattered greatly. Yugoslavs looked abroad, and especially to the European Community, for help in the transition from communism. The run-up to the much-vaunted single European market of 1992 was a time of idealism throughout the continent and optimistic Yugoslav commentators liked to compare the state of affairs in their country with that of Spain after Franco's death. For in Spain, as well as in Greece and Portugal, EC assistance had facilitated the transition to democracy after decades of dictatorship and Yugoslavs hoped the European Community could play a similar role on their behalf. Indeed, most parties contesting the country's 1990 elections aspired to membership and Slovenia's former communists campaigned under the slogan 'Europe Now' (*Evropa Zdaj*).

The European Community was certainly in a position to play such a role. However, one of the requirements for assistance was that Yugoslavia remain a unitary state. The European Community was loath to see Yugoslavia fragment into mini-states for two reasons: divorce was likely to be an exceedingly messy affair and it could become an unwanted precedent for the Soviet Union, which at the time also appeared to be on the verge of disintegration. Though the European Community expected a resolution of Yugoslavia's internal conflict without recourse to violence, its insistence on a single state inadvertently contributed to the deadlock in the country's constitutional talks. By refusing to concede even the possibility of a transition to a loose association of sovereign states and insisting on a single entity, the European Community wanted what Serbia and the JNA wanted and Milošević had no need to compromise.

The Slovene and Croatian envoys who lobbied the world's capitals in late spring and early summer 1991 aimed to raise awareness about

Yugoslavia and explain the reasons behind their forthcoming independence declarations. They were looking, above all, for a change in international attitudes, which they hoped might redress the balance of power within Yugoslavia. Without international support, Slovenia and Croatia believed they had no chance of persuading Milošević to temper his stance and feared that the only compromise they could look forward to was one condemning them to second-class citizenship. However, on their diplomatic tour, Kučan, Tudjman and their respective Foreign Ministers found themselves repeatedly cold-shouldered and effectively ordered to return to the negotiating table in Yugoslavia. Nobody wanted to listen to their point of view, let alone consider it. Yet, as far as both Slovenia and Croatia were concerned, they had already exhausted the negotiating process and had only chosen to declare independence because Milošević's tactics made further talks pointless.

While Slovenia and Croatia sought to internationalise Yugoslavia's internal conflict to improve their position *vis-à-vis* that of Serbia, what international intervention there was served to undermine their stance. Rather than condemning Serb violence in Kosovo, Vojvodina, Bosnia-Hercegovina and Croatia or urging moderation from Serbia and the JNA, diplomatic efforts focused on pressurising Slovenia and Croatia into abandoning their independence declarations. Though well-intentioned, such moves bolstered the resolve of the Yugoslav military and threatened to legitimise their use of force. Indeed, it was the eleventh hour intervention by US Secretary of State James Baker, designed avert Slovenia and Croatia's independence declarations, not the declarations themselves, which pushed Yugoslavia over the edge into war.

Five days before Slovenia was due to declare independence Baker, who was on an official visit to Albania, made an unscheduled stop-over in Belgrade to make the US position on Yugoslav matters categorically clear. During his one day visit he met with Yugoslavia's republican leaders and military chiefs and, before flying out, declared that the United States would not recognise Slovenia or Croatia 'under any circumstances'. Baker was effectively ordering Slovenia and Croatia to make a humiliating climbdown, without placing comparable pressure on Serbia and the JNA or offering the northern republics any form of carrot, such as his own good offices for mediation, as a face-saving alternative to their independence declarations. That night, as Kučan and Tudjman left Belgrade, both were extremely depressed. The message they had received from Baker, whether or not this was his intention, was that the United States was prepared to accept limited military intervention in the interests of holding Yugoslavia together.

Nevertheless, in the absence of an honourable alternative, both Kučan and Tudjman determined to press ahead with independence preparations. Indeed, as they got wind of JNA plans, both republics brought forward the date for their independence declarations to 25 June. A day later, Slovenia celebrated with an official ceremony and street parties throughout the capital, Ljubljana, as originally scheduled. But as revellers returned home in the early hours of 27 June JNA troops were already on the move. It was the beginning of the first European war since the Turkish invasion of Cyprus in 1975 and the bloodiest since the Second World War.

8

WAR

'Until the war broke out we could think about various options, even about whether some Yugoslav idea would succeed. But when war came it was clear to me that it was the end of it all' — Vasil Tupurkovski[1]

Slovenia fights

The JNA tanks which set off on 27 June 1991 did so on military, not civilian orders. It was a rash decision taken by a High Command which had convinced itself that military intervention was necessary to hold the country together and that, following James Baker's visit, the international community would sanction it. Strictly speaking, the action was also illegal since only the federal Presidency could authorise such a move, but in the absence of a President the military had taken it upon itself to make policy. Moreover, to demonstrate that the JNA was acting in the interests of all Yugoslavs, the forces deployed were commanded by a Slovene, General Konrad Kolšek, and ostensibly set out merely to secure the republic's borders.

The JNA justified its operations in Slovenia by reference to a series of federal resolutions in the two weeks leading up to the republic's independence declaration, which had been instigated by Prime Minister Ante Marković. What concerned Marković was future funding for the federal government since he was aware that Slovenia planned to take control of its international border crossings immediately after declaring independence and to hang on to future revenue from customs and excise duties. Hitherto, these receipts had been sent to the federal coffers in Belgrade and without them Marković's position and that of the federal government would be severely undermined. Nevertheless, Marković himself did not have the authority to order the JNA to secure Slovenia's borders or any desire to see the military deployed.

Instead of making straight for the nearest frontiers (as they

---

[1] Vasil Tupurkovski was Macedonia's representative on the federal Presidency, dubbed 'Kissinger of the Balkans' for his shuttle diplomacy during the summer of 1991.

presumably would have, had their sole intention been to secure border posts), JNA tanks criss-crossed Slovenia in a show of force. It was the culmination of three days of military manoeuvres aimed at exerting maximum pressure on the republic's leaders and persuading them to back down. But it achieved the very opposite. Slovenia's leaders refused to capitulate and, while fearful of the consequences, were so determined to extricate themselves from Yugoslavia that they were prepared to gamble their future on the successful prosecution of a war. As JNA troops attempted to seize control of Slovenia's border posts, Slovene forces engaged them in combat. Though the odds appeared stacked against a Slovene victory, Slovenia's leaders had made contingency plans and calculated that confronting the JNA was a risk worth taking.

During his year in office prior to the independence declaration Slovenia's Defence Minister, Janez Janša, had reorganised the republic's defences with the prospect of a limited war against the JNA in mind. He had also built up a network of Slovene officers sympathetic to the cause of Slovene independence, who kept him informed of JNA plans and enabled him to keep one step ahead of the military at all times. In addition to weapons belonging to the territorial defence force, Janša had managed to buy in sufficient arms to give him the firepower to bloody the nose of the JNA in a short war, though not enough to defeat it outright. However, he calculated that outright victory would not be necessary, given JNA commitments elsewhere in the country. He was essentially relying on conflict in Croatia and Bosnia-Hercegovina to shield Slovenia from a full-scale war. It was a high-risk strategy which very nearly backfired when Croatia's leaders decided not to fight.

In the run-up to the independence declarations Janša had been working closely with Martin Špegelj, his Croatian counterpart, and expected Croatia to come to Slovenia's assistance in the event of war. Indeed, as soon as the JNA clashed with Slovene forces, Špegelj wanted to join Slovenia in a full-scale independence war, but, in a stormy session of the Croatian cabinet, was overruled and sacked. Given Croatia's military weakness, Tudjman hoped to delay conflict for as long as possible and feared that a preemptive strike would prove counter-productive and give the JNA the excuse it had been looking for ever since he came to power to intervene and oust him. Tudjman believed that by declaring independence he had not crossed any point of no return and still hoped that, as long as he did nothing further to provoke Serbia or the JNA, he might be able to win international opinion round to the concept of an independent Croatia.

The independence declarations should be viewed within the context of eighteen months of futile dialogue on Yugoslavia's future, not in the light of subsequent military intervention. For, on 25 June 1991, Slovenia and Croatia were declaring independence from the federal concept of Yugoslavia as envisaged by Milošević; they were not seceding from all forms of Yugoslav union. Indeed, the only difference between Slovenia's status before and after its independence declaration was republican control of border posts and revenue from customs and excise duties, while in Croatia's case nothing of substance had changed. Moreover, to put the Slovene action which the JNA deemed grounds for intervention into perspective, Serbia had ceased paying its own customs and excise receipts to the federal government eight months earlier. The critical event, as far as Yugoslavia's disintegration is concerned, was not the independence declarations but the military's reaction to them.

Earlier the same year, the three Baltic republics had also declared unilateral independence from the Soviet Union without Western approval, yet there the declarations had not led to a war. Despite several potential conflict areas the Soviet military refrained from a hasty response, thus leaving the door open to peaceful settlement of differences. War hardens attitudes and destroys trust. The recourse to violence shattered the Yugoslav equation and dashed hope of reconciliation between Slovenia and the rest of the country. Before the declaration even the most fervent Slovene nationalists had not had a clear picture of what independence would entail, but as soon as the JNA chose to use force to keep Slovenia within the existing Yugoslav framework, independence came to mean total secession and nothing less. Slovenia wanted out and was no longer prepared even to remain within the confederal structure the republic's leaders had, hitherto, advocated.

The JNA High Command had hoped that a simple show of force would be sufficient to persuade the Slovene government to retract its declaration and, at the same time, act as a warning to the Zagreb authorities. However, they totally misjudged both the strength of feeling in Slovenia and the republic's military capacity. For, though short of heavy weaponry, Janša's army proved ready and willing to engage JNA forces at every opportunity. Perhaps ironically, Janša's tactics were those of General People's Defence, the strategy conceived by the JNA in the 1960s to deal with foreign invasion.

That the JNA performed so poorly in Slovenia was only partly a consequence of miscalculations about Slovenia's capacity to fight. More fundamentally, it should be attributed to a lack of morale among JNA troops and a reckless lack of preparation on the part of the High Command. Many of the soldiers despatched to secure Slovenia's borders were teenage conscripts, including some who had been in the JNA for less than a month, and of these most had not even been informed who their enemy was supposed to be and were shocked when Slovene units opened fire. Moreover, since the JNA only decided on intervention following Baker's visit to Belgrade on 21 June, the entire operation had to be organised within a week. After initial reverses the High Command considered a complete crackdown, but, by this stage, the JNA had already failed to achieve the limited intervention it believed Baker and the international community were prepared to sanction, and the European Community had set itself up as mediator.

Two days after fighting broke out the *troika* of Foreign Ministers coordinating EC foreign policy[2] flew to Belgrade and Zagreb to try to resolve the conflict, patched together a cease-fire agreement and flew out, their mission seemingly accomplished. The rapid response was motivated by fears of the potential fall-out from a war in a neighbouring country and especially the prospect of thousands of refugees streaming across the Italian border. However, to many European statesmen the conflict in Yugoslavia also appeared to offer an opportunity for the European Community to assert itself as an international force in the run-up to 1992 and the Single European Act. Indeed, Luxembourg's Foreign Minister, Jacques Poos, who headed the initial *troika* to Yugoslavia was bold enough to declare: 'This is the hour of Europe.'

The first EC-brokered deal failed to halt the fighting but on 7 July, after further shuttle diplomacy, all sides agreed in principle to the Brioni Accord, bringing the war in Slovenia to an end. In total, eight Slovene and thirty-nine JNA troops died and 111 Slovene and 163 JNA troops were wounded, while more than 2,500 JNA conscripts were taken prisoner.[3] The most spectacular damage was at the border

---

[2] EC foreign policy is guided by each of the Community's countries in turn for six-month periods on a rotational basis. To improve continuity the current Community President forms a *troika* with its predecessor and successor. When war broke out in Slovenia Luxembourg was head of EC foreign policy while Italy and the Netherlands made up the rest of the *troika*. On 1 July Luxembourg handed over the Presidency to the Netherlands and Portugal replaced Italy within the *troika*.

[3] Two Austrian photographers, eight foreign truck-drivers and two Slovene civilians were also killed.

posts, scenes of the heaviest fighting, and at Ljubljana airport, which had been attacked from the air. In addition, humiliated JNA officers shot up and looted the village of Gornja Radgona just before the final cease-fire. Slovenia appeared to have got off lightly, yet most Slovenes were reluctant to accept the Accord, which included a three-month moratorium on independence, and it took some cajoling from the President, Milan Kučan, to persuade the republic's parliament to sign up to it.

Nevertheless, Brioni was not an EC triumph. The agreement held because the JNA had lost interest in Slovenia. Indeed, eleven days later, on 18 July, the JNA decided unilaterally to pull out all its troops and equipment within three months. This was a victory for the Serb nationalists over the remaining Yugoslavists in the military, for by abandoning Slovenia the JNA was also discarding all visions of Yugoslavia in favour of a Greater Serbia. The three-month moratorium on independence was designed to buy the time to give Yugoslavia's leaders a second chance to resolve their differences, but in the absence of any new mechanism for conflict resolution the odds against a negotiated settlement of the country's future were greater than ever. Even at the height of the Slovene war the conflict in Croatia had been more intense and the fighting more savage, yet, at Milošević's insistence, the Brioni resolutions were restricted to Slovenia. As a result, EC observers who began arriving in Zagreb were there to monitor the cease-fire in Slovenia but had no mandate to extend their operations into Croatia.

The only sop to Croatia at Brioni was that Serbia and Montenegro were persuaded to accept Stipe Mesić as federal President. A rein-vigorated Presidency was supposed to contribute to a more auspicious atmosphere for a further round of inter-republican talks, but, given that the institution had not functioned for the past two months, Mesić could only be a lame duck President. Though nominally head of Yugoslavia's armed forces, he had no influence over the JNA. Meanwhile, the situation in Croatia, which had effectively been ignored at Brioni, was deteriorating by the day.

Croatia burns

Determining when a conflict escalates into a war or, more specifically, when the intensity of the Croatian conflict rose to a level constituting war is difficult. The first deaths were recorded on 31 March, while the first atrocity (at Borovo Selo) took place on 2 May. A day later Tudjman went on television to warn that war had begun, though he continued to attend the weekly inter-republican summits which were ostensibly aimed at finding a peaceful solution to the conflict. During the war in Slovenia there was constant skirmishing in eastern Slavonia in villages around the towns of Osijek, Vukovar and Vinkovci, while Serb rebels from Knin launched an offensive towards Banija and Kordun. By July the daily death toll had become so great that the Croatian media stopped listing fatalities by name and began reporting numbers of dead instead.

Nevertheless, the most critical war waged in July was fought not on the battlefield but in the media. Since Yugoslavia's complexity did not translate easily into journalism and since in-depth coverage of protracted inter-republican squabbling was unlikely to sell more newspapers or boost television ratings, the country had, hitherto, been largely neglected by the international media. But as war broke out in Slovenia, Yugoslavia could no longer be ignored and all of a sudden the country was swarming with journalists, many of whom had never been there before and had minimal knowledge of Yugoslav affairs. All were prime targets for rival republican media whose propaganda offensive, which had always been directed as much at international opinion as at the domestic public, went into overdrive.

The war for international sympathy in the 1980s could be seen on Cable News Network, the Atlanta-based, twenty-four hour television news station, which has a weekly slot turned over to reports prepared by other stations. *World Report* is one of CNN's most innovative programmes and enables journalists from all over the world to make reports on subjects of their own choice. These usually offer insight into otherwise little known parts of the world, but Belgrade television used the opportunity CNN offered to air programmes vilifying Yugoslavia's non-Serbs. These were first about alleged Albanian atrocities against Serbs in Kosovo and later about secessionists in Slovenia and the rebirth of fascism in Croatia. Naturally Slovenes protested and began sending some of their own reports to CNN, which the network was also happy to broadcast. But since the only satellite feed out of Yugoslavia went via Belgrade, Slovene programmes were blocked and Slovene journalists forced to send their reports out via another country.

In the absence of any great interest or expertise in Yugoslav affairs, Belgrade could not fail to win the propaganda war. The Serbian media were the beneficiaries of a sophisticated public relations apparatus built up under Tito to enhance his and Yugoslavia's esteem abroad, while foreign journalists and diplomats were concentrated in Belgrade and rarely visited other parts of the country. In addition, a veritable cottage industry churned out tracts in English cataloguing the alleged, on-going history of genocide against Serbs, which were liberally distributed to visiting journalists. From the beginning of the Serb revolt in Croatia its propaganda value was a major factor behind it. Indeed, the initial referendum on autonomy was deliberately scheduled to coincide with the 1990 European Athletics Championships, which were being staged 60 miles away in Split, and voting (for fewer than 50,000 people) was strung out over two weeks to attract maximum publicity. Nevertheless, come June 1991, Slovenia fought and won an exemplary media war.

In advance of its independence declaration Slovenia made meticulous preparations. An efficient, well-equipped press centre was set up beneath Cankarjev Dom, the cultural centre where twenty-eight months earlier the republic's communist leaders had first challenged Milošević, and foreign journalists were provided with as much information and access to Slovene decision-makers as they could want. Most Slovene leaders were likeable characters who naturally came across well in their dealings with the media and certainly bore no resemblance to the nationalist fanatics they had been portrayed as in Belgrade. Moreover, even less agreeable figures like Janša were shrewd enough to manipulate the media with war progress reports and casualty figures (often total fabrications) at junctures when nobody had any real idea what was happening.[4]

In contrast to Slovenia and Serbia, media relations in Croatia were a shambles. There was no press centre, a shortage of background literature for foreign journalists and a less-than-accommodating attitude to the media. In part, this was because the decision to declare independence was taken at the last minute and there was no time to prepare properly when the republic was already facing more problems than it could handle. But more fundamentally, it was symptomatic of Tudjman's inability to cope with anything but the most subservient media. Tudjman was adamant that since Croatia was a democracy, the

[4] So slick was Slovenia's media campaign and so consummate the victory that journalists joked that the last barricades to come down in Slovenia after the Brioni Accord were those around the Cankarjev Dom press centre keeping the media in.

international community should come to his aid, and could not understand the lack of sympathy abroad. As usual he was his own worst enemy and, with several other leading HDZ politicians, succeeded only in alienating many foreign journalists with the extremity of his denunciations of Serbia and the JNA.

For outsiders coming to Yugoslav matters for the first time in the middle of 1991, Serbia appeared to have a strong case, especially with reference to 1941. When Croat propagandists tried to explain their desire for independence by invoking the right of a nation to self-determination, Serb propagandists were able to retort that they had no problem with that as long as Croatia did not think it could also get away with Serb regions of Croatia. Serbian propaganda portrayed the conflict as fundamentally a question of Serb rights in an independent Croatian state and made a persuasive argument to justify Serb fears based on the Ustašas' track record. Nevertheless, in spite of Tudjman, the hopeless Croatian public relations set-up and the Ustaša legacy, in the course of the fighting Croatia came to win the media war.

What undermined the Serb cause, above all, was the way it was prosecuted. The actions of Serb irregulars and the JNA, and, in particular, the atrocities they committed cost them international sympathy. During the first three months of fighting, Croatia had virtually nothing to hide. Indeed, Croat fighters were so desperate they generally allowed foreign journalists to roam freely around their lines. At their own risk, reporters could effectively go wherever they wanted and thus became witnesses to the barbarity of Serb irregulars and the JNA.[5] It should be pointed out, however, that atrocities were committed by a relatively small number of Serbs, who were not representative of the wider Serb community in Croatia, most of whom simply wished the conflict would go away but found themselves reluctantly sucked in.

[5] The high number of casualties among journalists in the first months of war was, above all, due to the fact that Croatian soldiers let them wander wherever they wanted to go. Since most journalists in Yugoslavia had spent their entire careers in Europe, few had any combat experience and they were as a result more reckless than they might have been otherwise. I, too, was present in Glina, the scene of the first major battle of the war in Croatia, when the first journalist to die in Croatia, Egon Scotland, a forty-two-year-old reporter with the *Süddeutsche Zeitung*, was killed. By May 1994, fifty-nine journalists had lost their lives covering the Yugoslav wars, and two were missing.

Those responsible for atrocities and the principal instigators of violence in Croatia belonged to Serb extremist organisations, such as the Četniks or *Arkanovci*, which had been recruiting openly in Serbia since the late 1980s. These fanatical groups fed off the discontent and frustrations of young males and prospered in inverse proportion to the Yugoslav economy. Recruits were generally unemployed, with little education and even bleaker prospects. Most had attended Milošević's meetings during the 1980s and some had even been paid to travel from one rally to the next to ensure a high turn-out at every venue. By joining a fanatical nationalist organisation, they found companionship and a cause in life. They were indoctrinated with hatred for non-Serbs, obsessed with the notion that Serbs were perennial victims and believed that when committing atrocities they were merely righting historical wrongs.

The Serbs who organised the revolt in Croatia came from very specific communities. They were either from around Knin or from the Serb community which settled former German villages in eastern Slavonia after the Second World War. Unlike Serbs elsewhere in Croatia neither of these communities had any tradition of political cooperation with Croats. Knin had been a Četnik stronghold during the Second World War, and the recent settlers, or *došljaci* as they were called, came originally from eastern Hercegovina and Montenegro. The irregular units they formed were based on units of the territorial defence force that most of them already belonged to, which were designed to be integrated into the JNA in the event of war. Virtually none of the instigators of the revolt came from Croatia's urban Serb population or the more-established communities, the so-called *starosedeoci*, which had lived alongside Croats for generations.

In many parts of Croatia Serbs and Croats managed to remain on good terms despite the conflict raging around them. However, extremists like the Četniks and *Arkanovci* determined to shatter once and for all every last bond between communities. The mutilated corpses of Croatian policemen massacred at Borovo Selo represented not an isolated incident but the first of a series of premeditated atrocities committed by Serb irregulars in the summer of 1991. As the Croatian media magnified the impact of each killing with an equally gory report, the political temperature, which had been at fever pitch for many months, boiled further out of control. Each death increased the level of mistrust between communities and diminished the prospects of inter-communal tolerance. As the conflict escalated beyond hope of a peaceful settlement, it became virtually impossible to remain neutral and, increasingly, even moderate Serbs who had endeavoured not to take sides found themselves dragged into the war.

Fanatics were by no means confined to the Serb side. Some Croats were also itching for a fight—though because they lacked the weapons they were not in a position to cause much damage. Croat extremists were, again, essentially outsiders who did not belong to the established communities which had lived alongside Serbs for centuries. A few were *došljaci* who had migrated from western Hercegovina to eastern Slavonia since the Second World War (though in much smaller numbers than Serbs), while most were *émigrés* returning from abroad. Croat *émigrés* were an especially insidious influence, since they had not learned respect for the cultures of all Yugoslavia's nations at school in the way other Yugoslavs had and, critically, did not have to live with the consequences of their actions: if the worst came to the worst, they could always return to Toronto or Melbourne or wherever they had come from.

As Serb rebels registered their disapproval of Croatia's independence declaration with a series of offensives, the Croatian conflict moved up a gear at the end of June 1991. Even before the declaration, great swathes of Croatian territory had been beyond Zagreb's control and day-to-day crisis management in these regions was left to heavily out-gunned, local officials. The more level-headed of these worked tirelessly and at great personal risk to maintain some semblance of peace but found themselves fighting a losing battle as their efforts were repeatedly undermined by the actions of extremists on both sides.[6]

Though Croatia lacked weapons, the odds against a successful war of independence were not as great as it may have appeared in the summer of 1991. Ostensibly the JNA remained a multinational fighting force, though the attitude of non-Serbs in the military was ambivalent and the High Command unwilling to risk all-out war in case the JNA fell apart. Imminent disintegration, rather than any sense of Yugoslavism or desire for a negotiated settlement, had dissuaded the

[6] In eastern Slavonia, scene of the heaviest fighting, the local police chief kept a semblance of peace until the end of June by maintaining a constant dialogue with Serb rebels. However, he was gunned down days after Croatia's independence declaration by Croat fanatics whose patience had snapped and who wanted to fight back. The Mayor of Karlovac, an ethnically-mixed town 35 miles south-west of Zagreb, also managed to stave off war until October by playing a similarly skilful balancing act, but when it came the destruction was as great there as anywhere else.

military from intervening in Croatia during the January crisis and convinced Špegelj that the time to fight was when the JNA moved against Slovenia. This assessment proved accurate, as Slovenes in the JNA resigned *en masse* during the war in Slovenia, rapidly to be followed by their Croat colleagues.

The exodus of Croats and Slovenes cost the JNA more than merely the corresponding loss of manpower. On the one hand, it could no longer claim to represent any form of Yugoslavia other than a Greater Serbia. On the other hand, Croat and Slovene officers tended to have skills the JNA found it difficult to replace. Though Serbs and Montenegrins outnumbered Yugoslavia's other nationalities in the JNA, they were concentrated in the infantry, while Slovenes and Croats tended to be in more technically demanding areas. For example, General Anton Tus, who became Commander-in-Chief of the Croatian Army, had been in the air force, where the proportion of Croats was much greater. Moreover, since the latest military hardware required advanced technology, the JNA's leading research installations were in Slovenia and Croatia. It was also no coincidence that Yugoslavia's only plant servicing Mig fighters was in Zagreb.[7]

Croats who resigned their commissions enlisted in the Croatian National Guard (*Zbor narodne garde* or ZNG), an armed gendarmerie formed in May 1991 and organised on a republican basis to complement local police forces. Over the months this influx of professional soldiers enabled the ZNG to evolve into a fully-fledged army. As a result, officers on both sides had attended the same military academies, knew each other personally, and were aware of the tactics the other side was likely to adopt.

Croatia was not short of military expertise or motivated fighters, just weapons. So desperate were Croatian soldiers, they even used guns left over from the Second World War taken from museums and film sets.[8] Since few weapons were manufactured in Croatia the only way

[7] Mig fighters require a complete overhaul after a maximum of 250 flying hours. This proved a great blessing to Croatia. By December 1991 much of the Yugoslav airforce was grounded and in need of servicing.

[8] Since much of the best and most accessible central European architecture was in Ljubljana and Zagreb, Yugoslavia had long been a favourite location for films set during the Second World War, including *The Winds of War, The Dirty Dozen* and *Sophie's Choice*. As a result, the Yugoslav film industry possessed a large arsenal of vintage weapons including Bren guns and Sten guns which had originally been parachuted in to Tito's Partisans.

to acquire them was from abroad or from the JNA's own stockpile. While Croat *émigrés* set about procuring arms on the international market and workshops across Croatia began manufacturing munitions and basic arms such as mortars, the Croatian Army acquired most of its weapons from the JNA, using a plan Špegelj had drawn up with Janša in the run-up to the independence declarations. Croatian forces surrounded JNA barracks, cut water and electricity supplies and, using psychological pressure, persuaded the soldiers within to surrender and hand over their arsenal. On account of the JNA's dismal morale the strategy proved remarkably successful and in the course of September and October 1991 several major barracks surrendered.

JNA tactics reflected the prevailing lack of morale in the military. Officers relied on their superior firepower to bombard Croatian towns and villages into submission from afar rather than risk infantry in frontal assaults. The result was great devastation, though with comparatively few casualties since civilians, who were the ultimate targets of the bombardment, remained underground in cellars while their houses were systematically levelled above them. The final assault was left to irregulars whose brutal conduct served as a warning to other non-Serbs.

Ethnic cleansing was part of the Croatian war from the very beginning. It was neither a systematic slaughter of all non-Serbs nor a spontaneous and frenzied killing. It was a calculated action designed to maximise the conflict between Serbs and Croats and persuade non-Serbs to vacate their homes and flee. Moreover, the victims who were singled out for the most savage treatment by Serb irregulars were not Croats but Serbs fighting on the Croatian side. It can be argued that ethnic cleansing was more humane than the months of bombardment to which the JNA subjected civilians. If a handful of people were killed in an especially brutal manner, the rest were usually willing to abandon their homes without a fight and escaped with their lives intact. Indeed, when given an ultimatum from the JNA, more than 8,000 Croats from the village of Ilok, about 25 miles south-east of Vukovar, decided in October 1991 that their best option was to flee.

Serb victories came in the first months of fighting when Croatia was unarmed. Baranja, in north-east Croatia on the border of Hungary and Vojvodina, fell in August, while most of Banija and Kordun, regions to the south-east of Zagreb where Serbs formed a large percentage of the population, had also fallen by October. However, as Croats decided that the war was an attack on Croatia and everything Croat, they buried their political differences and rallied behind a war effort. At the beginning of August a government of national unity was formed which included two Serbs as well as representatives of all the major Croat political parties. As the professional soldiers who had left the JNA bolstered Croatia's defence, Serb forces found it increasingly difficult to capture further territory without incurring massive casualties.

The most celebrated battles were those for Vukovar and Dubrovnik: Vukovar was more typical of the way the war was fought and became to Croats a poignant symbol of their suffering; Dubrovnik was protected from a similar fate by its international reputation but did more than anything to destroy the Serb cause abroad. Vukovar was condemned by geography. It lay on the border with Vojvodina and could easily be swallowed by Serbia. Indeed, it appears that Tudjman was even prepared to barter the town away at his Karadjordjevo meeting with Milošević. According to the 1991 census, 84,024 people lived in the Vukovar district, of whom 43.7 per cent were Croats, 37.4 per cent Serbs and 7.3 per cent Yugoslav. Croats and Serb *starosedeoci* tended to live in the town itself while Serb *došljaci* lived in surrounding villages such as Borovo Selo. In August the town was encircled by the JNA and pounded mercilessly for eighty-seven days. When the thirteenth cease-fire of the war proved as ineffective as its twelve predecessors, the defenders surrendered and those who fell into the hands of Serb irregulars were executed *en masse*.

The decision to move against Dubrovnik was made primarily to keep Montenegro allied to Serbia and an active participant in the war. Hitherto, most of the fighting had taken place well away from Montenegro in Slavonia. As Montenegrin soldiers began returning home in body bags, the JNA found it increasingly difficult to mobilise further reservists for a cause Montenegrins could not relate to. By opening another front in southern Dalmatia, however, the JNA extended the Croatian war into Montenegro's backyard. Guided by JNA officers, Montenegrin reservists and Serb irregulars from eastern Hercegovina laid waste the 30 miles of Croatian coast between the Montenegrin border and Dubrovnik. The exercise was extremely lucrative as every building *en route* was plundered and within days the contents joined the spoils of the Slavonian war on sale in markets across Serbia and Montenegro. Since those weapons Croatia possessed were already deployed elsewhere, resistance was minimal until the JNA arrived at Dubrovnik's ancient city.

While the JNA attempted to justify its assault on Dubrovnik by alleging that the city's Serbs were victims of systematic persecution, the accusations had, by now, begun to ring hollow and the attack finally put the lie to Serbian claims that the war was about Serb rights in Croatia. Of Dubrovnik's 70,672 inhabitants only 6.7 per cent or 5,735 were Serbs, all fiercely proud of their ancient city and as committed to its defence as their Croat neighbours. Though hopelessly outgunned, Dubrovnik refused to surrender, as the JNA demanded, and appealed, instead, to the world for assistance.

To capture Dubrovnik the JNA would have had to destroy it in the same manner as it had obliterated Vukovar. No matter how desperate the conditions for Dubrovnik's inhabitants and no matter how great the destruction, the city was not going to surrender. Moreover, since the international community proved more concerned about the ancient city walls than it had been for the thousands of Croat lives lost in the preceding months, Dubrovnik became the key to Croatia's propaganda war. Zagreb was determined to make maximum capital out of the city's plight and, since no foreign journalists were present when the JNA originally encircled Dubrovnik, the first images were supplied by the Croatian media and naturally played up the threat to the ancient city.[9] Even after the foreign media had arrived, Croat defenders were quite prepared to provoke in-coming fire by shooting at the JNA from within the ancient city. That said, the pounding of Dubrovnik caused irreparable damage and was as gratuitous and unwarranted as the scorched earth policy pursued between the Montenegrin border and Dubrovnik, and the systematic levelling of Vukovar and much of eastern Slavonia.[10]

By this stage, the sole aim of Croatian diplomacy was to win international recognition, a panacea for which no sacrifice, not even Dubrovnik's ancient city, was too great. During the summer of 1991, as hundreds of poorly-armed Croatian soldiers were thrown into

[9] There are allegations that the most spectacular images of burning around the ancient city were achieved by setting fire to a pile of tyres behind the city walls. While this may have been the case, what was undeniable was that the JNA had systemically destroyed everything in its path betwen the Montenegrin border and Dubrovnik.

[10] Most of the destruction occurred on 6 December 1991 when once again there were no foreign journalists present. The decision to pound Dubrovnik that day was made by JNA officers on the ground who apparently wished to scupper an agreement to end the war which was being worked out under UN auspices.

battles they were totally unprepared for and could scarcely hope to come out of alive, the Zagreb authorities were already prepared to achieve this in blood. They calculated that following huge casualties the international community would be obliged to recognise Croatia as soon as the three-month moratorium on independence, agreed at Brioni, ended on 8 October. However, it was to no avail as even after the Presidential Palace in Zagreb was apparently rocketed by a Yugoslav warplane the day before the moratorium expired,[11] the international community refused to accept Yugoslavia's demise.

While propagandists made all sorts of claims about what was happening during the war in Croatia, an impartial record of events was compiled by the much-maligned EC observers. In September Milošević had been persuaded to extend their mandate to Croatia and off their own back they produced a confidential report on the war which was leaked to the media by diplomatic sources sympathetic to Croatia. The report accused the JNA and Serb irregulars of a systematic campaign of terror, killings, looting and ethnic cleansing across Croatia and pointed out that, whereas the Croatian authorities had allowed the observers to carry out their investigations freely in Croat-held territory, the JNA and Serb irregulars had barred access to many areas. It concluded that, though Croats had also committed atrocities, the overwhelming majority had been committed by Serbs against Croats; and, much to the embarrassment of EC governments, proposed four possible courses of action, including military intervention against Serbia and the JNA.

The destruction and brutality of the war inevitably spawned extremism in Croatia. As Croat casualties mounted and Serb forces laid waste great tracts of the republic, support for the neo-fascist Croatian Party of Right (*Hrvatska stranka prava* or HSP) grew to such an extent that Tudjman felt personally threatened. The HSP considered itself the successor of Ante Starčević's 19th century Party of Right

[11] Whether or not the Presidential Palace was rocketed from the air is a matter of some controversy. Serbs allege that it was blown up from the ground in an attempt to persuade the international community to recognise Croatia the next day. At the time of the alleged attack I was across the road in the Croatian parliament and was knocked to the ground by the blast. It seemed pretty convincing to me and so, within seconds, I telephoned the London radio station, LBC, to file a report. However, closer investigation threw up a host of unanswered questions, and I cannot say for sure whether an attack took place or not.

as well as of Ante Pavelić's Ustaša movement and was committed to the creation of a Greater Croatia including chunks of Bosnia-Hercegovina, Vojvodina and Montenegro. Though it had no seats in the Croatian parliament, the HSP formed a military wing, Croatian Defence Forces (*Hrvatske odbrambene snage* or HOS), and, as Croatia's position deteriorated, began attracting volunteers in increasing numbers.[12] Eventually, Tudjman moved to neutralise the HSP. In September the head of the party's military wing, Ante Paradžik, a student leader from 1971, was gunned down by Croatian police and in November the party's leader, former dissident Dobroslav Paraga, was arrested and charged with attempted armed revolt.

While the war came close to toppling Tudjman in Croatia, it breathed new life into Milošević's regime in Serbia. On 9 March Milošević had been on the verge of losing power; by July he was Serbia's undisputed leader at the head of a patriotic war. Any criticism was deemed unpatriotic and opponents were labelled 'enemies of the Serb nation'. Indeed, so firm was his grip on power he even began mobilising some of his most outspoken critics. In this way, Nenad Čanak, a Serb from Vojvodina and leader of Vojvodina's League of Social Democrats (*Liga socijaldemokrata Vojvodine*), found himself press-ganged into the JNA and despatched to eastern Slavonia, while many other opposition sympathizers of military age in both inner Serbia and Vojvodina chose to flee the country.

By the fall of Vukovar the military equation was very different to that in the summer when large-scale fighting first erupted. Though the balance of firepower was still heavily weighted against Croatia, there were no more soft targets and Croatian forces had begun recapturing lost ground in western Slavonia. To secure the territorial gains which had already been made, Milošević decided to shift the Serb population of western Slavonia to eastern Slavonia where the Croat and Hungarian majority had been ethnically cleansed. The JNA abandoned western Slavonia and the local Serbs were forced to flee in its wake. The broader, international equation had also changed as, largely on account of German pressure, the European Community appeared on the verge of recognising Croatia. As a result, Milošević decided

---

[12] The original HOS volunteers were trained and armed in Slovenia with, it seems, the blessing of Slovenia's Defence Minsiter, Janez Janša.

it was time to make a deal and called on the United Nations to prepare a peace treaty.[13]

The UN agreement was put together by the veteran US diplomat Cyrus Vance[14] and signed in Sarajevo on 2 January. It envisaged deployment of 14,000 peace-keepers and the demilitarisation of contested regions. Serb forces were to give up captured territory where Serbs did not reside, and the peace-keepers would, in time, enable all people to return to their homes. It was not a definitive solution of the Serb-Croat conflict because it left the final status of Serb enclaves vague, enabling Zagreb to understand that they remained within Croatia and Belgrade to believe that they would be independent and self-governing. The cease-fire, the seventeenth brokered by international mediators, came in as scheduled the following day at 6 pm after twenty-four hours of the heaviest Serb bombardment of the entire war.

The JNA made one last, desperate attempt to halt recognition, despatching Mig fighters to shoot down two EC helicopters as they entered Croatian airspace from Hungary on 7 January. It seems that the JNA hoped to pin blame for the attack onto Croatia and thus dissuade the European Community from recognising Slovene and Croatian independence. Indeed, had both helicopters been destroyed the ploy might have worked, since the attack took place above Croat-held territory. However, only one helicopter was destroyed. The other escaped unscathed and the survivors could testify to who was responsible for the deaths of five of their colleagues. The shooting proved counter-productive and recognition went ahead as scheduled on 15 January. That night Croats celebrated by firing wildly into the air, relieved that their struggle had been vindicated. Recognition brought the war in Croatia to an end but was not, on its own, a magic wand restoring stability to the region. As peace-keepers began arriving in Croatia, another, more destructive, conflict was already boiling over into war.

---

[13] Milošević looked to the United Nations for the settlement and not the European Community because he felt he would get a better deal out of the United Nations. The European Community had already made it clear that its sympathies lay with Croatia and Slovenia and had had enough of his deception.

[14] Though officially Vance represented the United Nations, both Serbs and Croats viewed him as a representative of the United States.

International recognition

In January the United States refrained from recognising Slovenia and Croatia since senior officials at the State Department continued to blame the independence declarations for the outbreak of war and remained fearful of upsetting Serbia and thus precipitating conflict elsewhere in the country. Yet three months later on 6 April the United States recognised Slovenia and Croatia and, together with the European Community, extended recognition to Bosnia-Hercegovina. Since Croatian recognition appeared to have halted the war in Croatia, international policy-makers hoped that by recognising Bosnia-Hercegovina they might prevent the conflict there from escalating into a full-scale war. However, when recognition only exacerbated the fighting, the international community chose not to come to the aid of what was a fellow member of the United Nations and instead indulged in mutual recriminations over which country was to blame for the diplomatic failure.

British politicians, in particular, attempted to explain the Bosnian war as the consequence of a premature decision to recognise Croatia forced on them by Germany. While this interpretation conveniently absolved Britain of any responsibility, it did nothing for the people of Bosnia-Hercegovina. Indeed, it said more about the prevalence of anti-German prejudice in Britain than any superior British under-standing of Yugoslav affairs. Nevertheless, the paths to recognition, first of Slovenia and Croatia and then of Bosnia-Hercegovina, are revealing and throw light on international involvement in Yugoslavia and the flaws in diplomatic efforts to end the conflict.

To the small band of professional Yugoslavia-watchers, the coun-try's disintegration became a possibility as soon as Milošević came to power. The signs had been ominous for many years before 1990 but in November of that year a leaked CIA document warned that the Yugoslav 'experiment' had failed and the country would fall apart violently within 18 months. Nevertheless, with the exception of Italy whose diplomats were constantly trying to draw attention to the danger, the international community did its best to ignore Yugoslavia right up until June 1991 in the hope that somehow Yugoslavs would resolve their differences and the problem would go away. This policy of neglect was facilitated by Iraq's invasion of Kuwait in August 1990 and the Gulf War, which eclipsed all other conflicts for the best part

of a year and dashed attempts by Slovenia and Croatia to internationalise Yugoslav affairs.[15]

In international law the internal affairs of a country are its own
prerogative and generally beyond the scope of the rest of the international community. While politicians may pontificate about democratic
values and justice, this rarely impinges on foreign policy, where ethical
and humanitarian considerations come a poor second to narrowly-
defined national interests. States are able to abuse their own citizens
with impunity and a large number do. Statesmen and diplomats
monitoring Yugoslavia during 1990 and the first half of 1991 were
not interested in a just settlement within the country; they were
simply looking for a way of holding it together. Policy was based on
two premises: that a unitary Yugoslavia was the best arrangement for
that part of the world and that its disintegration should be prevented
lest it serve as a precedent for the Soviet Union. Given that both
Milošević's Serbia and the JNA were committed to a unitary state, they
appeared to represent the best option.

The greatest diplomatic error in Yugoslavia was made before the
conflict degenerated into war. This was the failure to listen to anything
but the Serbian point of view. Slovene and Croatian envoys who went
abroad to canvass international opinion were cold-shouldered by
foreign ministries, while, astonishingly, foreign diplomats based in
Belgrade were prepared to write weighty reports on Yugoslavia
without visiting Zagreb or Ljubljana. Here Britain was the greatest
offender. While other EC countries were at least quick to despatch
diplomats to Croatia soon after war broke out, Britain took pains not
to hear the Croatian point of view and throughout six months of
fighting the Foreign Office chose not to send a single diplomat to
Zagreb. Given the amount of time and energy which would be devoted
to Yugoslav matters in succeeding years and the gravity of the decisions
the international community would be taking regarding Yugoslavia,
the complacency was remarkable.

The countries which could claim that their diplomatic services kept
them well informed on Yugoslavia were Germany, Italy, France and
the United States, which all had consulates in Zagreb as well as

[15] At the height of Yugoslavia's January crisis Tudjman wrote to the US President
George Bush, pleading for his support in defence of the young democracies of Slovenia
and Croatia. Bush never answered since at the time operation Desert Storm had just
under way and he had other matters on his mind.

embassies in Belgrade. However, in the case of the United States, top officials chose to override the advice of the State Department to the extent that the senior diplomat on the Yugoslavia desk, George Kenney, eventually resigned in protest. Policy came from Deputy Secretary of State, Lawrence Eagleburger, and National Security Adviser, Brent Scowcroft, who had both been diplomats in Yugoslavia during the 1960s, spoke fluent Serbo-Croat and retained close contacts with the country. In the late 1970s Eagleburger returned to Belgrade as Ambassador, during which time he got to know Slobodan Milošević, then a banker and a man he believed the United States could do business with. More than a decade later this assessment formed the backbone of US policy on Yugoslavia, to the extent that when Secretary of State James Baker flew to Belgrade on 21 June 1991 he ordered Slovenia and Croatia to abandon their planned independence declarations rather than exert comparable pressure on Serbia.

Baker's eleventh-hour intervention was part of a flurry of diplomatic activity on the eve of the independence declarations aimed at holding Yugoslavia together. A day earlier, the Conference on Security and Cooperation in Europe reiterated support for Yugoslavia's continued territorial integrity and on 23 June EC Foreign Ministers voted unanimously not to recognise the independence of Slovenia and Croatia if they seceded unilaterally from Yugoslavia. Earlier, at the end of May, an EC delegation to Belgrade headed by Commission President Jacques Delors promised Prime Minister Ante Marković generous financial aid if the country remained together, though by this stage Marković no longer had any influence. A year and a half earlier, when he launched his reform programme, financial aid might have made a difference, but, at that time, no money was forthcoming.

When war broke out in Slovenia the United States left Yugoslav affairs to the European Community, which rapidly demonstrated that it was not up to the mediation role it had taken on and was powerless to prevent the conflict in Croatia escalating into another war. During July and August 1991, as Serb forces made the bulk of their territorial gains, the European Community had no coordinated strategy and left mediation efforts to the new head of EC foreign policy, Dutch Foreign Minister, Hans van den Broek, without giving him any official mandate. Meanwhile, Macedonia's representative on the federal Presidency, Vasil Tupurkovski, organised another series of inter-republican meetings which again went nowhere. It was not until 7 September, two months after the Brioni Accord, that the European

Community established in the Hague its Peace Conference on Yugoslavia under the chairmanship of the former British Foreign Secretary, Lord Carrington.

The EC Peace Conference was, in theory, exactly what Yugoslavia needed, since it aimed to consider the country as a whole and to develop a coordinated approach to all the region's conflicts rather than merely deal with immediate flash-points, such as that in Croatia, in isolation. All Yugoslav peoples, including the Albanians of Kosovo and the Hungarians of Vojvodina, were able to make their own representations to the Conference, while the condition of Bosnia-Hercegovina and Macedonia was supposed to be as much part of the agenda as that of Slovenia and Croatia. However, in spite of the Conference's admirable aims, it was fundamentally flawed, for it lacked military clout and could thus never be anything more than a talking shop.

The fundamental reason for the fighting in Yugoslavia in September 1991 was the imbalance in firepower between the country's Serbs and the JNA, on the one hand, and the country's other peoples, on the other. Militant Serbs possessed a huge military capacity which they were determined to use to achieve their aims, whereas the country's other peoples were essentially defenceless and no amount of talking would alter the military equation. The European Community did briefly consider despatching a force to Croatia, but the British Foreign Secretary, Douglas Hurd, ruled it out on 19 September at a meeting of EC Foreign Ministers in Brussels and with it all thoughts of wider military intervention in Yugoslavia. Yet, without military intervention, the imbalance in firepower would not be redressed and the fighting would continue.

Ironically, by their actions, both the European Community and the United Nations ensured that the imbalance in firepower became a permanent feature of the conflict. By banning arms sales to any part of Yugoslavia as soon as war broke out in Slovenia the European Community was ostensibly trying to contain the conflict, as was the UN Security Council when on 25 September it imposed an arms embargo on the whole of Yugoslavia. However, the impact of the arms embargo was more sinister. Since Yugoslavia was a net exporter of weapons and the arms factories were concentrated in Bosnia-Hercegovina and Serbia, the embargo had no impact on the military capacity of the JNA; it merely made it more difficult for Croatia, whose territorial defence force had been disarmed in May 1990, and later Bosnia-Hercegovina, to fight back.[16]

Lord Carrington may or may not have been the right man to resolve Yugoslavia's problems, but he was never provided with the military back-up which might have given the EC Peace Conference the authority to have a real impact. Nevertheless, he remained at all times the consummate diplomat. Whereas van den Broek had repeatedly singled out Slobodan Milošević as the obstacle to his mediation efforts, Carrington preferred to blame all sides equally.

Despite mounting evidence that Serb forces and the JNA were committing systematic atrocities in Croatia, the European Community was loath to accept Yugoslavia's demise, and the Peace Conference worked to patch together a compromise to keep Slovenia and Croatia within Yugoslavia. Ironically, the EC proposals were for a loose association of states closely resembling the blueprint for Yugoslavia put forward by Slovenia and Croatia more than a year earlier, which the international community had not been prepared to consider at the time. It was accepted by five Yugoslav republics but rejected by Serbia, since as far as Milošević was concerned it presupposed the disappearance of Yugoslavia as an independent state. Nevertheless, all sides were deemed equally responsible for the conflict and for repeated failures to implement cease-fires, and, as fighting showed no signs of abating, first the European Community and then the United States introduced sanctions against all six Yugoslav republics.

As agreements signed in the Hague failed to have any impact on the fighting in Croatia, the EC mediation efforts descended into farce, while the war and mounting death toll made it increasingly difficult to reach a compromise. Milošević was able to sidestep discussion of Vojvodina and Kosovo, both deemed internal Serbian matters, and continued to insist on Yugoslavia's territorial integrity. In the absence of a military alternative, the EC Peace Conference could only aspire to appeasing Serbia and then persuading Yugoslavia's other republics to accept whatever settlement Serbia agreed to. It was an approach which became the basis for international mediation even after the United Nations became involved and war spread to Bosnia-Hercegovina.

---

[16] Despite the war and the demand for weapons at home, Yugoslavia managed to increase its arms sales during 1991. Total sales of military equipment in the year amounted to $460 million.

International attitudes to the war in Yugoslavia were based not on an analysis and understanding of Yugoslav affairs but on domestic political considerations and each country's own selective experience of conflict. In the case of the United States this meant Vietnam and in the case of Great Britain this meant Northern Ireland, both powerful reasons to avoid entanglement. Politicians had to balance media-generated pressure for intervention against the likely casualties from an indefinite military presence in Yugoslavia. Those countries whose armies could have made a difference decided the risks of military intervention outweighed the potential benefits and chose, instead, to ridicule the notion. As fighting escalated, a rift emerged within the European Community between countries like Germany, which believed the way to end the war was to stand up to Serbia, and those like Britain, which preferred to stay out of the conflict and consider all sides equally guilty, irrespective of evidence to the contrary.

German attitudes were also largely dictated by domestic political considerations for public opinion was influenced by large numbers of resident Croat workers and the influx of Croat refugees.[17] Before the war, Germany was as committed to Yugoslavia's territorial integrity as any other country in the European Community. Two days before Slovenia and Croatia declared independence Hans Dietrich Genscher, the veteran Foreign Minister, voted with his EC counterparts not to recognise them as independent states if they seceded from Yugoslavia unilaterally. However, the fighting changed Genscher's opinion, since he considered the recourse to violence and the manner in which the JNA prosecuted the war far graver offences than the independence declarations. Moreover, the lesson he drew from Germany's own past was the failure of appeasement and the importance of nipping aggression in the bud.

Germany was not the only country which sympathised with Croatia and Slovenia—Ireland, in particular, felt a certain affinity on account of its own colonial past while Italy was especially concerned at the prospect of thousands of refugees fleeing across its borders—but for Genscher the issue became a personal crusade. Since Germany was unable to deploy troops in Yugoslavia for constitutional reasons,[18]

[17] Many Croat refugees arriving in Germany were children whose parents had packed them off to relatives already living and working in Germany.

[18] Mindful of the history of the Hitler era, Germany's post-war founders took steps to ensure that no future armed force could be similarly misused, and enshrined the military's role in the constitution. Article 87a restricts its deployment to defending Germany and the territory of Nato against outside attack.

the most Genscher could offer Croatia was international recognition and this rapidly became the principal goal of German diplomacy. As early as 5 July, Genscher went on record saying he believed the European Community should threaten to recognise Slovenia and Croatia if the JNA refused to halt its aggression.

Increasing evidence of Serb atrocities and the failure of Carrington's Peace Conference won most EC countries over to Genscher's point of view, though Britain and to a lesser extent France remained sceptical. At the time, British objections had less to do with hypothetical fears for Bosnia-Hercegovina and more with practical military considerations. Britain was not opposed to the concept of recognition itself but was concerned about Croatia's borders and reluctant to recognise Croatian sovereignty over territory under Serb occupation. Nevertheless, after a nine-hour meeting of EC Foreign Ministers which began on 16 December and finished on 17 December, Britain backed down in return for earlier German concessions over the Maastricht Treaty on European Union. To maintain a united façade the European Community agreed that recognition would not occur before 15 January 1992 and established a five-member judicial commission, under the French constitutional lawyer Robert Badinter, to consider applications from any Yugoslav republic seeking independence.

Bosnia erupts

In addition to Slovenia and Croatia, both Macedonia and Bosnia-Hercegovina applied to the Badinter Commission before the EC-imposed 20 December deadline, as did the unofficial Albanian government of Kosovo. In the case of Slovenia and Croatia, recognition was a formality and Badinter duly recommended that both republics be recognised, though Zagreb was asked to improve its legislation concerning treatment of minorities.[19] The Commission also recommended that Macedonia be granted recognition, but ignored the Albanian application since Kosovo was not a republic. Bosnia-Hercegovina was deemed more complex and the Commission decided

[19] The Arbitration Committee later found that Croatian law did largely take account of the reservation expressed in January and that although constitutional provisions concerning the status of its minorities 'sometimes fall short of the obligations assumed by Croatia. . .it nonetheless satisfies the requirements of general international law.'

that a referendum should be carried out there to assess public opinion before considering the matter further. Meanwhile, another conference was set up within the EC Peace Conference on Yugoslavia specifically to mediate between the nations of Bosnia-Hercegovina, again under the chairmanship of Lord Carrington.

Bosnia-Hercegovina was far more ethnically mixed than the rest of Yugoslavia. While all six Yugoslav republics contained more than one people, a single nation, nevertheless, formed an absolute majority in each of the other five, with minorities concentrated in specific regions. In Bosnia-Hercegovina, by contrast, no nation formed an absolute majority and all three constituent nations were distributed reasonably evenly throughout the republic. According to the last census which was carried out in April 1991, 43.6 per cent of the 4,354,911 population declared themselves Muslim, 31.3 per cent Serb, 17.3 per cent Croat and 5.2 per cent Yugoslav.[20] Of 109 municipalities, thirty-seven had an absolute Muslim majority, thirty-two an absolute Serb majority and thirteen an absolute Croat majority. A further fifteen municipalities had a simple Muslim majority, five a simple Serb majority and seven a simple Croat majority. With the exception of Croat-populated western Hercegovina, even in those municipalities where one nation did form an absolute majority it rarely accounted for more than 70 per cent of the population, and as often as not neighbouring municipalities had majorities of one of the republic's other peoples. Bosnia-Hercegovina could not fragment neatly along ethnic lines because there was no ethnic line to fragment along. Dividing Bosnia-Hercegovina into ethnic territories would inevitably be messy and require massive population transfers.

Recriminations over diplomatic failure in Bosnia-Hercegovina are essentially redundant, since persuasion alone could not prevent the Bosnian conflict escalating into another war and the only strategy which might have averted bloodshed, namely timely military intervention, had been ruled out during the war in Croatia. As in Croatia, the fundamental cause of fighting was the imbalance in firepower between militant Serbs and the JNA, on the one hand, and the republic's other citizens of all nationalities, on the other. But since no country was prepared to deploy its own troops to neutralise the

---

[20] In practice Yugoslav meant the children of mixed marriages. Another 2.2 per cent of the population did not belong to any of these categories.

military imbalance, diplomats could only observe how the imminent catastrophe, which all Yugoslavia-experts were predicting, unfolded.

While EC policy towards Bosnia-Hercegovina and Yugoslavia in general was not especially enlightened, it is, nevertheless, ridiculous to suggest, as Serb propagandists do, that EC actions made war in Bosnia-Hercegovina inevitable. The conflict predated international attempts at mediation, and, in the absence of a credible military threat, the European Community could only cajole the republic's political leaders into a compromise; it was never in a position to impose a settlement. Indeed, EC mediators were so impotent they could be virtually ignored. The disintegration of Bosnia-Hercegovina was in many ways a rerun of the break-up of Yugoslavia since the republic came to the brink of war and went over the edge for internal Yugoslav reasons. The difference was that this time the international community was unable to claim ignorance. The European Community's real failure was less its inability to prevent the war breaking out than its refusal either to protect innocent communities or even to allow them to defend themselves.

Both Carrington and Vance opposed recognition of Slovenia and Croatia in January 1992, and the Bosnian President, Alija Izetbegović, requested it be withheld for fear of the impact on his own republic. Bosnia-Hercegovina had been on the brink of war for many months and all three men feared Croatian recognition might be the detonator for an eruption of violence, though in the event it was not. Despite hysterical threats from Serb politicians and the Serbian media, the fighting in Croatia came to an end and the conflict in Bosnia-Hercegovina remained on the edge without spilling over into bloodshed. Moreover, recognition did not scupper any wider political settlement within Yugoslavia since Carrington's Peace Conference had never come even remotely close to one. Since Bosnia-Hercegovina remained calm for almost three months after fighting ended in Croatia, it is perverse to attribute the outbreak of war to the recognition of Croatia. An act of aggression is necessary for any war to break out and that was still missing in Bosnia-Hercegovina. A more plausible explanation requires examination of the manner in which the republic came to the brink of war and the events surrounding the first act of aggression which proved to be the turning-point.

Under communist rule the great divide in Bosnian society had not been between peoples but, as throughout Yugoslavia, between city and countryside. The urban population, especially that of the capital,

Sarajevo, tended to be relatively sophisticated and cosmopolitan, while their rural counterparts of all nationalities who formed the majority of the population were much less sophisticated. With the exception of Sarajevo, Bosnia-Hercegovina was underdeveloped by Yugoslav standards and the proportion of the total population living in the countryside far greater than in Slovenia, Croatia, Vojvodina or Serbia, and even much of the urban population consisted of first generation city-dwellers. On account of their ascribed backwardness Bosnians had a reputation for being rather simple and were the butt of many jokes.[21]

Historically, all three Bosnian peoples had lived in harmony — though, according to the Ottoman system of rule, each separate and within its own religious community. Under the Habsburgs Bosnian society began to modernise itself and the religious divisions began to break down. However, in 1918 as the Empire disintegrated, inter-communal violence erupted, especially in eastern Bosnia between Muslims and Serbs. Between 1941 and 1945, when Yugoslavia's state infrastructure disappeared, Bosnia-Hercegovina again descended into anarchy. In the absence of traditional authority and in a climate of fear, it was kill or be killed. Yet, out of the chaos, a multinational fighting force, Tito's partisans, emerged as the victors. Under communist rule Bosnian society leapt forward and inter-marriage became increasingly common especially in the capital Sarajevo, which by 1991 had a population of 525,980, of whom 56,280 — or 10.7 per cent — considered themselves primarily Yugoslav and not Serb, Croat or Muslim.

As communism disintegrated, Bosnians again sought security within their own ethnic group and 75 per cent of those who voted at the November 1990 elections (about 50 per cent of the total electorate) opted for nationalist parties, the Muslim SDA, Serb SDS and Croat HDZ. Nevertheless, they were not voting for the wholesale destruction of their homeland. The nationalist parties were broad coalitions and local candidates reflected the very different concerns of communities spread throughout the republic. Moreover, all three parties joined together in government. Indeed, had the fate of Bosnia-Hercegovina been left to Bosnians there was still a chance that they could have come to an understanding among themselves. But it

---

[21] Bosnian jokes in Yugoslavia were very similar to Irish jokes in England. Instead of Mick and Paddy they featured Mujo and Haso, both Muslim names.

was not left to Bosnians and conflict was imported from outside, principally from Serbia.

Serbian secret police and nationalist agitators began stirring up Bosnia-Hercegovina's Serb communities in 1989 as soon as Milošević was victorious in Vojvodina, Montenegro and Kosovo. The tactics were identical to those in Croatia and even before the elections Milošević's proxies, the SDS, had established two Serb *krajinas* within Bosnia-Hercegovina which rejected Sarajevo's authority. A Serb National Council was set up in Banja Luka and Belgrade was systematically arming the Serb population. As in Croatia, Milošević's xenophobia struck a chord among the more backward Serb communities and since Bosnia-Hercegovina was so much less developed than Croatia this meant a far greater proportion of the total Serb population. By November 1991, six *krajinas* had been established across Bosnia-Hercegovina in all regions that Serb nationalists claimed as part of a Greater Serbia, each with its own Serb administration.

While the SDS acquired a powerful military wing, its Muslim and Croat rivals as well as the official Bosnian government were defenceless. In the run-up to the elections the JNA disarmed Bosnia-Hercegovina's territorial defence force in the same way it had disarmed those of Slovenia and Croatia six months earlier. Consequently, as in Croatia, the SDS was able to act with impunity, secure in the knowledge that it was the only political party with its own army and would in any case be supported by the JNA in the event of war. From the very beginning Radovan Karadžić, the SDS leader in Bosnia, openly consorted with both Milošević and Vojislav Šešelj, the Četnik leader.

Given their military weakness, the only tactics open to Bosnia's Muslim and Croat leaders were those of appeasement. On the whole they were responsible politicians terrified by the prospect of war. They considered Bosnia-Hercegovina indivisible and the very notion that ethnic states could be carved out of it ridiculous. Yet that was Karadžić's sole aim and even before the elections he was demanding that the republic's education system, media and police force be divided into separate ethnic entities. Perhaps it was significant that, though practising psychiatry in Sarajevo, Karadžić was originally from Montenegro, not Bosnia, and, like Serb *došljaci* in Croatia, quite happy to destroy what was not his own.

Since the republic's government was a coalition of all three leading parties, including the SDS, Karadžić could and did sabotage its operations, making sure there was no progress towards a negotiated compromise.[22] At the same time, the SDS trained its own army and stoked the fears of ordinary Serbs with images of an Islamic fundamentalist dictatorship. The allegations were based on a tract written twenty years earlier by Alija Izetbegović, the Muslim leader and Bosnian President, in which he had extolled the superiority of Islam over Christianity and Communism, and the virtues of an Islamic state. As a result of this 'Islamic Declaration', Izetbegović was imprisoned, but in the two intervening decades he mellowed into a tolerant, albeit naive, politician. In 1991 the allegations were nonsense, but the character assassination was so intense that ordinary Serbs were taken in and as the Serbian media churned out stories about the imminent slaughter of Serbs in Bosnia-Hercegovina, they lived in genuine fear of Islamic fundamentalism.

During the months of fruitless inter-republican negotiations preceding Slovenia's independence declaration, both Bosnia-Hercegovina and Macedonia appeared prepared to agree anything which would keep the country intact. The leaders of both republics feared that the consequences of Yugoslavia's disintegration would be greatest in their own republics, though they were powerless to halt the slide towards civil war. On 3 June 1991 Izetbegović and Kiro Gligorov, his Macedonian counterpart, presented the rest of the federation with their own compromise model for Yugoslavia in a last-ditch attempt to stave off disintegration. But, by this stage, Slovenia was unwilling to back down from its independence declaration for yet another round of inter-republican talks without a guarantee that they would be any more productive than the earlier rounds.

Though the SDS was clearly working to destroy Bosnia-Hercegovina, Izetbegović refused to prepare for war. He considered the potential carnage too horrendous to contemplate and decided, instead, to avoid any step which the SDS might conceivably construe as provocation. Bosnia-Hercegovina became the home of Yugoslavia's peace movement as Muslims, Serbs and Croats came together to denounce war-mongers elsewhere in the federation and as the Bosnian media, the Sarajevo daily newspaper *Oslobodjenje*, Bosnian television and the independent Yugoslav station *Yutel*, refused to take any nationalist position. During the war in Croatia this attempt at neutrality went to absurd lengths. Rather than condemn Serb atrocities in Croatia, the Bosnian

---

[22] Even after war had broken out SDS representative remained in the Bosnian government.

media chose to ignore them. They also chose to ignore the way in which the JNA was using Bosnia-Hercegovina as a base for its attacks on Croatia and the increasing number of armed incidents taking place within Bosnia-Hercegovina itself, for fear of enraging Serbia.

Nevertheless, from the very beginning of fighting in Croatia, Bosnia-Hercegovina was deeply involved. Bosnians were conscripted into the JNA, Bosnian factories manufactured munitions for the JNA and JNA weapons withdrawn from Croatia and Slovenia were deployed in Bosnia-Hercegovina. Indeed, many of the big guns which were to reduce Sarajevo and Mostar to rubble during the spring and summer of 1992 were dug in around the cities in September and October 1991. At the same time, Croats from western Hercegovina flocked to enlist in the Croatian Army and fought the JNA throughout Croatia from Dubrovnik to Vukovar. Since the principal victims of early clashes in Bosnia-Hercegovina were Croats from Hercegovina it was easy for the Sarajevo media to play down their significance. But each shooting raised the political temperature and brought the republic closer to war.

Yugoslavia's disintegration put Bosnia-Hercegovina in an extremely awkward position for only within some form of Yugoslav entity could all three of its constituent peoples feel truly secure. Izetbegović hoped to avoid the issue by putting his faith in the international community and accepting whatever it decided the republic's future should be. In October 1991 the EC Conference on Yugoslavia asked Bosnia-Hercegovina and Macedonia whether they, too, wanted to be independent states. Since neither Muslims nor Croats could stomach becoming a minority within a Greater Serbia, the HDZ and SDA as well as the republic's minor parties opted for independence. In protest, Karadžić withdrew the SDS deputies from the Sarajevo parliament warning that moves towards Bosnian independence were leading the republic 'into a hell in which the Muslims will perhaps perish'.

A month later, after an exclusively Serb referendum within the six Bosnian *krajinas*, the SDS duly proclaimed the formation of a Serb republic within Bosnia-Hercegovina.[23] The new republic had all the trappings of an independent state with its own government and currency. However, it also contained a large non-Serb population and its

[23] In the referendum 99 per cent of voters in an estimated 85 per cent turn-out backed the creation of a Serb republic within Bosnia-Hercegovina if the republic tried to break away from Yugoslavia.

six entities were separated from one another by territories populated
by Croats and Muslims. More than four months before war broke out,
the creation of the Serb republic effectively destroyed Bosnia-
Hercegovina, for Karadžić was not offering a discussion document—he
was delivering an ultimatum. The republic's Croats and Muslims could
either join with Serbia in a rump Yugoslavia or their society would
be destroyed. The SDS's military might and the weakness of its
opponents ruled out any need for compromise or even consideration
of alternative points of view.

For the same reasons that Slovenia and Croatia could not remain
within a Serb-dominated Yugoslavia, Bosnia-Hercegovina's Muslims
and Croats could not join a rump Yugoslavia and, despite Karadžić's
threats, applied to the Badinter Commission for recognition.
Izetbegović hoped that, if he complied with everything the European
Community asked of him, it would not stand by and allow Karadžić
to destroy Bosnia-Hercegovina.

Since the Badinter Commission wanted a referendum in Bosnia-
Hercegovina, the government duly organised one for 28 February and
1 March. The result was 99 per cent support for independence.
However, the SDS rejected the referendum in advance and ensured that
Serbs boycotted it. Consequently, only 63 per cent of Bosnia-
Hercegovina's total population turned out to vote. Before the results
came through, a Serb attending a wedding in Sarajevo was shot dead
by an unidentified assassin and within the hour masked Serb gunmen
erected barricades around the city. A dozen people died that day as
Karadžić presented the government with six demands, including
separate, ethnic police forces and media, and Izetbegović rushed to
fudge a compromise. The referendum had achieved nothing; it had
merely reaffirmed the gulf between the minimum position of the SDS,
on the one hand, and the republic's other parties, on the other.

The European Community was not looking for justice within
Bosnia-Hercegovina; it was merely hoping to dispose of the problem
by facilitating some form of compromise between the republic's three
peoples. As in Croatia, this effectively meant discovering the minimum
settlement acceptable to the Serbs and persuading the Muslims and
Croats to agree to it. Carrington's solution was cantonisation, that
is the division of a sovereign Bosnia-Hercegovina into 'three constituent units, based on national principles and taking into account the
economic, geographic and other criteria'. On 18 March representatives
of the SDS and HDZ signed up to it as did a reluctant Bosnian govern-

ment. However, the agreement was as worthless as the EC-brokered cease-fires during the Croatian war. Though Karadžić had supposedly agreed to preserving Bosnia-Hercegovina as a single entity, he was not about to dismantle his Serb state. Cantonisation was merely partition by another name and as this became clear to Izetbegović, he reneged on the agreement.

During March the number of armed incidents grew daily yet a full-scale war did not break out, since it remained difficult to shatter bonds between communities which had lived side by side for centuries. For that outsiders were required. As in Croatia, the principal instigators of violence belonged to Serb extremist organisations, especially the *Arkanovci*. War erupted on 2 April as *Arkanovci* raided Bijeljina, a small town on the Serbian border, claiming that they were preventing a massacre of Serbs but murdering several dozen Muslims in the process. Three days later Serb gunmen fired indiscriminately from the top of the Holiday Inn Hotel in Sarajevo at anti-war demonstrators who had gathered to profess their commitment to a multinational Bosnia-Hercegovina and that evening Serb heavy artillery began its bombardment of Sarajevo. The next day, the European Community and the United States recognised Bosnia-Hercegovina as an independent state, only to stand by as Serb forces and the JNA laid waste the new country.

Bosnia betrayed

Serb military action in Bosnia-Hercegovina had been prepared many months in advance. It was coordinated with the JNA, which was determined to hang on to its Bosnian munitions factories, and aimed to seize the entire republic for the rump Yugoslavia, or, failing that, to forge land corridors between the six *krajinas* linking them together within a single Serb entity. It was designed as a *blitzkrieg* so that Karadžić would be able to present the international community with a *fait accompli* and within the first month of fighting his forces came to control about two–thirds of the republic. However, that was effectively the end of Serb territorial gains. Despite Izetbegović's refusal to make military preparations prior to the outbreak of war and the obscene imbalance in firepower, the Muslims, Croats and those Serbs who remained loyal to the Sarajevo government refused to capitulate.

Though Serb apologists consider the recognition of Bosnia-Hercegovina the spark which ignited the conflict, this explanation ignores the order of events. The war had already begun before the international community recognised Bosnia-Hercegovina; the events were not the other way around. Moreover, the decision to recognise Bosnia-Hercegovina was not the considered outcome of months of deliberation but a reflex action aimed at halting the fighting. At the time, the European Community was smarting from criticism that it had exacerbated the war in Croatia by refusing to recognise Slovenia and Croatia in the summer of 1991 and hoped that simply by recognising Bosnia-Hercegovina it might persuade the Serbs to back down. But there was little conviction behind recognition and neither the European Community nor the United States had any intention of coming to Bosnia-Hercegovina's aid. Instead, as in Croatia they aimed merely to contain the war and ensure it did not spread beyond Bosnia-Hercegovina.

Containment consisted of further mediation and the legally dubious extension of the UN arms embargo on Yugoslavia to include Bosnia-Hercegovina. With Resolution 713 the UN Security Council had in September 1991 imposed an embargo on arms sales to an extant Yugoslavia.[24] However, the embargo did not necessarily apply to Yugoslavia's internationally-recognised successor states, Slovenia, Croatia and Bosnia-Hercegovina which by April 1992 had all become members of the United Nations in their own right. Moreover, it ran counter to the spirit of the UN Charter since, under Article 51, a member state has the right to self-defence. Nevertheless, and contrary to the wishes of the UN General Assembly, which voted repeatedly for the embargo to be lifted, the Security Council chose to maintain it on the explicit insistence of two of its permanent members, Britain and France.

Since the arms embargo effectively awarded the Bosnian Serbs permanent superiority in military hardware, Bosnia-Hercegovina's legally-constituted and internationally-recognised government felt betrayed. While Serb forces were systematically levelling Bosnian cities and cleansing the countryside of non-Serbs, the Croat and Muslim populations were deprived of the means to fight back, yet the international community refused to intervene to protect them. Izetbegović in particular felt aggrieved because, unlike his Croatian and Slovene

---

[24] The resolution had actually been passed with the approval of the Belgrade authorities since the JNA's monopoly of heavy weaponry made it easier to defeat Croatia.

counterparts, he had done his utmost to comply with the wishes of the international community. His attempts to defuse areas of conflict had been sincere, and despite provocation he had refused to arm his people. Nevertheless, as soon as war broke out, Izetbegović was treated as simply the leader of one of Bosnia-Hercegovina's 'warring factions'.

In fact, the European Community betrayed Izetbegović as soon as it accepted cantonisation as the basis of a settlement within Bosnia-Hercegovina. Although desperate to agree virtually anything which might avoid a war, Izetbegović could not endorse cantonisation since that meant abandoning the concept of civil society — that is, a society in which all citizens were treated equally irrespective of nationality — and sanctioning the national principle as the basis of a settlement in Bosnia-Hercegovina. Cantonisation envisaged the republic's division along ethnic lines even though ethnic lines did not exist at that stage. Yet it did not address the actual causes of Bosnia-Hercegovina's instability, namely the huge imbalance in firepower and the alacrity with which the SDS was prepared to resort to violence.

Recognition appeared to give Izetbegović a lifeline, but, as the international community refused to intervene to protect Bosnia-Hercegovina's Muslims and Croats and, at the same time, denied them the means of self-defence, it proved worthless. From the European Community's perspective recognition had held out the possibility of a quick-fix solution at no cost and had therefore been worth trying. But when it failed to halt the fighting, the fact that Bosnia-Hercegovina had officially become a fully-fledged member of the international community was conveniently forgotten. Recognition made no effective difference to Bosnia-Hercegovina's status and as Carrington resumed his mediation efforts the Sarajevo government was deemed no more than a 'warring faction' on a par with the SDS in a civil war. However, given the nature of the war in Bosnia-Hercegovina, the entire mediation process was fundamentally flawed.

Since Izetbegović had refused to prepare for war, Bosnia-Hercegovina's Muslims and Croats found themselves at the mercy of bands of militant Serbs such as the *Arkanovci* as soon as fighting broke out. The result was the catastrophe all Yugoslavia experts had been predicting for months. Having triggered the war with their raid on Bijeljina the *Arkanovci* rampaged across the east of the republic, leaving a trail of death and destruction in their wake. Elsewhere in Bosnia-Hercegovina further groups of Serb irregulars carried out an identical campaign of atrocities against defenceless Muslim and Croat communities, while, as in Croatia, the JNA contented itself with bombarding cities from afar. Consequently, a very large, though incalculable, proportion of the total dead from the war in Bosnia-Hercegovina were killed in the first three months of fighting, if what was taking place can be described as fighting.

Both the scale of the killing and the logic behind it were uncannily reminiscent of June, July and August 1941 when the Ustašas descended on defenceless Serb villages. The difference was that this time Serbs were the perpetrators of the atrocities, and Croats and especially Muslims were the victims. The Serb forces which overwhelmed two–thirds of Bosnia-Hercegovina in April 1992 set out systematically to erase all trace of ncn-Serb culture from lands earmarked for a Greater Serbia. Given the number of Muslims and Croats who lived either within or between the six Serb *krajinas*, the undertaking was enormous and the killing had to be on a massive scale to have any chance of succeeding. Ethnic cleansing was not a by-product of the war; it was its principal aim. As one 'warring faction' attempted to exterminate or expel the two–thirds of Bosnia-Hercegovina's population who were essentially defenceless, the very prospect of mediation seemed farcical.

Sarajevo became the focus of media attention because reporters could get there and it had been a magnificent city, not because the suffering of its inhabitants was greater than anywhere else. Most of the initial killing took place in rural areas well away from the prying eyes of foreign journalists, who could only piece together what was happening in Serb-held regions from the accounts of refugees.[25]

Serb tactics in Bosnia-Hercegovina were identical to those pursued in Croatia, though the scale was greater and the consequences more gory. Atrocities were fundamental to the war effort and served to shatter any remaining trust between peoples and force non-Serbs to abandon their homes. The more barbaric the killing, the greater the incentive for other Muslims and Croats to flee and, sure enough, within days of the outbreak of war, refugees began flooding into Croatia. Those who stayed put were stripped of their possessions and

[25] Roy Gutman, foreign correspondent of the New York paper *Newsday*, won a Pulitzer prize for his despatches from Bosnia-Hercegovina, which were based on the testimonies of survivors of Serb-run detention camps. His investigations remain the most comprehensive, if controversial, account of ethnic cleansing and form the content of his book, *Witness to Genocide*.

herded into detention camps. The terror was not confined to Muslims and Croats since Serbs who dared side with the Bosnian government or merely oppose the war were dealt with in an equally brutal fashion. Most rural Serbs were confused by the war but so indoctrinated with fear of Islamic fundamentalism that they genuinely believed theirs was a defensive struggle against Muslim extremists. Many were dragged reluctantly into the conflict and some were even forced to participate in atrocities, aware that if they refused they too would be killed. Others, most of whom had been misfits in peacetime, actually revelled in the orgy of violence during the spring and summer of 1992.

Despite compelling press reports of ethnic cleansing, the international community turned a blind eye and left Carrington to continue his futile shuttle diplomacy. Not until television journalists from Britain's Channel Four got inside the Omarska detention camp on 6 August 1992 did the world wake up to the horror of what had already been taking place for four months. Television footage of cadaverous prisoners cowering in terror and ringed by barbed wire conjured up images of Nazi death camps and provoked public outrage on an unprecedented scale. The outcry could not be ignored and forced Britain's Prime Minister, John Major, who had recently taken the chair of the European Community, to organise an international conference on Bosnia-Hercegovina in conjunction with the United Nations.

By the time the London Conference came together at the end of August the territorial position within Bosnia-Hercegovina had hardly changed for about two months, though fighting was far from over. Despite their overwhelming superiority in weaponry, Serb forces had failed to conquer the entire republic and were unable to present the world with a *fait accompli*. The two–thirds of Bosnian territory seized in the first month of war remained in Serb hands and had been largely cleansed of Muslims and Croats. But the remaining third was held by the mainly Muslim Bosnian Army and the Croat Defence Council (*Hrvatsko vijeće odbrane* or HVO).

Resistance to the Serb onslaught was of necessity improvised but eventually proved remarkably successful. Since Karadžić's army was predominantly drawn from rural areas, it had no problem taking control of large tracts of the Bosnian countryside, but the offensive came unstuck in the cities and regions with a predominantly Croat population. In many respects the war was as much between city and countryside as between Serb and non-Serb. Since Muslims had belonged to the political élite in Ottoman times, they had historically formed a greater proportion of the urban population, and, even in the 1990s remained the most urbanised of Bosnia-Hercegovina's peoples. That said, since the Second World War ethnic divisions had largely disappeared in the cities and intermarriage was so common that in Sarajevo, for example, it was almost impossible to find someone without relatives from a different ethnic background. As urban Serbs joined with Croats and Muslims in defence of their homes, they proved less a potential fifth column and more a source of optimism for the prospects of a multinational Bosnia-Hercegovina.

The urban population was also swelled by an influx of Muslim and Croat refugees from the countryside. Though lacking weapons, the Bosnian government was not short of manpower or commitment and, despite appalling conditions, the cities refused to surrender. As it became clear to Serb forces that they would not be able to capture urban centres without incurring massive casualties, they chose to bombard them from afar, as in Croatia, rather than launching frontal assaults. The result was a series of sieges, most notably that of Sarajevo where the daily carnage was broadcast almost simultaneously around the world via satellite links.

The tide of battle first turned in western Hercegovina, a region adjacent to Croatia where Croats actually formed a greater proportion of the population than in Croatia proper. In the first months of fighting Serb forces were able to inflict great damage, but without the support of an indigenous Serb community, could not sustain the offensive and were gradually pushed back. Many Croats from western Hercegovina had been volunteers in the Croatian Army during the war in Croatia and returned home to join the HVO as soon as war broke out in Bosnia-Hercegovina. They could rely on Croatia for military supplies, as well as on the Croat community abroad, much of which came originally from Hercegovina. By the end of June they had even pushed Serb forces out of Mostar, the capital of Hercegovina and the city which suffered the heaviest destruction in the whole of Bosnia-Hercegovina.

With images of the Omarska detention camp and more revelations of ethnic cleansing fresh in the minds of world leaders, they talked tough at the London Conference. Bosnia-Hercegovina's territorial integrity was reaffirmed, the republic was treated as a sovereign state with the legal right to defend itself against aggression[26] and a framework for resolving the war was drawn up. Huge international

---

[26] Though, significantly, the arms embargo was not lifted.

pressure forced Serb leaders to adopt a conciliatory stance and agree, among other things, to end hostilities, place heavy weapons under UN supervision and allow the free passage of humanitarian relief to civilian population centres. Cyrus Vance and Lord Owen, a former British Foreign Minister, were appointed on behalf of the United Nations and European Community, respectively, to oversee a negotiated settlement based on the principles agreed in London to be worked out at a new Conference on Yugoslavia to take place in Geneva. However, as soon as public outrage over detention camps died down, the London principles were conveniently forgotten and not one element of the agreement was implemented.

Bosnia abandoned

The London Conference was a watershed for international involvement in Yugoslavia. Hitherto, the international community's role had hardly been honourable, but Bosnians, nevertheless, clung to the hope that as soon as the West understood what was happening, it would come to their assistance. On account of Channel Four's report and the parallels between Omarska and the Nazi extermination camps of half a century earlier, pressure for intervention to halt a repetition of the Holocaust was enormous. In London, world leaders spoke of war crimes trials and how they would never recognise a settlement based on ethnic cleansing. The principles agreed as a framework for ending the war effectively entailed reversing the results of ethnic cleansing and neutralising Serb military superiority and thus appeared to provide the basis for a lasting settlement. But, despite the rhetoric, no country was prepared to commit the resources necessary to turn such aspirations into achievable goals.

Quite simply, the London agreement appeared too costly, both financially and politically, for the international community to implement. It required a credible military threat to force Serbs to give up their territorial gains, which, if successful, would have had to be followed by an indefinite policing role. It was a greater commitment than any statesman was prepared to make. Yet without such a commitment the Geneva Conference found itself in the same position as its EC predecessor. Like Carrington before them, Vance and Owen could only aspire to finding the minimum settlement acceptable to the Serbs and then bullying non-Serbs into agreeing to it. As promises made in London failed to materialise, Bosnians stopped deluding themselves that help was just around the corner and decided that the only way to achieve a just settlement was to maximise their own war effort.

The London Conference was typical of the international response to the war in Bosnia-Hercegovina. Without the irrefutable proof of systematic Serb brutality towards Croats and Muslims provided by Channel Four, and the ensuing public outcry, it would never have taken place. Before the film from the Omarska detention camp was transmitted, the European powers had done everything possible to treat the conflict as a purely civil war in which all belligerents were equally guilty, irrespective of evidence to the contrary.[27] Unless the war came to threaten their own interests directly, Britain and France, the two countries with the military might to make a difference, were determined to stay out, and thus international involvement was restricted to measures aimed at ensuring that fighting did not come to threaten western European interests. The arms embargo enabled the European powers to manage the war, while humanitarian aid stemmed the flow of refugees to western Europe.

To justify their inaction, statesmen and diplomats chose to interpret the war as a peculiarly Balkan phenomenon. It was allegedly the result of ancient and irrational animosities, inherent in Balkan peoples, who had seemingly been at each others' throats since time immemorial and were all as bad as each other.[28] Fighting was supposedly part of

---

[27] It is hard to believe that senior Western diplomats and politicians did not know about Bosnian detention camps many months before Channel Four filmed inside Omarska. Moreover, given the amount of money countries spend on intelligence and today's satellite technology, it is highly improbable that in the 1990s journalists could have uncovered a scoop of such magnitude had the intelligence community known nothing of it. In fact, UN officials had been reporting the existence of these camps since June 1992 but the information was suppressed for political reasons.

[28] The most vocal advocate of this point of view was General Lewis MacKenzie, the Canadian officer in command of UN forces in Bosnia-Hercegovina between March and August 1992, whose opinions were eagerly seized upon by those opposed to intervention. MacKenzie had been greeted as a saviour when he entered Sarajevo in June to open the city's airport to relief flights but his name became a term of abuse as he insisted that all sides were equally to blame. He was eventually removed but continued to play an active role in Yugoslav affairs, taking advantage of the reputation he had acquired in Bosnia-Hercegovina with a series of speaking engagements, some of which were organised by SerbNet, a Serb-American lobby group. On one such trip to Washington in May 1993 he told the House Armed Services Committee: 'Dealing with Bosnia is a bit like dealing with three serial killers — one has killed fifteen, one has killed ten, one has killed five', and asked 'Do we help the one who has only killed five?'

Balkan culture and Bosnia-Hercegovina ideal guerrilla country, in which any international force would inevitably become bogged down with no prospect of getting out.

Mediators were still hoping to end the fighting but the settlement had to be cheap. Talk of war crimes trials or reversing ethnic cleansing got in the way of a negotiated settlement and was rapidly discarded. The War Crimes Commission which was set up after the London Conference proved totally ineffective as Britain and France systematically hampered its operations.[29] Meanwhile, Owen and Vance worked to make Izetbegović and his government accept the ethnic division of Bosnia-Hercegovina; and, to make the deal more palatable, attempted to persuade the Bosnian Serbs to relinquish some of their territorial gains. Owen claimed he was simply being a realist but Bosnians felt that the West had abandoned them—everyone, that is, but the media. While diplomats tried to wash their hands of Bosnia-Hercegovina, journalists determined to keep the war at the very top of the international agenda.

Coverage of Yugoslav affairs improved steadily as the media came to know more about the region. By the time war broke out in Bosnia-Hercegovina, journalists who had covered the war in Croatia were no longer willing to write the fighting off as tribal warfare. Bosnians were white, they were Europeans and they were accustomed to a reasonably high standard of living. Moreover, in urban centres, and especially the capital, they were often extremely sophisticated and articulate. A great proportion of Sarajevo's population spoke at least one foreign language and could communicate easily with the foreign media. Indeed, when visiting journalists discovered how well-read and informed many Sarajevans were, they were frequently embarrassed by their own ignorance of Bosnian affairs. It was, as UN Secretary-General Boutros Boutros-Ghali pointed out,[30] a rich man's war and, consequently,

---

[29] While the War Crimes Commission was originally starved of funding, the Special Rapporteur appointed to the Commission, Cherif Bassiouni, was, nevertheless, able to begin compiling a war-crimes data-base with donations from the Soros foundation, the charitable trust set up by the billionaire investment guru, George Soros. Though Bassiouni, a Muslim professor of law at Chicago's De Paul University, was probably the most suitably qualified candidate for the post of prosecutor, his appointment was blocked by Britain and France because they feared he would do too good a job.

[30] Boutros-Ghali made this infamous remark on a visit to Sarajevo in July 1992, suggesting that there were other more deserving causes and that the massive media attention given to Bosnia-Hercegovina was diverting resources away from the Third World.

Western reporters found it exceptionally easy to relate to the agony of Bosnians whose lives were disintegrating around them.

Journalists who spent time in Bosnia-Hercegovina experienced some of the hardships ordinary Bosnians had to contend with, albeit only on a temporary basis. They shared many of Sarajevo's worst moments and made good friends in the city from all three ethnic groups who remained committed to the ideal of a multinational Bosnia-Hercegovina. Over months of fighting they came to respect the resilience and dignity of Bosnians and inevitably grew emotionally involved in the conflict. Many foreign reporters became the most ardent advocates of intervention, with the result that, as the world turned its back, they came to feel the same sense of betrayal as the Bosnians themselves. Meanwhile, the carnage of war made spectacular television, which networks were eager to screen.

In essence, international policy toward Bosnia-Hercegovina boiled down to a series of reactions to television pictures. Under intense pressure from the media, world leaders had to be seen to be doing something but remained unwilling to take any of the steps which might have actually contributed to a resolution of the war. Reactions were typically hasty and designed to assuage domestic public opinion, not to do anything for the Bosnians themselves. Moreover, measures taken in response to a particular outrage frequently ran counter to what had, hitherto, been the prevailing wisdom as to the best way to reach a settlement, and were invariably watered down as soon as the initial public outcry subsided.

The decision to recognise Bosnia-Hercegovina was itself a response to the first images of fighting and flew in the face of the prevailing diplomatic opinion. Until war actually broke out, the European Community had consciously chosen not to extend diplomatic recognition to Bosnia-Hercegovina for fear of incensing Serbia and precipitating war. Only after the policy of non-recognition had manifestly failed was it changed. But when the act of recognition did not immediately have the desired impact, it was watered down so that the Sarajevo government remained simply a 'warring faction', and not the legitimate representative of a sovereign state. Recognition suggested taking sides and, above all, EC diplomats wished to remain neutral, so as to be in a position to mediate. But given the nature of the war and the pressure of public opinion neutrality was untenable.

The UN Security Council eventually imposed sanctions against rump Yugoslavia, that is Serbia and Montenegro, on 30 May 1992.

The move again came in response to television images, this time from the notorious Sarajevo bread queue massacre which had killed sixteen people three days earlier. However, it was not until 27 April 1993 — eleven months later and shortly after another outrage — that the Security Council approved a mechanism for enforcing the sanctions. It was the same story for the no-fly zone above Bosnia-Hercegovina. On 9 October 1992 the Security Council banned all military flights over Bosnia-Hercegovina but again did not impose an enforcement mechanism until 7 April 1993 — six months and 465 flights later.

Television images of refugees led to humanitarian palliatives. When reporters demonstrated how humanitarian aid was habitually blocked and failed to reach its destination the Security Council adopted a resolution authorising the use of force to ensure deliveries. Months later, UN troops began cautiously to implement it. Images of horrendous suffering in the town of Srebrenica led to the establishment of so-called safe havens there and in five other besieged Bosnian towns and cities. However, despite UN protection, these enclaves remained subject to Serb shelling. The pathetic image of Irma Hazimuratović, a five-year-old Sarajevo girl lying in her death bed with meningitis, embarrassed the British government into flying a handful of the most acutely ill patients out of Bosnia-Hercegovina to Britain amid a tasteless fanfare of publicity.

The few diplomatic breakthroughs were all achieved by massive threats of force against the Serbs, though Milošević or Karadžić were invariably able to defuse seemingly tense situations with a minimum of concessions. Rather than try the patience of the international community, Milošević withdrew the JNA from Bosnia-Hercegovina in May 1992. However, before departing it left its equipment with the Bosnian Serb Army which continued to pursue identical tactics. Two months later, further threats enabled UN troops to reopen Sarajevo airport for relief flights. But since the United Nations repeatedly failed to implement its own resolutions, the threats became less and less credible and Serb forces were increasingly prepared to flout them. It was not until 28 February 1994 — nearly three years into the war — that the international community took its first direct military action against Serbs forces when US jets, under Nato command, shot down four war planes in breach of the no-fly zone.

NATO intervention appeared to open a new chapter in the Yugoslav conflict and restore some credibility to international attempts to end the fighting. But it, too, was essentially a response to the greatest individual outrage of the war, the Sarajevo market massacre in which sixty-eight people were killed by a single mortar shell. This event, on 5 February 1994, jolted the West into belated military action against the Serbs, enabling Nato to issue an ultimatum ordering Serb forces to remove their heavy weaponry from around Sarajevo within ten days or face air strikes. After initial foot-dragging and much posturing, the Serbs complied rather than call NATO's bluff. Within days, life began returning to Sarajevo after nearly two years of siege, though the wider war in Bosnia-Hercegovina was still far from over.

Issuing an ultimatum again ran counter to the prevailing wisdom among diplomats as to the best way of reaching a settlement within Bosnia-Hercegovina, but its success was incontrovertible and in marked contrast to the months of deadlock which preceded it. Despite regular claims from the mediators that they were on the verge of a breakthrough, the Geneva Conference had achieved nothing positive in 18 months of negotiations. The Bosnian government refused to accept the consequences of ethnic cleansing, the Bosnian Serbs refused to give up as much land as the mediators wished and the mediators lacked the muscle to make them yield more. The most equitable distribution of territory they could come up with became known as the Vance-Owen plan. It envisaged the division of Bosnia-Hercegovina into ten provinces—nine ethnically-denominated and one mixed—linked together under a weak central government in Sarajevo, and was touted around the world as a panacea. However, despite months of talks, in which both Milošević and Karadžić were persuaded to endorse the plan, the Bosnian Serb parliament rejected it, and the plan was finally scuppered by a lack of international support.

The real result of the Vance-Owen plan was the destruction of the Croat-Muslim alliance and the creation of a three-way conflict. Necessity had forced Croats and Muslims to join forces during the first months of war, but the two peoples had never constructed a formal alliance. It was a marriage of convenience which proved extremely effective in repelling the initial Serb onslaught but began to come unstuck over diverging conceptions of Bosnia-Hercegovina's future as soon as the tide of battle turned. By autumn 1992 cracks had appeared in the alliance which required great sensitivity on both sides if they were to be bridged. However, the Vance-Owen plan, and the alacrity with which the Croats signed up to it, turned disagreement into full-blown conflict. By the following spring, the former allies were fighting among themselves over the third of the republic which Serb forces had failed to grab.

Relations between Muslims and Croats within Bosnia-Hercegovina were complex and differed widely across the republic. Croats who lived in regions also populated by Serbs and/or Muslims—essentially central Bosnia—tended to consider themselves as much Bosnian as Croat and found it easy to ally themselves with Muslims and even Serbs fighting in the Bosnian Army. By contrast, Croats who lived in regions where Croats formed an overwhelming majority—essentially western Hercegovina—considered themselves primarily Croat and were eager to forge closer ties with Croatia proper rather than Bosnia-Hercegovina's other peoples. Official relations between Muslims and Croats depended on which Croat faction held sway and were complicated by external influences—that is, interference from Zagreb and, in particular, Croat *émigrés* from Hercegovina.[31]

Since only about a third of Bosnia-Hercegovina's Croat population came from Hercegovina, the moderate faction performed better in the elections and dominated the HDZ until about two months before the outbreak of war. Led by Stjepan Kljuić, a farsighted politician from Sarajevo, the party cooperated with the SDA in the Bosnian parliament and worked hard to maintain the republic's integrity. However, after an acrimonious battle within the HDZ, Kljuić was forced to resign and, with Zagreb's backing, Mate Boban, a Croat from Hercegovina, took control of the party. Kljuić moved to Sarajevo where he joined Izetbegović's cabinet and remained committed to an integral Bosnia-Hercegovina. Meanwhile, Boban based himself in Hercegovina where he worked to carve out a Croat mini-state, christened Herceg-Bosna.

Few Croats from Croatia proper had territorial aspirations against the neighbouring republic. A unitary Bosnia-Hercegovina formed a useful buffer state between Croatia and Serbia and most Croats were aware that its dismemberment might serve as a precedent for Serb-occupied regions of Croatia. Moreover, western Hercegovina was sparsely-populated and barren, offering Zagreb no material gain. However, to Tudjman, strategic and economic considerations came a

---

[31] Croat *émigrés* had provided much of the HDZ's finance and thus formed a powerful interest group at the centre of government. At the head of the Hercegovina lobby was Gojko Šušak, a former pizza parlour owner in Canada, who became Croatia's Defence Minister.

poor second to nationalist dreams and the annexation of a chunk of Bosnia-Hercegovina formed a fundamental part of what he increasingly considered his historic mission of uniting all Croats within a single Croatian state. Tudjman and Milošević had discussed the division of Bosnia-Hercegovina at Karadjordjevo, and, even at the height of the Serb onslaught, he sponsored talks between Boban and Karadžić at which they, too, considered the contours of a possible carve-up.[32]

The informal Croat-Muslim alliance was hampered from the outset by Croat resentment at the way the Bosnian government had refused to acknowledge Serb aggression in Croatia and turned a blind eye to JNA operations against Croats in western Hercegovina during the war in Croatia. Since Sarajevo had made no preparations for war, it was not in a position to offer assistance to the rest of the country and effectively abandoned Croat-populated regions. To survive the initial Serb onslaught, Croats from Hercegovina had had to organise their own defence and looked to Croatia for supplies and Croat *émigrés* for financial support. As a result, it was the HVO and HOS, not the Bosnian Army, which halted the Serb advance across Hercegovina and then began liberating territory seized in the first month of fighting. However, having incurred heavy casualties, Croat forces were unwilling to turn their gains over to the Sarajevo government and resented the way Izetbegović avoided placing the alliance on a formal footing, yet expected them to take in Muslim refugees from elsewhere in Bosnia-Hercegovina.

The war altered both the ethnic and the political equation in western Hercegovina and especially in Mostar, the region's principal city, exerting a great strain on the Croat-Muslim alliance. Before the war, Croats and Muslims had formed roughly the same proportion of Mostar's population[33] and the municipal council had been finely balanced between Croats, Muslims and Serbs. However, after the HVO expelled Serb forces from the region and life began returning to the city, Croats monopolised political power, even though, following an influx of Muslim refugees, they were now in the minority.

As soon as the Vance-Owen plan was unveiled, the Bosnian Croats signed up to it since it awarded them more territory than perhaps they

[32] Boban and Karadžić met in Graz, Austria, on 6 May 1992.

[33] According to the 1991 census, Muslims formed 34.8 per cent, Croats 33.8 per cent, Serbs 19 per cent and Yugoslavs 10 per cent of Mostar's population.

were entitled to in strictly proportional terms. When the international mediators bullied a reluctant Sarajevo government into following the Croats and agreeing to the plan, the Croat authorities in Mostar and other Croat-designated provinces began implementing it, irrespective of Muslim opinion. However, the Vance-Owen plan was not the answer. As with cantonisation, it was but a smoke-screen for ethnic partition and, as Croats took the plan to its logical conclusion, the Muslims objected. After several months of tension the Croat-Muslim conflict escalated into full-scale war in spring 1993. Since a large proportion of the HVO and especially HOS were actually Muslims who had enlisted in Croat units because Croat forces were generally better armed than the Bosnian Army, soldiers who had fought side by side to repel the Serb onslaught now fought each other.

The fighting between Croats and Muslims was some of the most brutal and sustained of the entire war, largely because the combatants were reasonably well matched. It was a battle for survival and conditions resembled images from the First World War. Without doubt, the lowest point was reached in November 1993 when Croat forces destroyed Mostar's historic landmark, the bridge linking the eastern and western halves of the city and giving Mostar its name.[34] As a result of this wanton act of violence and media revelations of Croat atrocities and the existence of Croat-run detention camps in western Hercegovina, Croatia lost much international sympathy and there were calls, especially in Britain, for sanctions against Croatia. However, the major battles of the Croat-Muslim war actually took place in central Bosnia, where the Croat position was weak and a rejuvenated Muslim military notched up an impressive series of victories.

After more than eighteen months of war Bosnia-Hercegovina had descended into anarchy. It was a struggle for existence in which, as in every war, all sides could point to atrocities committed by the other sides. As central authority disintegrated, the war degenerated further into several mini-wars. In parts of Bosnia-Hercegovina the Croat-Muslim alliance remained intact, while elsewhere Croats actually turned to the Serbs for help in their fight against the Muslims. In Banja Luka, the largest Serb-held Bosnian city, Serb forces rebelled against their own leadership, and in Cazinska Krajina, the Muslim enclave in

---

[34] Mostar straddles the river Neretva and before the war had five bridges joining the two halves of the city. The Serbo-Croat word for bridge is *most*.

western Bosnia around Bihać, there was fighting between Muslims loyal to the Sarajevo government and other Muslims loyal to Fikret Abdić, a maverick local politician and business tycoon.[35]

The three-way war was exactly what international statesmen who opposed intervention were looking for. As Bosnians faced a second winter at war and a negotiated settlement was as elusive as ever, several prominent European politicians threatened to withdraw their own country's troops unless the 'warring factions' accepted the latest package that Owen and, since Vance stepped down in May 1993, his new co-mediator — the former Norwegian Foreign Minister, Thorwald Stoltenberg — were offering. In essence, the Owen-Stoltenberg proposals were an attempt to win Serb approval with a more explicit carve-up of Bosnia-Hercegovina than envisaged under the Vance-Owen plan which also aimed to make some form of Muslim state viable. However, though Karadžić appeared to look on the new plan favourably, the Muslims could not be bullied into accepting something they considered not only impractical but ridiculous. In addition to extra troops, the Owen-Stoltenberg plan required the construction of a series of fly-overs and tunnels to ensure that Muslims and Serbs should never meet!

As the Geneva Conference stalled yet again, diplomats and statesmen indulged in a pathetic quest to find a scapegoat. This time the whipping boy was no longer Germany, whose diplomats had been careful to take a back seat in the negotiation process, but the United States. US ambivalence towards the various peace proposals allegedly encouraged the Muslims to hold out for more in the hope that eventually the international community would provide them with the material support necessary to achieve their aims. US interference supposedly prevented Muslims facing up to reality. However, as far as the Muslims were concerned, irrespective of US or any other outside intervention, the terms of the deal on the table were so dishonourable that they considered the continuation of the war a better option.

In fact, the entire Geneva Conference and especially Lord Owen stuck in American throats. US diplomats were embarrassed to be associated with the mediation process to such an extent that three key men on the Yugoslavia desk at the State Department resigned in

---

[35] Fikret Abdić had been Managing-Director of Agrokomerc, the food-processing company based in Cazinska Krajina, which had gone bankrupt with debts of $900 million in 1987 (see chapter 5) and had been jailed for his part in the scandal.

protest. That said, US policy had not always been so altruistic. The Bush administration continued to appease Serbia right up until it became clear that Bill Clinton would win the 1992 elections. Until then, the State Department had placed its hope for peace on Milan Panić, a Serb-American businessman of dubious credentials, whom Milošević was happy to appoint the unelected Prime Minister of Serbia in order to avoid more onerous sanctions without making any change in policy. However, the Bush administration was on its way out and no longer regarded Yugoslavia as its responsibility. Eagleburger, now Secretary of State,[36] named Milošević, Karadžić, Mladić, Šešelj and Arkan, among others, as war criminals.

The Clinton administration came into office promising a more hands-on approach to the Yugoslav conflict but found its initiatives stymied by the Europeans, especially the British. The United States wanted to lift the arms embargo and strike Bosnian Serb positions from the air, but the European powers argued against intervention on behalf of the Bosnian Muslims on the grounds that it would place their troops who were already deployed in Bosnia-Hercegovina at unacceptable risk and jeopardise the humanitarian effort. In frustration, the new Secretary of State, Warren Christopher, let slip that John Major had even told him he feared his government might fall if the United States succeeded in lifting the arms embargo against the Bosnian Muslims. As far as the Americans were concerned, the European powers appeared more interested in securing US troops to implement a dishonourable peace than in a just settlement. Though Clinton's most ambitious projects were shelved by European opposition, whatever action the international community did take — airdrops to besieged Muslim communities, the NATO ultimatum ordering the Serbs to pull back from Sarajevo, the shooting-down of four Serb war planes and the Croatian-Bosnian Accord — was all US-inspired.

The Sarajevo marketplace massacre silenced those who had been calling for the withdrawal of UN troops and brought both the United States and Russia to the forefront of the diplomatic effort to end the war. The NATO ultimatum achieved what close to two years of mediation had not, and forced the Serbs to lift the siege of Sarajevo. While Russian involvement helped the Bosnian Serbs save face, it was clearly the threat of military action and, in particular, the credibility

[36] Eagleburger succeeded Baker when the latter went to organise the Bush election campaign.

of that threat in the absence of dissenting voices, which persuaded them to back down. But it was not a new dawn for Bosnia-Hercegovina. As soon as public outrage subsided the ambitious projects of UN officers on the ground were watered down. As Bosnian Serb leaders saw the international community again in disarray over its policy towards Bosnia-Hercegovina and, critically, witnessed its reluctance to send additional peacekeepers, they renewed their offensive. With UN troops effectively maintaining Serb gains around Sarajevo, the Bosnian Serb Army turned its guns on the remaining Muslim enclaves, even though they had supposedly been designated 'safe havens' by the United Nations.

The one genuine diplomatic breakthrough of the entire war was the Croatian-Bosnian Accord, brokered in secret by US diplomats and signed in Zagreb on 25 March 1994. Whereas the Geneva Conference had attempted to exploit Croat-Muslim divisions in pursuit of a three-way deal and had consistently fuelled the conflict, the United States concentrated on resurrecting the Croat-Muslim alliance as the first step towards a lasting settlement. Instead of attempting to find an equitable division of territory between Croats and Muslims, US diplomats worked to unite both peoples within a single state and underwrote the agreement with the promise of financial aid for post-war reconstruction. The outcome of weeks of secret talks was an end to fighting between Croats and Muslims in Bosnia-Hercegovina and the establishment of a confederation between Croatia and the new federation of Bosnia-Hercegovina.

9

PROSPECTS

'Men and nations will act rationally only when they have exhausted all other possibilities.' — Franjo Tudjman[1]

Serbia: the key

Even before Yugoslavia disintegrated the country had an ominous capacity to worry its neighbours and frequently featured in apocalyptic scenarios. In the 1970s best-seller, *The Third World War: a future history* by General Sir John Hackett, the Third World War was set to break out in Yugoslavia days after Soviet intervention.[2] While this scenario became dated as soon as the Cold War ended, alarmists on both sides of the interventionist debate have attempted to play on wider fears for world security to justify their respective stances. Since the First World War began in Sarajevo, both sides have argued, the Third World War may also begin there, unless, according to the interventionists, the international community takes military action to ensure that it does not, or, according to the non-interventionists, the international community keeps well clear of the conflict.

Though both Russia and the United States have been drawn into the war in Bosnia-Hercegovina, fears of a super-power clash are clearly exaggerated. Since the end of the Cold War, the region is quite simply no longer sufficiently important to merit such a confrontation. Nevertheless, the prospect of further bloodshed remains great and a settlement in Bosnia-Hercegovina, if one could be found which satisfied all parties, would not, by any means, end all conflict in the former Yugoslavia. While it is foolhardy to speculate on the outcome of any conflict, the fact that the course of the Yugoslav wars has, hitherto,

---

[1] Tudjman became President of Croatia a year after *The Impasses of Historical Reality*, his most controversial historical work from which this citation is taken, was published in 1989.

[2] Hackett had been one of the most senior generals in the British Army. In his *The Third World War: A Future History*, published in 1978 by Sidgwick & Jackson, he envisaged that the Third World War would break out in 1985 and that the initial clash between NATO and Warsaw Pact forces would take place in Slovenia.

been depressingly predictable and the violence has followed a clear pattern does offer pointers to the future.

Prospects vary greatly from republic to republic: from those of Slovenia, which nobody could realistically have hoped in the late 1980s to be in as healthy a position as at present; to those of Kosovo, where slaughter on a similar scale to Bosnia-Hercegovina is a serious possibility. The one factor common to all three wars which have already been fought, as well as every other conflict area in the former Yugoslavia, is Serbian involvement, suggesting that the evolution of all these conflicts depends, above all, on developments within Serbia, or, to be precise, on the political future of Slobodan Milošević, who, during seven years in power, has moulded Serbian society in his own image.

Today, Milošević is very different from the puritanical *apparatchik* who, in 1987, launched the anti-bureaucratic revolution. The Zastava car and modest flat have been replaced with the privileged lifestyle for which Milošević used to criticise his colleagues in the Party hierarchy, including limousines and one of Belgrade's finest villas. Indeed, despite economic sanctions, he has even taken to smoking expensive foreign cigars. Rumours that Milošević has stashed away a small fortune in Cyprus in case his position in Serbia becomes untenable have been rife in Belgrade for several years. However, many critics fear that he has no intention of ever leaving office alive, and that, like his parents (who both killed themselves), he suffers from an urge to destroy himself and, in the process, is leading Serbia towards national suicide.

If Milošević were suddenly to retire from politics, the shock waves would cripple the Serb war effort in Croatia and Bosnia-Hercegovina and might even unleash civil war in Serbia. There is no obvious successor, or even mechanism for succession, and, in Milošević's absence, Serbian society would be deeply divided. However, this scenario is highly unlikely. Despite military failures in Slovenia, Croatia and Bosnia-Hercegovina, the imposition of sanctions, runaway inflation and economic collapse, Milošević remains popular at home and his lust for power appears undiminished. The key to his grip on Serbian society and enduring popularity is his control of the media and security apparatus, which remains as firm as ever.

The Serbian opposition is weak and divided. Milošević's most articulate and outspoken critics are celebrated individuals whose liberal opinions and cosmopolitan outlook may charm foreign journalists but cut little ice with the Serbian electorate. The largest single opposition party remains Vuk Drašković's Serb Renewal Movement (*Srpski pokret obnove*), whose by now moderate nationalist alternative picks up most protest votes but is unable to make a decisive breakthrough at the polls without access to the media. Since the 1990 election Drašković has attempted to dissociate himself from the nationalist excesses of his past and has matured into a reasonably distinguished, though maverick, political leader. Meanwhile, since falling out with Milošević, Vojislav Šešelj, the Četnik leader, has taken over the mantle of the extreme nationalist opposition figure. In addition, since May 1992, when it became clear that Milošević had failed to achieve a Greater Serbia in Croatia and Bosnia-Hercegovina, the Serbian Orthodox Church has withdrawn its support and joined the chorus clamouring for his resignation.

Both the media and the security apparatus, including the armed forces, are regularly purged to ensure their continuing loyalty to Milošević. The JNA is a shadow of its former self, all Yugoslavists have been dismissed and, in any case, Milošević prefers to use the police to maintain his rule. Veljko Kadijević, the Defence Minister during the war in Croatia, resigned immediately after the shooting-down of an EC helicopter in January 1992. Four months later, after the creation of a new Yugoslav federation consisting of just Serbia and Montenegro, another forty senior generals were pensioned off and replaced with younger and more nationalistic officers. In a subsequent purge, General Momčilo Perišić, the most notorious JNA officer of the war in Bosnia-Hercegovina, responsible for the destruction of Mostar, was appointed Chief-of-Staff.

While the JNA bequeathed the new Yugoslav federation great reserves of military hardware, its bloated bureaucracy and lines of patronage are a financial liability Serbia could do without. The cost of maintaining military personnel, pensioners and their dependents has compounded an already desperate economic situation. Average annual income has crashed from about $3,000 in 1989 to below $300 in 1994, while inflation rocketed in 1993 above 50,000 per cent. In shops prices are changed most days, black marketeers control much of the economy, and even the well-to-do find it increasingly difficult to make ends meet. Nevertheless, despite huge privations and given Milošević's record, remarkably few Serbs blame the Serbian President for their predicament.

Between December 1990 and December 1993 Milošević called four general elections. On each occasion he won with ease and demonstrated that it is he alone who pulls the strings in Serbian society, a fact that erstwhile rivals Milan Panić, Dobrica Ćosić and Vojislav Šešelj have all learned to their cost. At times, Milošević has entered into temporary alliances with all three men. Panić, the Serb-American businessman who was appointed unelected Prime Minister of Yugoslavia in May 1992, shielded Milošević from a tougher international response to the war in Bosnia-Hercegovina with his comical quest for peace. Ćosić, the writer and intellectual father of modern Serb nationalism, offered Milošević some respectability at home. And Šešelj, the Četnik leader, used his paramilitary forces to terrorise Milošević's opponents. However, as soon as each man parted from the course Milošević had set for him, Milošević withdrew support and, after a slander campaign in the media, they all fell from grace.

The power of the media within Serbia cannot be over-estimated, especially when no alternative opinions have been expressed for the best part of a decade. Belgrade's opposition newspapers, the daily, *Borba*, and the weekly, *Vreme*, are tolerated so that Milošević can demonstrate to the world the existence of an independent press in Serbia. However, few Serbs can still afford the luxury of buying a newspaper and must rely on state television for their news.[3] Given the intensity and duration of Milošević's propaganda offensive, it is hardly surprising that most Serbs unquestioningly accept the bizarre conspiracy theories served up by the official media. To many, Milošević remains the saviour of the Serb nation and few have any idea what has taken place in Croatia and Bosnia-Hercegovina. Serbia is fighting the good fight against the combined forces of Islamic fundamentalism, the Vatican, the Third Reich and their allies, and is a misunderstood and innocent victim.

Instead of harming him, sanctions have contributed to Milošević's enduring popularity by shielding him from the consequences of his own economic blunders and isolating Serbs further from the outside world. Since Yugoslavia was never a great trading nation and, before the war, Serbia was as self-sufficient as a modern state can be, sanctions should have made relatively little difference. Indeed, other pariah states have managed to live comfortably with sanctions for decades.

[3] Serbia does have one independent radio station, B92, and one independent television and radio station, Studio B. However, both are short of money and cannot broadcast beyond Belgrade. Moreover, in the run-up to elections or at the time of key events, both stations find that their freedom to broadcast is curtailed.

However, the Serbian economy was already teetering on the brink of collapse as a result of several years' economic mismanagement and the cost of the wars in Slovenia, Croatia and Bosnia-Hercegovina, and police rule in Kosovo and the Sandžak. Sanctions have merely helped push it over the edge. Nevertheless, the state media have turned economic collapse to Milošević's advantage by blaming all Serbia's economic problems on the economic 'genocide' which the world is allegedly waging against Serbs.

Ironically, it is on account of his control of the media that Milošević may actually be in a position to come to a settlement with Croatia and Bosnia-Hercegovina. Peace entails the abandonment of the Greater Serbian vision which has, hitherto, formed the core of Milošević's approach towards the rest of the former Yugoslavia. But, with the media backing him to the hilt, Milošević can probably pull off a volte-face the like of which no politician in the democratic world could even contemplate. Moreover, he is far more concerned for his own future than dreams of a Greater Serbia, and has been aware of the threat that the continuation of the war in Bosnia-Hercegovina poses to his own position ever since sanctions were imposed against the rump Yugoslavia. As a result, he has become genuinely committed to a settlement, even if it effectively means selling out the Croatian and Bosnian Serbs.

Early in 1993 Milošević threw his weight behind the Vance-Owen plan, since the agreement was generous to Serb aspirations and, more importantly, ensured his own political survival. During months of fruitless negotiations he was even able to pose as a peacemaker, helping the mediators cajole Radovan Karadžić and the Bosnian Serbs into accepting the plan. However, while Milošević had tired of the war and knew he had nothing more to gain from it, his proxies on the ground refused to make the necessary concessions. The Bosnian Serbs believed they were still winning the war and had no intention of giving up any of their territorial gains. At the time, it appeared a re-run of the Croatian peace settlement. For, in Croatia, too, the Serb rebels had been reluctant to sign up to the UN agreement ending the war, but found they were dependant on Belgrade's continued support and had no choice but to come on board. However, in Bosnia-Hercegovina rebel Serbs possessed the firepower to fight on, irrespective of Milošević's wishes, and chose to defy their mentor.

While Milošević wants a settlement with Croatia and Bosnia-Hercegovina to ensure his own political survival, it is hard to envisage

Serbia at peace with Milošević still at the helm. Serbia has effectively been at war ever since he came to power, and national hysteria remains the essence of Milošević's rule. Conflict has been the key to his government and, apart from conflict, it is difficult to see what he has to offer. Indeed, many in the Serbian opposition fear that as soon as Milošević extricates himself from the war in Bosnia-Hercegovina he will have to open up another national crusade to revive his political fortunes and divert attention away from Serbia's economic predicament. With a Pandora's box still to be opened in the rest of the former Yugoslavia, he will not have to look far.

Vojvodina, Montenegro and the Sandžak

Vojvodina and Montenegro were the first two Yugoslav federal units to fall to Milošević's offensive in October 1988 and January 1989, respectively, and have, hitherto, remained largely loyal. However, as a result of military failure, economic collapse and the isolation imposed on them by international sanctions, opposition to the link with Serbia has begun to take on epidemic proportions. Close relations were fine while Vojvodina and Montenegro felt they were deriving some benefit from the link, but as its disadvantages have come to outweigh the advantages, both have sought to distance themselves from Milošević. Essentially, both Vojvodina and Montenegro would prefer their relationship with Serbia to be viewed in a similar light to that between Austria and Germany after the Second World War — that is, they wish to portray themselves as the first victims of Serbian aggression, and not accomplices to that aggression. Meanwhile, the Sandžak, which is a region of strategic importance straddling south-western Serbia and northern Montenegro, populated principally by Muslims, is almost certain to become another flashpoint.

Relations between Vojvodina's many peoples came under strain as soon as pro-Milošević demonstrators toppled the province's government and began an anti-bureaucratic revolution. All Vojvodina's non-Serbs complain that, since hardline nationalists seized power, rights they had, hitherto, taken for granted have been slashed to such an extent that they now face systematic and institutionalised oppression. According to the 1981 census, 56.6 per cent (1.15 million people) of Vojvodina's population were Serbs or Montenegrins, and the remaining 43.4 per cent were a mixture of peoples, including Hungarians, Croats, Slovaks and Romanians. At that time, Hungarians formed about 19 per cent and Croats 5.4 per cent of the population. However, in the intervening years Vojvodina's non-Serb population has declined sharply. The decline is partly due to natural demographic factors which have been at work since the Second World War, but since 1989, and especially 1991, non-Serbs attribute it to direct pressure on their communities to move out.

In the 1991 census, Vojvodina's Hungarian community had declined to 340,000, from 385,000 a decade earlier, and the decline accelerated that summer as Hungarians of military age fled across the border to avoid conscription. As the war gained momentum, Croats also left, or were forced out, in droves, and non-Serbs who remained found their presence increasingly unwelcome. Nevertheless, the political party representing the interests of Vojvodina's Hungarians, the Democratic Union of Hungarians in Vojvodina (*Demokratska zajednica Vojvodjanskih Madjara*), is one of the largest opposition parties in the Belgrade parliament and, despite hysterical media campaigns against its activities, lobbies hard for minority rights in Vojvodina.

In fact, Vojvodina's minorities also have considerable support within the province's Serb community, which is itself divided between Serbs loyal to Milošević and those who oppose him. The divide is, essentially, as in Croatia, that between *starosedeoci*, the established community which has lived in harmony with Vojvodina's other peoples for generations, and *došljaci*, the settler community which has colonised the province this century. The *starosedeoci* are highly embarrassed by modern Serb nationalism and the alliance with Serbia, but have been sidelined since 1988. Moreover, since the adoption of Serbia's most recent constitution in 1990, Vojvodina's autonomy and parliament have disappeared, making it more difficult for regionalists to manifest their disaffection. Nevertheless, as Vojvodina's economic position deteriorates, they are becoming increasingly vociferous. Indeed, in this context, it is worth noting that a major reason that Vojvodina acquired autonomy from Serbia in 1945 was the attitude of the province's Serb community who objected to what they considered economic exploitation in the interwar period.

For Montenegrins, too, the Serbian alliance has become increasingly embarrassing to such an extent that even the nationalists whom Milošević installed in power in 1989 have publicly dissociated themselves from Belgrade. Though smaller than Vojvodina, Montenegro was a fully-fledged republic in Tito's Yugoslavia and is now officially an equal partner with Serbia in the new Yugoslav federation. As a result, the Podgorica[4] leadership has considerable room for manoeuvre which it is using to mend fences with its neighbours, both Croatia and Albania, and to ingratiate itself with the international community in the hope that sanctions may be lifted.

The nature of the relationship between Montenegro and Serbia and whether a separate Montenegrin identity exists or not, are perennial questions in Montenegrin politics. According to the 1991 census, about 380,000, or 61.8 per cent, of the republic's 615,000 population considered themselves Montenegrin, while about 57,000, or 9.2 per cent, declared their nationality as Serb. In many ways, the relationship is akin to that between Austria and Germany, and Austrians and Germans. Serbs and Montenegrins speak the same language and officially belong to the same Church,[5] but have different historical experiences and have thus evolved two separate identities over the centuries. The precise nature of the relationship depends not on historical and cultural ties but on whether it is mutually advantageous, and as far as many Montenegrins are concerned they now have little to gain from the alliance and much to lose. However, they are aware that they have to tread warily because Serbia is land-locked and will not easily give up its last remaining outlet on the sea.

Podgorica first broke ranks with Belgrade in October 1991 when it backed EC proposals to create independent republics, based on existing borders, out of the ruins of the Yugoslav federation. Hitherto, Momir Bulatović, the Montenegrin President, had appeared, if anything, more nationalistic than Milošević and the Montenegrin media had been fuelling the conflict as aggressively as their Serbian counterparts. At the time of the rift, however, the JNA was besieging Dubrovnik, diplomatic pressure on Serbia and Montenegro was at its height and, critically, as Montenegrin reservists began returning home in coffins, the war was proving highly unpopular at home. Amid Serbian charges of treason, Bulatović cautiously began to distance himself from Milošević and to chart an independent course for Montenegro.

To many Montenegrins the Dubrovnik campaign is the blackest page in their history and proof of the folly of their alliance with Serbia.

[4] After more than four decades as Titograd, Montenegro's capital reverted to its original name of Podgorica in 1991.

[5] One manifestation of Montenegro's increasing dissatisfaction with the Serbian alliance is the establishment of a separate Montenegrin Orthodox Church. However, it is too early to tell whether the new Church will prosper.

At the time, both the Serbian and Montenegrin media portrayed the assault as self-defence to preempt an alleged Croatian offensive against the northern Montenegrin coast[6] and halt alleged Croat massacres of Serbs in southern Dalmatia. In the intervening years, however, Montenegrins have learned that the allegations were simply a pretext to draw them into the Serb-Croat war and are especially ashamed of the role played by Montenegrin reservists in the campaign. Since the JNA withdrawal from around Dubrovnik and the normalisation of relations with Croatia, Podgorica has repeatedly come into conflict with Serbia and the military over its attempts to rebuild trust with their Croat neighbours. Indeed, Bulatović has even appeared on Montenegrin television to refute JNA claims of Croatian border incursions. Moreover, whereas during the Dubrovnik campaign the Montenegrin daily, *Pobjeda*, used to publish names of deserters, the numbers are now so great that the JNA has stopped releasing figures for Montenegrin draft-dodgers.

Podgorica's new, more moderate course is essentially enlightened self-interest. Serbia is no longer the power it was when Milošević brought down Montenegro's Titoist government in January 1989, and Croatia is no longer the weakling it was when the JNA laid waste southern Dalmatia in October, November and December 1991. Moreover, since close to 30 per cent of Montenegro's population belong to the Croat, Muslim and Albanian minorities, Podgorica has belatedly become as hostile to any change in republican borders as Zagreb, where the borders in question are Croatian, and Sarajevo. At the same time, Bulatović has adopted a conciliatory approach towards his non-Montenegrin subjects, including banning Šešelj from addressing the Montenegrin parliament, and the Montenegrin media have been quick to follow suit. Nevertheless, the threat of ethnic conflict remains, especially in the Sandžak.

The Sandžak is a former Ottoman province sandwiched between Bosnia-Hercegovina, Serbia, Montenegro and Kosovo, with a predominantly Muslim population which was conquered in the First Balkan War and divided between Serbia and Montenegro. It is significant, in particular, for its geography since it separates Serbia from Montenegro and in the past has been used to keep the two apart. At the Congress of Berlin in 1878, for example, the Habsburgs decided

---

[6] The region is called Boka Kotorska and is claimed by Croat nationalists on both ethnic and historic grounds.

to station a garrison in the Sandžak to prevent the unification of Serbia and Montenegro. Since about 250,000 Muslims form more than 80 per cent of the Sandžak's current population, Belgrade alleges that they aim to break away and join their co-religionists in Bosnia-Hercegovina. As Belgrade resorts to increasingly strong-armed tactics to maintain Serbian rule, the accusation is becoming self-fulfilling since the Muslims feel no other option is open to them.

Conditions for the Sandžak's Muslims depend on which side of the Serbian-Montenegrin border they live. In the six Montenegrin municipalities which form part of the Sandžak, Muslims have few gripes about their status as Muslims but are suffering economic hardship like all Montenegrin citizens as a result of sanctions and economic collapse. Since Bulatović embarked on an independent course from Belgrade, Montenegrin Muslims have had the right to take their grievances to a Council for the Rights of National and Ethnic Groups and have become increasingly involved in mainstream Montenegrin politics. In the fifteen Serbian municipalities which form part of the Sandžak, by contrast, Serbian police administer arbitrary justice and have totally alienated the Muslim population from Belgrade.

The upsurge of Serb nationalism which accompanied Milošević's rise to power in the mid-1980s first made the Sandžak's Muslims conscious of their vulnerability in Serbian society. As communist rule disintegrated in 1990, they formed their own branch of the Bosnian Muslim political party, the SDA, and, in an attempt to match the Croatian Serbs, set up their own Muslim National Council, demanding the same rights for Muslims in Serbia as granted to Serbs in Croatia. In October 1991 the Muslim National Council organised an unofficial referendum on Muslim autonomy, which, like the equivalent Serb referendum in Croatia, received virtually unanimous support. However, Belgrade rejected any comparison between the Muslims of Serbia and the Serbs of Croatia and chose instead to expand the security apparatus to enforce strict Serbian rule.

As war erupted in Bosnia-Hercegovina, relations between Belgrade and the Sandžak deteriorated further and the Serbian police presence was again reinforced. In August 1992 Serb extremists began ethnically cleansing a corridor beside the Bosnian border to prevent the Sandžak's Muslims aiding their beleaguered co-religionists in the neighbouring republic. It is a scenario which Muslim leaders fear may be repeated elsewhere in the Sandžak as fabricated stories of imminent Muslim rebellion are a regular feature in the Serbian media, especially around election time. They only hope that, if Serbia does decide to move against them, the international community will not sit by and watch them slaughtered in the same manner as it did with the Muslims of Bosnia-Hercegovina.

The Kosovo conundrum and Macedonian question

No matter how grim the situation in the Sandžak, it cannot be compared to that obtaining in Kosovo. Since the province was forcibly stripped of its autonomy in March 1989, order has been maintained by a massive police and military presence, and relations between Albanians and Serbs have continued to decline, to such a degree that it is difficult even to imagine a peaceful resolution of the conflict. Two entirely separate societies, one Serb, the other Albanian, now exist in parallel, with as little contact as possible. Where they meet, they collide and the outcome is violence. Since Albanians form more than 90 per cent of the population and Serbia is committed on many fronts, the situation is unlikely to endure. Eventually, the Albanians must achieve a settlement which reflects their overwhelming numerical preponderance. However, it was in Kosovo that Milošević first made his mark in Serbian politics and it is in Kosovo that he cannot afford to make any compromise, whatever the circumstances.

At the time of the 600th anniversary of the Battle of Kosovo Polje, when Serb national euphoria was at its height, Milošević unveiled ambitious plans to kickstart the Serbian economy with a recolonisation of Kosovo. Unemployed Serbs from the rest of Yugoslavia were to be encouraged to migrate to the province with guaranteed accommodation and jobs, and, to make way for the new generation of Serb settlers, Albanians would be systematically dismissed from state employment. In the course of 1990, Kosovo's Serb authorities began administering this new national policy without any regard for Albanian opinion. Serbs began moving into the province to fill newly-created posts in the Kosovo bureaucracy and the bloated security apparatus, while, at the same time, about 70 per cent of Albanians in employment were sacked. The result was total and irreconcilable Albanian alienation from Serbia.

Inter-communal trust disintegrated to such an extent that, when, in March 1990, Albanian schoolchildren began mysteriously to fall ill, rumours started circulating to the effect that the children were being poisoned by the Serb authorities in an attempt to reverse the province's ethnic balance. The cause of the illness was never discovered but in panic Albanians withdrew their children from school. A year later, all Albanian-language schools, as well as the Albanian-language departments at Priština University, were effectively shut down after Albanian teachers and lecturers refused to accept new educational directives determined in Belgrade.

While the Serbian media have been filled with stories of imminent Albanian revolt ever since Milošević came to power, the likelihood of insurrection is minimal. Given the scale of the Serbian police presence and the fact that Albanians are unarmed, their leaders fear that to organise a revolt would be tantamount to suicide. Instead, under the guidance of the writer and pacifist Ibrahim Rugova, they have adopted an approach towards the Serbian authorities modelled on that pursued by Mahatma Gandhi towards the British in India, but even more cautious. Albanians avoid any form of protest that the Serbs might conceivably construe as provocation, for fear that the authorities will use it as a pretext to begin slaughter on a scale greater even than in Bosnia-Hercegovina, and they refuse to retaliate no matter how great the aggravation. The Gandhian policy is yet to yield any tangible dividends but, as far as Rugova is concerned, the very fact that an Albanian society still exists in Kosovo at all is an achievement in itself.

If Belgrade was aiming, as Albanians allege, to deprive the Albanian population of the economic means of existence, it came close to success in 1990 and 1991, but failed as Albanians rallied behind Rugova. Whereas, before Milošević's clampdown, blood feuds between rival Albanian families had been a common feature of life in Kosovo, Serbian oppression has led to a remarkable homogenisation of Albanian society and enabled even sworn enemies to come to terms with each other. Albanians are now united against the common oppressor and systematically pool resources, including remittances from the Albanian community abroad, to make sure that all their co-nationals have sufficient food, clothing and fuel to survive. Few people can afford anything more than the bare essentials — though, ironically, Belgrade's oppressive rule has also boosted local capitalism by forcing Albanians to establish their own cottage industries.

Since the 1990 sackings Albanians have managed to construct their own parallel society by setting up their own clinics, businesses, newspapers, schools, and universities within private houses. Teachers, doctors and nurses do not receive salaries, but, like most Albanians, are remunerated in kind with just enough to survive on. The Serbian security apparatus continues to make life as difficult as possible, confiscating vital equipment, and robbing and imprisoning Albanians for no other reason than that they are Albanian. However, since virtually every single Albanian family in Kosovo has had at least one member jailed, imprisonment has come to be viewed merely as an integral part of growing-up and no longer has any deterrent effect. Albanians have become remarkably resilient, disciplined and focused on the national struggle, as if their lives will only begin once they have rid themselves of Belgrade's tyranny. It is a veritable *intifada* which, if necessary, could continue for years and years.

Since the disintegration of Yugoslavia, Albanian demands have risen from autonomy within a federation of eight units to full independence from the Serb-dominated rump state. Whereas it was possible for Albanians to be Yugoslavs, no amount of coercion can turn them into Serbs, and no amount of concessions can erase the memory of what has taken place in Kosovo since 1989. Albanians reject the constitutional order which was imposed on them by force and boycott the parliamentary process. While Serbs are no longer as triumphalist as at the time of the 600th anniversary of the battle of Kosovo, they remain as committed to the land as ever, and are certainly prepared to fight to keep the 'cradle of the Serb nation' within Serbia. Serbs and Albanians have diametrically opposite aims in Kosovo, which both sides must achieve in full. Given the circumstances, it seems a tragedy cannot be averted.

In the event of war in Kosovo, the possibility that fighting spreads beyond the territory of the former Yugoslavia is greater than in any other Yugoslav conflict. Kosovo is essentially one great plain so there are no logistical impediments to intervention. Moreover, since some form of union with Albania proper is undoubtedly the ultimate aim for Kosovo's Albanians, Albania has a direct stake in the province's future. Indeed, Albania's President, Sali Berisha, has warned on many occasions that, if fighting breaks out in Kosovo, his country cannot remain a bystander and, though militarily weak, he is confident of support from Turkey and much of the Islamic world. While the West is aware of the threat that Kosovo poses to the stability of the southern Balkans, there has been no attempt to mediate between Serbs and Albanians or moderate the excesses of Serbian rule other than repeated warnings to Belgrade not to begin ethnic cleansing in Kosovo. Since even under the 1974 constitution Kosovo was an integral part of Serbia, in international law it is considered a purely internal matter.

As a result, Kosovo's destiny may yet depend on Milošević's position in Serbia which, given his track record, may well require another war against another defenceless people.

To the south of Kosovo, Macedonia, or, to give it the title under which it was admitted into the United Nations, the Former Yugoslav Republic of Macedonia (FYROM), lies in almost as precarious a position. As in Bosnia-Hercegovina, affection for Titoism and the Yugoslav state survived in Macedonia long after it became unfashionable in the rest of Yugoslavia because Macedonians had been among the greatest beneficiaries of Tito's state and had most to lose from its demise. In the wake of Yugoslavia's disintegration, Macedonia's tragedy is that it is poor, ethnically-divided, militarily weak, landlocked and surrounded by aggressive neighbours. While the new country's President, Kiro Gligorov, has, so far, managed to avoid bloodshed, this should not be a reason for complacency. Almost everything about Macedonia, from its borders, to its language, history, flag and even its name, is controversial.

At the turn of the 20th century the Macedonian question boiled down to a power struggle between Serbia, Bulgaria and Greece over the vestiges of the Ottoman Empire in Europe, each with its own historic claim to the land. In the first Balkan War of 1912 an alliance of all three states defeated the Ottomans, and in the second Balkan War, a year later, Greece and Serbia claimed the lion's share of the spoils at Bulgaria's expense. Macedonia, a purely geographic entity with a mainly Slav-speaking population, was thus divided three ways. Greece helped itself to 51 per cent, the so-called Aegean Macedonia, Serbia took 39 per cent, the so-called Vardar Macedonia (today's FYROM), and Bulgaria the remaining 10 per cent, the so-called Pirin Macedonia. Today's Macedonian question is still a power struggle between Serbia, Bulgaria and Greece, but is further complicated by an Albanian dimension, since at least 21 per cent of Macedonia's population are ethnic Albanians, as well as a Turkish angle, since Turkish diplomacy has been quick to capitalise on Greek insecurity in Macedonia, and the evolution of a distinct Macedonian Slav identity in the course of the 20th century.

According to the 1991 census, 64 per cent (about 1.31 million people) of Macedonia's 2.03 million population registered as Macedonians, 21 per cent (about 427,000 people) as Albanians, 4.8 per cent (about 97,000 people) as Turks and 2.2 per cent (about 44,000 people) as Serbs. However, the number of Albanians, who are concentrated in western Macedonia along the borders with Albania and Kosovo, is probably somewhat higher, perhaps even as high as 700,000, since many Albanians chose to follow the example of their co-nationals in Kosovo and boycott the census. The critical internal relationship between Macedonians and Albanians has been tense ever since the 1980s when Macedonia's then communist rulers supported and then aped Belgrade's crackdown on Albanians. The advent of democracy brought an end to state-sanctioned discrimination and saw the creation of a multinational government in which Albanians hold several key posts. Nevertheless, Albanians remain wary and relations between Skopje and Tirana have been strained by a number of border incidents and by Albanian opposition to Macedonian membership of various international organisations without additional constitutional guarantees for the rights of Albanians. Since Albania is also weak, it is unlikely to precipitate military confrontation. However, in the event of fighting in Kosovo, the Albanians of western Macedonia may eventually choose to throw in their lot with their co-nationals across the border.

Whereas Albania is weak, the same cannot be said for Macedonia's other neighbours. An indication of Macedonia's plight is that, of its neighbours, Serbia is probably the least threatening. Serbs have, for the most part, come to terms with the concept of a separate Macedonian nationality and, in any case, Serbia is too preoccupied elsewhere to meddle in Macedonia. Though extreme Serb nationalists and some elements within the Serbian Orthodox Church[7] are lobbying for Serb autonomy within Macedonia (and claiming that there are some 300,000 Serbs living there), the JNA had pulled out of the republic by April 1992. Nevertheless, Milošević has taken to calling Macedonia 'Skopje' in an attempt to curry favour with Greece, his sole potential ally in the European Union, as the European Community has been known since 1 January 1993.

Greek politicians and diplomats have done their utmost to make life difficult for Macedonia, and have generally succeeded. Athens' fierce opposition to Macedonian statehood is based on disputed ethnic territory but essentially reflects domestic political needs as well as Greece's shameful treatment of its own minorities. While Macedonia is at present weak, Macedonian nationalists (whose political parties are

---

[7] The Macedonian Orthodox Church was established under communist rule with Tito's blessing, but without the accepted canonical procedure of the Orthodox communion of Churches. As a result, the Serbian Orthodox Church considers it an artificial creation and refuses to recognise it.

represented in Skopje's parliament and have been in and out of government) do, nevertheless, harbour ambitions of one day uniting Macedonia's three constituent parts. This must be a matter of concern to both Greece and Bulgaria, who both refuse to recognise the existence of a Macedonian nation, since, to achieve their aims, Macedonian irredentists would have to alter international borders. However, the matter should also remain in perspective. The way to ensure against Macedonian irredentism is surely to help the fortunes of the moderates, like Gligorov, who are currently in power, not to undermine their position at every opportunity, nor to treat them like international pariahs.

The ethnic composition of Macedonia, the geographic entity, has changed markedly in the course of the 20th century. Whereas Slavs formed the majority and Muslims, both ethnic Turks and Slavs, made up a sizeable minority in Ottoman times, the numbers of both peoples in Aegean (Greek) Macedonia have dwindled as a result of forced assimilation and expulsions in the aftermath of the Second World War and the Greek Civil War, to such an extent that today Slavs form a relatively small, unrecognised minority, and the Muslim population has disappeared. Greece's record towards non-Greeks living in Greece is essentially identical to that of pre-communist Serbia to non-Serbs living in Serbia. Indeed, it was Greek and Serbian misrule in Aegean and Vardar Macedonia, respectively, during the interwar period which spawned the Internal Macedonian Revolutionary Organisation, whose terrorist actions included the assassination of King Alexander in 1934. Before the Second World War, Macedonians tended to move to Bulgaria to escape Greek tyranny, but after the creation of the republic of Macedonia in Tito's state, Yugoslavia became the preferred destination.[8]

Even before Yugoslavia fell apart, Greece was highly sensitive to any mention of the name Macedonia. When Yugoslavs visited Greece they had to declare their ethnic origin on the border and anybody who answered 'Macedonian' was turned back. Greek claims on Macedonia are akin to Serb claims on Kosovo, based not on the region's present ethnic composition, but on historic right. Because Alexander the

---

[8] From the Macedonian point of view the Greek Civil War was a disaster. The Greek communists were largely funded by Tito and included a high proportion of Macedonians in their ranks. When the tide of battle turned and, on account of pressure from Stalin, Tito abandoned the Greek communists, many Macedonians fled to Yugoslavia to escape reprisals, leaving their land behind.

Great's Empire was centred on Macedonia, Greek nationalists believe that Greece is eternally entitled to possess this territory as well as its name and everything else associated with it.[9] As a result, Athens has done its utmost to force Macedonia to change its constitution, flag and even name.

When Macedonia applied to the European Community for recognition in December 1991, the EC Arbitration Commission could see no impediment and recommended that it be granted forthwith. However, though the European Community recognised both Slovenia and Croatia on 15 January 1992 and even Bosnia-Hercegovina on 6 April 1992, in Macedonia's case it held back on Greek insistence. Meanwhile, Greek statesmen and diplomats lobbied world capitals and even launched advertising campaigns abroad to add to the pressure on Macedonia. The outcome was a wait of nearly two years before the European Community recognised Macedonia—two years in which the economy deteriorated alarmingly and the United Nations decided to deploy precautionary peacekeepers, supplied by the United States. In the event, 11 members of the European Union extended recognition to Macedonia in December 1993, just before Greece took over the EU chair, though only under the temporary name of FYROM.

Since admittance into the United Nations, FYROM has become a member of both the International Monetary Fund and the World Bank and an austerity plan has been prepared to reverse the country's economic decline, which has seen annual average incomes crash from about $2,000 in 1990 to below $800 in 1993. However, economic reform is being hampered both by international sanctions against the rump Yugoslavia and a trade embargo imposed unilaterally by Greece in February 1994. Since Macedonia's oil supplies have traditionally come via the Greek port of Salonika, the Greek embargo has been especially savage. Indeed, just to survive, Skopje has been obliged to forge closer links with both Bulgaria and Turkey, which, given Bulgarian attitudes towards Macedonia and Macedonians, may not be in its best long-term interests. As in other contemporary conflicts in the Balkans, negotiations are characterised by intransigence, and it is difficult to envisage a peaceful resolution, satisfactory to all parties.

---

[9] Ironically, whether or not Alexander the Great was himself Greek is a matter of historical debate. It would appear that in Alexander's time Greeks considered Macedonians, if not as Barbarians, then as something less than Greek.

Bosnia-Hercegovina: savage reality

Of all conflicts in the former Yugoslavia the most intractable is, without doubt, that in Bosnia-Hercegovina, where, after more than two years of fighting, a settlement is as elusive as ever. That it has been so difficult to end the fighting there is hardly surprising, since the time for a negotiated compromise in any conflict is before it escalates into war, certainly not after one side has attempted, and failed, to exterminate the other. Moreover, the longer fighting continues, the more difficult it is to reach a lasting settlement. Each death diminishes the prospects of reconciliation and intensifies the desire for vengeance. In such conditions extremists flourish and, far from tiring of the fight, they grow addicted to it.

There are essentially two issues to consider: how the war on the ground is likely to evolve; and how the international community is likely to react to it; and clearly the two issues will affect each other. Though the Bosnian war is more than two years old, the debate surrounding it, as far as the international community is concerned, has hardly changed since the initial Serb offensive ground to a halt in May 1992. All arguments and counter-arguments were already thrashed out at the London Conference in August 1992, when the principles on which a settlement was to be based were supposedly drawn up. The fact that no settlement has been reached in the intervening years is the result not of any fundamental disagreement over what should constitute the ideal solution for Bosnia-Hercegovina, but of a lack of political will to put the principles agreed in London into practice.

Although the international community, and especially the United Nations, has been repeatedly humiliated by the Bosnian Serbs, the essence of international policy towards the war in Bosnia-Hercegovina as well as the wider conflict in the former Yugoslavia is unlikely to change. The reason is quite simple. While Western diplomats and statesmen consider events in the former Yugoslavia, and especially the reporting of those events, a nuisance, they do not view them as a direct threat to their national interests. As long as the fighting can be managed and confined to the territory of the former Yugoslavia, it is an inconvenience that western Europe can live with. However, if the international community was to become a combatant in Bosnia-Hercegovina, events there would come to threaten the national interests of the countries whose troops were to be deployed, as well as the political futures of the statesmen who decided to despatch them. It is a risk which the European powers, essentially Britain and France, are not prepared to take, and hence their sustained efforts to avoid entanglement.

Military intervention in Bosnia-Hercegovina is limited to securing deliveries of humanitarian aid, and, in the absence of a peace agreement, it is highly unlikely that this role will be expanded. At the same time, despite threats from some Western politicians to withdraw their troops, UN forces are there to stay, since the UN presence and, in particular, its humanitarian operations, allows the international community to contain and manage the conflict. In this context it should be noted that when the United Nations began its relief work in Bosnia-Hercegovina, the Bosnian government had no desire for humanitarian aid. Bosnian leaders asked only that the United Nations lift the arms embargo and give them the means of self-defence, but their pleas fell on deaf ears. For the international community, the focus on humanitarian aid was an ideal strategy, since it enabled statesmen to appear to be doing something to alleviate suffering without being drawn into the conflict as a combatant,[10] and, critically, it stemmed the flow of refugees to western Europe. While humanitarian aid has not necessarily kept Bosnians alive, it has certainly kept them in Bosnia-Hercegovina.

Whatever the original logic behind the arms embargo, it has not facilitated any form of settlement, or dampened the flames of conflict. Indeed, if anything, the embargo has achieved the opposite, since, by awarding Serbia and the Serb diaspora throughout the former Yugoslavia a massive superiority in firepower, it has enabled Serb forces to act with impunity, secure in the knowledge that their enemies do not have the resources to fight back. Nevertheless, and despite repeated demands from the Muslim bloc within the UN General Assembly to arm the Bosnian Muslims, the UN Security Council, or

[10] The visit of the French President, François Mitterrand, to Sarajevo in June 1992 was critical to launching humanitarian operations in Bosnia-Hercegovina. At the time, Sarajevo had been besieged and bombarded for nearly three months and the international community was at a loss how to react. Sarajevans greeted him as a saviour and were convinced that his arrival would usher in military intervention against the Bosnian Serbs. But it did not. Instead, Mitterand's presence in Sarajevo demonstrated that it was possible to enter the city by air, and soon after the first relief flights began bringing in humanitarian aid.

at least its permanent members from Europe, remains determined to maintain the arms embargo. For, as far as the European powers are concerned, lifting the embargo would only prolong the war by encouraging the Bosnian Muslims to attempt to recover lost territory and would also entail giving up control over the conflict.

Since the arms embargo has effectively deprived the Bosnian Muslims of the means of self-defence, the United Nations has found itself obliged to step in to moderate Serb excesses. However, without the political will where it matters, UN envoys have no choice but to continue appeasing Serbia and the Bosnian Serbs. It is easy to talk tough and draw up impressive-sounding declarations at venues far away from the former Yugoslavia, but, without the courage to back them up on the ground, all threats and resolutions are worthless. The recklessness with which the international community has been prepared to issue, but not implement, threats and ultimatums has merely contributed to UN impotence and encouraged Serb brinkmanship. As a result, Serb leaders have been able to call the world's bluff again and again, and until the United Nations actually carries out one of its threats, the cycle will not be broken.

Repeated humiliations at the hands of the Bosnian Serbs may try international patience, but not enough for the international community to reverse the territorial gains by force. Instead, damage-limitation is the order of the day and, to minimise further embarrassment and present a united front, the key countries — Britain, France, Germany, Russia and the United States — have begun to coordinate their policies towards the war. As diplomats and statesmen agree that Bosnia-Hercegovina is a no-win situation, they wish only to wash their hands of the conflict, but find that it continues to haunt them, as the media refuse to let it lie. While no statesman will go on record to say that he supports the principle of ethnic cleansing or that it should form the basis of any peace agreement in Bosnia-Hercegovina, the reluctance to stand up to Serb aggression and refusal to lift the arms embargo speak louder than any words. The goal remains a negotiated settlement and this boils down to persuading the Bosnian Serbs to make some territorial concessions and forcing the Bosnian Muslims to accept the resulting deal.

Ironically, mediators may eventually find it easier to persuade the Bosnian Serbs to sign up to any peace agreement than the Bosnian government. The Bosnian Serbs already possess more territory than they can hold, and want a way of cementing together their most strategic gains—in particular, the corridors linking what are now exclusively Serb enclaves. They are prepared to trade land for a settlement but nowhere near enough to satisfy the Bosnian government, which remains wedded to the concept of a single, multinational Bosnia-Hercegovina. Bosnian leaders fear that the division of their republic will merely create two unviable mini-states dependent on foreign aid, whose borders will require permanent UN policing. Moreover, they feel they have been abandoned by the international community and that their prospects of securing a just settlement are greater if they continue to prosecute the war, irrespective of world opinion and the arms embargo.

Bosnian leaders are certainly entitled to resent the international community and to prefer their chances on the battlefield to the negotiating table. The deal which mediators hope to bully Izetbegović into accepting will divide Bosnia-Hercegovina into two roughly equal territorial units, one Serb, the other a Croat-Muslim federation. It will not, however, enable people who have been ethnically cleansed to return home, nor will it establish any mechanism for bringing war criminals to justice, principles which have essentially been written off by the mediators but on which the Bosnian government will not compromise. Moreover, given the number of innocent Muslims who have been killed and the manner in which many of them died at Serb hands, Bosnian leaders find even the idea that they should sit down and negotiate with men of Karadžić's and Mladić's ilk nauseating. Although the outgoing Bush administration in the United States named many of the leading Serb politicians as war criminals as early as 1992, the much-vaunted War Crimes Commission and International War Crimes Tribunal, set up soon after media revelations about Serb detention camps, have yet to compile the evidence, let alone bring a case, against anybody.

Meanwhile, despite the arms embargo, the military equation is shifting slowly in favour of the Bosnian government. Arms and munitions factories within Bosnia-Hercegovina are working around the clock to equip the Bosnian Army, and weapons trickle in from sympathetic countries, especially from some of the wealthier Muslim states of the Middle East. While Serb forces retain superiority in heavy weaponry, they lack manpower, discipline and morale. In more than two years of fighting they have failed to defeat what was originally a defenceless enemy and, as the war drags on and Serb soldiers are unable to return home, potentially destructive rifts are emerging within the Bosnian

Serb military.[11] By contrast, the Bosnian Army, which contains a core of soldiers who were cleansed from their homes by the initial Serb offensive, has evolved into an exceptionally motivated and mobile fighting force, determined to win back lost territory.

Serb offensives essentially amount to massive and protracted bombardment of densely-populated urban areas, which, on account of the number of civilian casualties, invariably attract both media attention and international condemnation. But the Bosnian Army, too, launches its share of offensives, which, while never as brutal, are often more effective and have come to terrify isolated Serb communities. Without heavy weaponry, the Bosnian Army relies on its greater mobility to launch lightning strikes against strategic Serb targets, and, especially during the winter when the weather neutralises the Serb big guns, has frequently achieved spectacular inroads into the corridors linking Serb territories together and disrupting lines of communication.

In the very long term the Bosnian Army's greater numbers and motivation will count for more than the superior firepower which the Bosnian Serbs currently possess, and the Bosnian government is well aware of this. Moreover, the Bosnian Army is psychologically prepared for the long haul. The only people who talk of war-weariness are outsiders who have not lived through a war themselves. While war appears ghastly when it first breaks out, human beings gradually grow accustomed to it. The struggle for existence is the most powerful of causes and it is often easier to continue fighting than to have to deal with post-war reconstruction, especially if the settlement on offer is so unsatisfactory. It is only after wars end, when the day-to-day battle for survival and the intense camaraderie that accompanies it is over, that people begin to suffer the full psychological impact of the trauma they have just lived through. Indeed, it is since the siege of Sarajevo was lifted that Sarajevans have had the time to realise how much they have lost.

The Bosnian government's hand is strengthened by the resurrection of the Croat-Muslim alliance. Since Muslim and Croat leaders signed

[11] Serb soldiers in Banja Luka, the largest Serb-held city in Bosnia-Hercegovina have already organised a revolt over their living conditions. They resent risking their lives every day for a pittance, while, at the same time, war profiteers are able to drive around in BMWs.

a truce on 1 March 1994 the cease-fire has held and this has enabled the Bosnian government to redeploy forces to Serb fronts. The creation of a Bosnian federation within a loose Croatian-Bosnian confederation has much to recommend it to both Croats and Muslims and its prospects are good. The Croat-Muslim war was a very different affair to that involving the Serbs since it may be attributed to an unfortunate series of events and misunderstandings. Though the Croat-Muslim war, too, had its unsavoury moments, there was no premeditated attempt by either people to exterminate the other. Moreover, its only beneficiaries were the Bosnian Serbs. As a result, both Croats and Muslims are able to view their war as an unfortunate episode which they now wish to put behind them. The healing process began even before the Croatian-Bosnian Accord was signed, as extremists on both sides, including the Bosnian Croat leader Mate Boban, found themselves unwelcome among their own people and were dismissed. Nevertheless, as after any war, reconciliation requires great tact and understanding, which have, hitherto, been in short supply, and the relationship between Croats and Muslims will inevitably remain delicate for some years.

The resurrection of the Croat-Muslim alliance has given the Bosnian Serbs good reason to be worried. As it is, despite their initial military victories, they have not done well out of the war, yet still have a lot to lose. While the Bosnian Muslims know they can rely on the Muslim world for financial and military aid and the Bosnian Croats know they will be supported by Croatia and Croat *émigrés*, the Bosnian Serbs can only look to Belgrade for support, and even Belgrade's attitude is lukewarm. If the Bosnian government does choose to continue the war and the tide of battle begins to turn, the Bosnian Serbs will rapidly find themselves isolated and friendless. Milošević is far more concerned about his own future than the fortunes of the Serb diaspora who have just about exhausted their usefulness to him and are increasingly viewed as a liability. Serb communities in much of Bosnia-Hercegovina and also in Croatia find themselves stranded a long way away from Serbia proper, surrounded by hostile Muslims and Croats.

Croatia: the new regional power

Since January 1992 an uneasy truce has held in Croatia, maintained, in part, by UN peacekeepers. While most of the provisions contained in the Sarajevo Accord, the peace agreement ending the Serb-Croat war, have not been implemented, Croatia has used the intervening years to rebuild and, in the process, has constructed professional armed forces, complete with a standing army. As a result, the military equation is now very different from that obtaining in August 1990 when rebel Serbs first cut Croatia into two. Croatia is no longer defenceless, the JNA is a shadow of its former self and rebel Serbs can no longer count on patronage and weapons from Serbia. As sanctions, economic mismanagement, and the expense of the wars in Slovenia, Croatia and Bosnia-Hercegovina, as well as police rule in Kosovo and the Sandžak, all take their toll on Serbia, Croatia is the ultimate beneficiary. Despite having a smaller population than Serbia and a comparatively under-developed defence industry, it is Croatia which is evolving into the region's new power.

The arms embargo has made it difficult for Croatia to purchase weapons abroad, but not impossible. Weapons continue to come in, though more slowly and at greater cost than if the embargo were to be lifted, and gradually the military scales are tipping in Croatia's favour. The military build-up is for one reason alone, namely to recapture lost territory. On account of Croatia's geography, the republic has to reimpose sovereignty over Serb-held regions merely to be able to function properly as a state. At the time of writing, the 25 per cent of Croatia in Serb hands effectively splits Zagreb from Dalmatia and impedes communications between the capital and much of Slavonia. In addition, Serb forces are still in a position to shell many Croatian cities at will. As a result, the overriding issue in Croatian politics is the return of all territory lost during 1991.

International mediators hope for a negotiated compromise but, as in Bosnia-Hercegovina, the omens are poor. Indeed, the Croatian conflict is no closer to resolution than it was when the terms of the truce were ostensibly agreed, and the possibility of a return to large-scale hostilities is very real. In more than two and a half years the cease-fire is virtually the only provision of the Sarajevo Accord to have been implemented. No territory has been yielded voluntarily, nobody has been able to return to their homes as envisaged and the contested regions of Croatia remain militarised. In effect, the agreement has merely turned what were the front lines of January 1992 into borders, thus cementing Serb gains. While this suits the Serb rebels, it is anathema to Zagreb, whose patience with the negotiating process has all but run out.

In January 1993 Croatia flexed its newly-acquired muscles with a lightning strike against strategic targets in Serb-held territory. In military terms the offensive was highly effective and within days Croatia had recaptured Zemunik airport, the Maslenica bridge and the Peruča dam, all critical to internal communications and, in particular, the Dalmatian economy.[12] In diplomatic terms the exercise was rather less effective since it incurred the wrath of the international community and provoked calls for sanctions against Croatia in some quarters. In the event, Croatia held onto its gains and international anger rapidly died down as media attention reverted to events in Bosnia-Hercegovina.

Under the terms of the Sarajevo Accord, Zemunik airport, the Maslenica bridge and the Peruča dam were all due to be handed back to Croatia. But since no amount of negotiations or diplomatic activity was going to persuade rebel Serbs to give them up, after more than a year of waiting, Zagreb chose to seize them back by force. The offensive placed Croatia in a strange position. While Zagreb cannot be realistically denied the right to try to restore Croatian authority over such territory, any attempt to achieve this by force is regarded by the UN Security Council as a unilateral breaking of an international agreement, so that, under international law, Croatia finds itself an aggressor on its own territory. Nevertheless, the international community is already stretched to the limit in the former Yugoslavia and is not about to reverse any Croatian gains.

Like Sarajevo, Zagreb's hand has been strengthened by the Croatian-Bosnian Accord. Indeed, the agreement is probably of greater significance to Zagreb than to Sarajevo since it has saved Croatia from the consequences of a foolhardy foray into the Bosnian war. From Zagreb's point of view the Croat-Muslim war was an unmitigated disaster which only served to sully Croatia's reputation abroad, yet Tudjman was unable to extricate himself from what was a conflict of his own making. By the end of 1993 economic sanctions against Croatia appeared imminent, while, at the same time, Zagreb's apparent eagerness to carve up Bosnia-Hercegovina and annex predominantly Croat regions was setting a precedent for predominantly Serb regions of Croatia. Croatia was in serious danger of becoming an international

---

[12]Zemunik airport is just outside the Dalmatian port of Zadar. The Maslenica bridge is the coastal road link between Dalmatia and northern Croatia but was destroyed by Serb forces in August 1991. The Peruča dam is the key to a hydoelectric plant which supplies Dalmatia with power.

pariah like Serbia, but has been rescued by US diplomatic intervention ending the Croat-Muslim war.

Despite official denials, units of the regular Croatian Army had been actively engaged in Bosnia-Hercegovina against Muslim forces. Their presence was not premeditated Croatian aggression against Bosnia-Hercegovina but a desperate attempt to reverse the military setbacks suffered by their co-nationals in the neighbouring republic. In the course of 1993 the rejuvenated Bosnian Army notched up a series of impressive victories against the Bosnian Croats and appeared to be on the verge of driving the HVO out of central Bosnia. Remaining Croat enclaves were surrounded and the HVO was suffering heavy casualties it could not afford in defending them. To stem the tide, Zagreb decided it had no option but to despatch reinforcements to bolster the HVO.

The Croatian-Bosnian Accord gave Tudjman a face-saving alternative to continuing the war in Bosnia-Hercegovina, which he was eager to take. Under the agreement, federal Bosnia-Hercegovina consists of five mainly-Muslim cantons and four mainly-Croat cantons with a complex system for power-sharing, including strict rotation of offices, between Croats and Muslims. Local authorities are responsible for policing, education and housing, while foreign affairs, defence, finance and energy matters remain the prerogative of the Sarajevo government. The loose confederation with Croatia is expected to include customs and monetary union with possible military cooperation but details will only be finalised when the eventual contours of the region become clearer. Both Bosnia-Hercegovina and Croatia can look forward to US aid for reconstruction and believe that the renewed alliance will speed up the rate at which weapons come in from abroad.

Since the signing of the Croatian-Bosnian Accord Croatia's Serb rebels have also shown a willingness to negotiate with Zagreb. However, it is a willingness born of desperation and weakness. When the boot was on the other foot the Serb attitude was very different. At the beginning of 1992 the then Serb leader in Knin, Milan Babić, was determined to continue the war with Croatia and only accepted the Sarajevo Accord under duress after a series of personal visits from the British UN envoy, Marrack Goulding, and Belgrade's withdrawal of support. As a result, the Serb rebels cannot expect a very conciliatory attitude on the part of Zagreb.

If the Croatian media are anything to go by, the only settlement acceptable to Zagreb is unconditional Serb surrender. Since the war, Croat attitudes have hardened and the majority of Croatia's Serbs who stayed put and refused to join the rebels have borne the brunt of this national anger. As far as Croatian opinion-makers are concerned, rebel Serb leaders had the opportunity to negotiate in good faith during 1990 and 1991 but opted for war and must now live with the consequences of that decision. Zagreb thus favours a military solution and is simply waiting for a good moment to strike, which will presumably be when Serbia becomes militarily embroiled in yet another conflict. In the event of a resumption of war, UN peacekeepers will simply be withdrawn since they are only there on Croatian sufferance and Croatia can easily revoke their mandate.

To capitalise on his successful prosecution of the Serb-Croat war Tudjman called snap elections soon after the arrival of UN peacekeepers in Croatia, in which both he and his party, the HDZ, were triumphant, thanks, in part, to a fiercely partisan media. Since reelection, the media-generated climate of war has not eased despite the formal end of hostilities and Tudjman has moved to stamp out all internal opposition. The purge of the press, in particular, has been vicious. In the summer of 1992 Croatia's most respected weekly, *Danas*, was forced out of business and the independent-minded daily, *Slobodna Dalmacija*, was taken over by HDZ sympathizers, while, as recently as 31 December 1993, the editor of the satirical fortnightly, *Feral Tribune*, was drafted against his will into the Croatian Army. Since the issue of occupied territory eclipses all others, there is no prospect of real democracy in Croatia until every inch of Croatian soil is recaptured and the borders Croatia possessed as part of federal Yugoslavia are restored.

While Zagreb has largely been reacting to events outside its control for most of the Yugoslav wars, it is now in a position to take the initiative and, as a result, Tudjman is becoming an increasingly critical figure. Like all politicians who have been in power for too long, Tudjman is convinced that what is good for him must also be good for Croatia and confuses his own interests and those of his party with the national interest. Moreover, he genuinely believes that he is on a historic mission to forge a powerful Croatian state. Yet Tudjman is impressionable and vain and wants, above all, to be viewed abroad as an accomplished and distinguished head of state. As a result, international opinion matters to him and, as with the Croatian-Bosnian

Accord, he will respond favourably to diplomatic initiatives with only minor incentives, as long as he is treated with deference. Croatia's borders, alone, are non-negotiable.

Though Tudjman considers himself indispensable to Croatia, he may be in for a nasty shock come the next elections. The HDZ, which has always been a broad coalition rather than a conventional political party, has already begun to disintegrate as a result of Tudjman's handling of the Bosnian conflict. Moderates in the party, led by Stipe Mesić, Yugoslavia's last President, and Josip Manolić, the former Interior Minister, have broken away to form the Croatian Independent Democrats (*Hrvatski nezavisni demokrati*) and accuse Tudjman of creating great humanitarian suffering and damaging Croatia's reputation abroad with his misguided Bosnian policy. The new party argues that Zagreb has a vested interest in a unified and strong Bosnia-Hercegovina and is highly critical of Tudjman's moves to muzzle the press and his human rights record in general.

In addition, as economic questions become more central to Croatian politics, the HDZ's populist nationalism will appear increasingly dated and, in Dražen Budiša, the leader of Croatia's Social Liberal Party (*Hrvatska socijalno-liberalna stranka*) and a student leader from 1971, Tudjman already has a serious rival. Economic reconstruction is as great an undertaking in Croatia as anywhere in former communist Europe and the nettle is yet to be grasped. Since Yugoslavia's disintegration, ordinary Croatian citizens have seen their living standards and prospects plummet and only drastic restructuring can reverse the trend. While Croatia is blessed with many natural assets, not least the Adriatic coast, which, especially in Istria, has continued to attract tourists despite the war, the economy is burdened by huge military spending and a massive refugee population. The road to recovery is long and there may not be an upturn for many years.

Slovenia moves on

Economic questions have already come to dominate political life in Slovenia where the republic's own ten-day war is but a memory and post-communist reconstruction more advanced than in any other former communist state. Most of the politicians who led Slovenia to independence, with the notable exception of the President, Milan Kučan, have since fallen from power. Nevertheless, almost everything which has taken place in the intervening years, both in Slovenia and in the rest of what was Yugoslavia, has vindicated their decision to turn their backs on the unitary south Slav state and press ahead with independence.

The contrast between Slovenia's fortunes and prospects and those of the rest of the country could not be greater. While ethnic conflict and war ravage seven out of the former Yugoslavia's eight federal units and will continue do so for the foreseeable future, Slovenia has emerged virtually unscathed from the carnage and can look to the future with confidence. Indeed, given the devastation and despair in so much of the former Yugoslavia, it is almost as though Slovenia never belonged to the same country. However, the contrast should not come as too great a surprise since Slovenia has always been a special case. With Slovenes making up more than 90 per cent of the republic's population, the danger of ethnic strife was minimal. Moreover, in the absence of a Serb minority, Slovenia could not be a target for Serb nationalists and never formed part of the Greater Serbian vision of Yugoslavia.

Ironically, the long-term impact of Slovenia's war and also of the wars in Croatia and Bosnia-Hercegovina has been, on balance, beneficial to the Slovene economy. Before war broke out, Slovenia was in much the same position as the rest of eastern Europe's former communist states. Though certain aspects of the free market had already been introduced as early as the 1960s, the economy was still, in essence, planned. Whether or not Slovenia remained part of Yugoslavia, major restructuring was necessary to transform the economy from planned to free market and this would almost inevitably entail a decline in living standards and a jump in unemployment. In the wake of economic restructuring a prolonged period of labour unrest and strikes appeared on the cards, with potentially destabilising political consequences. However, as a result of the war, Slovenes were much better prepared psychologically to deal with the pain of restructuring and, in contrast to the rest of eastern Europe, labour unrest never materialised.

War instilled a sense of discipline and national pride in the Slovene labour force which have helped facilitate a remarkably smooth economic transformation. Just ten days of fighting was more than enough to convince Slovenes to count their blessings. No matter how alarming the decline in living standards, it was still preferable to living at war. Moreover, the conflict in the rest of the former Yugoslavia was never far from Slovene minds. The Croatian and Bosnian cities which were being systematically destroyed were cities Slovenes knew well and, though many miles from the carnage, Slovene children, too, were reported to be suffering war-related trauma simply as a result of the barrage of images they witnessed, day in day out, on television.

In the short-term the war compounded Slovenia's economic difficulties by depriving the republic of its traditional markets in the rest of Yugoslavia. While the Brioni Accord, the peace agreement which officially ended the war in Slovenia, was followed by a three-month moratorium on independence, it effectively gave Serbia, via the National Bank of Yugoslavia, three months in which to sabotage the Slovene economy. It was a continuation of war by other means and the economic downturn in Slovenia was immediate and sharp. However, this, too, proved a blessing in disguise, since it provided Slovenes with a perfect scapegoat for the economic crisis and, at the same time, compelled Slovene businesses to force the pace of reconstruction and aggressively seek out new markets. As soon as the moratorium expired, Slovenia left Yugoslavia's monetary system and introduced, in coupon form at first, a new currency called the *tolar*.

By 1993 the worst was already over and the economy had begun to pick up. GDP grew again for the first time in five years and inflation fell to its lowest level for fourteen years. Since then, *per capita* income ($6,100 per annum in 1993) has begun to edge up, and unemployment, which was almost unheard-of in the 1980s, has stabilised at roughly the Western European average. At the beginning of 1993 Slovenia joined the International Monetary Fund and World Bank after agreeing to take on $2.3 billion of Yugoslavia's $15 billion federal debt. After more than two years of intense and often acrimonious debate, privatisation legislation was pushed through, which effectively enables each enterprise to select its own method of privatisation. The law was supposedly designed to reflect the ownership structure which existed in Yugoslavia under Worker Self-Management but it has also proved fertile ground for a number of business scandals. Nevertheless, the level of financial gerrymandering is no greater than in any other former communist country, though this is small comfort to the majority of Slovenes, who, after a couple of years of virtual silence, have again begun to indulge in the national pastime of complaining.

Surveys of public attitudes since independence have revealed profound changes. The idealism which characterised Slovene society in the 1980s, and which motivated a generation to campaign for a host of issues including the environment, gay rights and a civilian alternative to military service, and eventually to stand up to Serbia over human rights violations in Kosovo, has largely disappeared and been replaced by hard-nosed realism and a virtual obsession with work. The cultural excitement and sustained creativity of the years running up to independence may never be matched. Where once anything and everything went, now Slovenia is far more conservative, and hence a nostalgia for Yugoslavia has again swept Slovenia after a period in which most Slovenes appeared to wish to have nothing to do with their former compatriots. Serb pop singers, in particular, have been embraced by the Slovene public and charity concerts featuring artists from throughout the former Yugoslavia are always well attended.

In the long-term, Slovenes of all political persuasions aspire to full membership of the European Union and, in the process, to raising living standards to western European levels. Both goals are achievable — though, realistically, not before the beginning of next century at the earliest. A host of obstacles to EU membership complicates matters, not least the resurgence of fascist respectability in Italy. Since the international agreements demarcating the frontier between Slovenia and Italy were signed in the name of Yugoslavia, Italian irredentists have called for a revision of the borders. Though the probability of border revision is extremely unlikely, the very fact that elected Italian politicians have chosen to raise the issue highlights the greatest drawback of independence. With a population of just over 2 million, Slovenia can only ever be a minnow in a great sea.

10

CONCLUSION

'The line separating good and evil passes not through states, nor between political parties—but right through every human heart.' Alexander Solzhenitsyn[1]

Limited intervention, huge expense, total failure

In retrospect, it is difficult to envisage a worse strategy towards the Yugoslav wars than that which the international community has thus far pursued. While Yugoslavs are responsible for creating the conflict, international attempts to halt the fighting have been farcical. Indeed, even had the great powers set out to manufacture a state of permanent turmoil in the Balkans, it is unlikely that they could have created a greater quagmire. Yet the level of failure should not come as a surprise, since at no stage has there been any attempt to deal with the Yugoslav wars on their own merits or to address the causes of conflict. Instead, the running has been made by statesmen who had made up their minds in advance that the order of the day was damage limitation, not conflict resolution.

In its defence the international community cannot plead ignorance. Yugoslavia did not fall apart without due warning, nor have the manner and course of the disintegration been anything but predictable. Many years before Yugoslavia formally broke up, symptoms of the country's malaise were clearly evident and Western intelligence agencies had alerted their governments to the potential danger in good time. Moreover, as a result of saturation media coverage since the outbreak of hostilities, spurred in large part by a sense of shame among Western journalists at the cynicism and inaction of their own governments, anybody wishing to discover more about the conflict has certainly had the opportunity and should have a good idea of what has taken place in the former Yugoslavia.

The international response to the Yugoslav wars is a case study in the way the world is ordered and illustrates, above all, how ethical

---

[1] Solzhenitsyn, eminent novelist and former Soviet dissident, returned to Russia after twenty years' exile in 1994.

considerations play no part in the foreign policies of the great powers. The overriding aim has not been to bring about a just settlement, but to manage the conflict and make sure that the violence does not spill over into neighbouring countries. Indeed, as far as the great powers were concerned, the ideal solution for Yugoslavia in 1991 was almost certainly a rapid victory for the JNA. For, had the JNA succeeded in crushing Slovenia, Croatia and Bosnia-Hercegovina, Yugoslavia would never have become a diplomatic headache. No matter how brutal the resulting repression, the international community would have been able to wash its hands of the country with a series of carefully-worded condemnations at the United Nations and public expressions of profound concern all round. However, despite an overwhelming superiority in firepower, which was further boosted by the UN-imposed arms embargo against Yugoslavia, the JNA failed first in Slovenia, then in Croatia and then again in Bosnia-Hercegovina.

The refusal of Slovenes, Croats and Bosnians of all nationalities loyal to the Sarajevo government to lie down and die, coupled with heart-rending television images of the war have made events in the former Yugoslavia, and the international community's response to those events, a vital political issue across much of the world, and forced the international community reluctantly to become directly involved in the Yugoslav conflict. However, the sense of outrage among world public opinion at the horror and injustice of what has taken place in the former Yugoslavia has not persuaded those statesmen in positions of influence to alter the essence of their approach to the conflict. The fundamental reason for the international community's failure to halt the fighting is quite simple, namely that the great powers have not considered their national interests sufficiently threatened by the conflict to merit the political risk involved in a more ambitious strategy. Though the Yugoslav wars are undoubtedly an inconvenience, they are an inconvenience which the great powers feel they can live with as long as the conflict is contained within the territory of the former Yugoslavia.

The central plank of the international peace effort has, from the beginning, been mediation, based on the premise that all sides to the conflict shared equal responsibility. Perhaps, had all sides been both equally guilty and well-matched, this policy might conceivably have enabled international mediators to broker some form of compromise settlement. But in the Yugoslav context mediation was fundamentally flawed by the nature of the conflict and was never likely, on its own, to end the bloodshed. The Yugoslav wars were not the consequence of an unfortunate series of events and misunderstandings, but of a calculated attempt to forge a Greater Serbia out of Yugoslavia. Moreover, the principal factor fuelling the fighting was the massive imbalance in firepower between militant Serbs and the JNA, on the one hand, and Yugoslavia's other peoples, on the other, which enabled one side, Serbia, to act with impunity and to pursue all its goals, including the elimination of non-Serb culture from those lands earmarked for a Greater Serbia, without recourse to arbitration. And until either Serb military superiority was neutralised, or the Serb war effort came unstuck, negotiations would inevitably be meaningless.

Despite the military imbalance, the UN Security Council decided to impose an arms embargo against the whole of Yugoslavia in September 1991, and then to maintain it while Serb forces laid waste and ethnically cleansed great tracts of Bosnia-Hercegovina and Croatia. Whatever the original thinking behind the embargo, its only effect has been to make Serb military superiority a permanent feature of the conflict and to facilitate Serb victories. Yet, having made it as difficult as possible for non-Serbs to organise effective resistance, the great powers refused to protect defenceless communities or even to acknowledge what was taking place in the former Yugoslavia. And it is this indifference to the fate of the innocent victims of the conflict on the part of the UN Security Council, which has bordered on complicity in ethnic cleansing, that has brought shame on the great powers and brought the entire mediation process into disrepute.

Though a series of UN Security Council resolutions have expressed disgust and horror at ethnic cleansing, the great powers have, nevertheless, done their best to play down its true extent. For, in both Croatia and Bosnia-Hercegovina, ethnic cleansing was not simply a byproduct of the war, it was, in fact, the principal aim, and, as unpalatable as it may be to international mediators, ethnic cleansing is but a euphemism for genocide. Yet to admit that what has taken place constitutes genocide would carry with it an obligation to intervene against the perpetrator; and, above all, the great powers have sought to avoid military entanglement. Indeed, had it not been for the courage of a handful of journalists and filmed evidence of atrocities, the international community would have continued to turn a blind eye to the many Serb-run detention camps across Bosnia-Hercegovina. Moreover, in the interests of a quick settlement, the proceedings of the War Crimes Tribunal, which was ostensibly founded to prosecute war criminals from the former Yugoslavia, have been repeatedly under-mined to ensure that nobody is ever brought to trial.

Despite going to ridiculous lengths to avoid any condemnation of Serb aggression, international mediators have failed to come even remotely close to an overall settlement. At the same time, their impact on the broader Yugoslav equation has been highly pernicious. By pandering to extremists in both Belgrade and Zagreb, the mediators have reinforced the nationalists' claims to speak on behalf of all of their respective peoples and, in the process, have legitimised the results of ethnic cleansing. To be fair to the individuals in question, they have not had much choice in the matter. Without the political will among the great powers to reverse Serb territorial gains, there has never been a credible military threat, and, given the imbalance in firepower, the mediators could only aspire to discovering Serbia's minimalist position and then exerting pressure on all other parties to the conflict to accept it.

Media-generated pressure and the threat of a massive influx of refugees into western Europe have forced the international community to take on a more active role in the former Yugoslavia, though damage limitation has remained the order of the day. The provision of humanitarian aid is no less than a cruel deception which has addressed some of the symptoms of the conflict, but not the causes, as if Bosnians were victims of a natural disaster. When UN troops first opened Sarajevo airport to relief flights they were greeted as saviours, but Sarajevans rapidly came to realise that their presence was no more than a sop to Western public opinion. By placing troops on the ground in a humanitarian role, rather than as peace-keepers or peace-makers, the international community could be seen to be doing something, even though that something was not going to have any impact on the war itself. In addition, the provision of humanitarian aid has enabled Britain and France, the principal troop-contributing nations, to control the conflict more effectively and ensure that it does not come to threaten their own national interests. As a result, media coverage has shifted towards the humanitarian operation and away from politics, and, at the same time, the humanitarian operation has even been used as an argument against more concerted military action to halt the war.

The cost of the Yugoslav conflict to the international community is virtually impossible to calculate and, in any case, the bill is rising by the day. In purely financial terms the UN budget for peace-keeping and humanitarian operations has soared to about $2 billion a year. But even this is only a fraction of total costs and the wider implications of the failure to end fighting may yet prove infinitely more expensive. The Yugoslav wars have made a mockery of western European pretensions to a greater role in world politics and severely undermined the credibility and reputation of international institutions and great powers alike. At the same time, the West has wasted a great opportunity to build bridges with the Islamic world and, in the process, has created a reservoir of potential terrorist recruits in Europe. The international community wants only to wash its hands of the entire affair, but the conflict refuses to go away and seems destined to haunt world leaders for the foreseeable future, if not in Bosnia-Hercegovina then almost certainly in the host of remaining trouble spots which are currently on the verge of bloodshed.

Myth and reality

Despite several years' saturation media coverage of the Yugoslav wars in most of the Western world, understanding of the conflict among the public at large is generally poor. This is partly because Yugoslav affairs are indeed complex and do not translate easily into journalism; partly because, as in any war, matters have been obscured and distorted by the propaganda of the belligerents; and partly because of what can only be described as a deliberate campaign to confuse the issue by Western commentators and statesmen seeking, above all, to justify the policy of inaction and exonerate their own positions, irrespective of what has, or has not, actually taken place in the former Yugoslavia.

From the outset the great powers have appeared to devote more time to developing the case against military intervention than analyzing the conflict, and more energy to finding scapegoats for their own diplomatic failures than attempting to halt the war. Hence persistent attempts to deem all sides to the conflict equally guilty, and even to pin blame for the war on the victims of aggression: Slovenia and Croatia for declaring independence against the wishes of the great powers, and the Bosnian government for rejecting the European Community's plan for the cantonisation of Bosnia-Hercegovina. Hence also attempts to attribute the failures of mediation first to German and then to US diplomatic interference, and, at the same time, to bend over backwards, on the one hand, to consider the Serbian point of view and, on the other hand, to exaggerate Serbia's military prowess. Statesmen and diplomats have generally chosen to interpret the war as a peculiarly Balkan phenomenon, the result of ancient and irrational animosities, which cannot be understood, much less resolved, by intervention from the outside and clearly more civilised world. Though superficially compelling, the 'ancient hatreds' thesis does not stand up to serious examination. At best, it conceals great ignorance, at worst, it is downright disingenuous.

While there is clearly a great deal of hatred in the former Yugoslavia, it is hardly ancient or irrational. Indeed, it is only this century and, in particular, since the creation of the Kingdom of Serbs, Croats and Slovenes in 1918, that the south Slavs have had sufficient dealings with each other to fall out and come to blows. The wars fought in the Balkans in past centuries were not fought between the south Slavs, but between and against the multinational empires of the Habsburgs and the Ottomans, which held sway there for the best part of 500 years. Far from being perennial enemies, Serbs from Serbia and Croats from Croatia were, until very recently, essentially strangers. Moreover, Serbs who lived within the Habsburg Empire had more in common with their Croat neighbours than they did with Serbs from Serbia, and Serbs, Croats and Muslim Slavs from Bosnia-Hercegovina had far more in common with each other than they did with either Serbs from Serbia or Croats from Croatia.

During the centuries of Habsburg and Ottoman rule, relations between the many peoples living in the two empires were regulated from above and the south Slavs had little say in their own affairs. It was only with the demise of the great multinational empires and the emergence of an independent south Slav state that they began to take control of their own destinies, and only then that they had to come to terms with the ethnic complexity of their lands. Given the separate traditions and identities of the various Yugoslav peoples, south Slav union was bound to be a difficult process, but there was no inherent animosity between Serbs, Croats and Slovenes damning the Kingdom bearing their name from its inception. The hatred which is now so overwhelming is, in fact, a very recent phenomenon and reflects the failure of the south Slavs to develop a durable formula for national coexistence in the course of the 20th century. It is a hatred bred of fear which is rooted not in history, but in contemporary interpretations of the past and can be dated to the 1980s and the media offensive which accompanied Slobodan Milošević's rise to power in Serbia.

Slovenes, Croats, Muslim Slavs, and even Hungarians and Albanians were no more blood enemies of Serbs than Jews were of Germans in the 1930s and 1940s. Yet, from the moment that Milošević launched his anti-bureaucratic revolution, that is how they were portrayed in the Serbian media, and that is what ordinary Serbs, who were on the receiving end of the media offensive, came to believe. What had, or had not, actually taken place in the distant past, during the Second World War and even during the four decades of communist rule, ceased to matter as the Serbian media dredged up and distorted every conceivable event from Serb history. Yugoslavia's non-Serbs were simply scapegoats for the economic and political failings of communist society in the 1980s and a convenient tool which Milošević was able to exploit to further his own political ambitions. However, the xenophobia cultivated by the Serbian media was very real and, in time, it destroyed Yugoslavia.

When Milošević crushed Kosovo in March 1989, the Titoist vision of Yugoslavia as a country in which every nation could feel at home, was already dead and buried. By this time, Milošević had come to control four out of Yugoslavia's eight federal units and his ambitions could no longer be blocked at the federal level by a coalition of the republics which remained beyond his influence. Moreover, he was now able to use his newly-acquired federal muscle to turn up the pressure on those republics and generally make life as difficult and unpleasant as possible for the country's non-Serbs. The omens for the future of the Yugoslav state were terrible. In fact, the only reason that a full-scale war had not already broken out was that Kosovo's Albanians did not have the weapons to fight back. Yet, at this stage, Franjo Tudjman and Alija Izetbegović had played no part in the Yugoslav drama whatsoever and were but relatively celebrated dissidents in their respective republics.

To try to equate Tudjman with Milošević or Croatia with Serbia is absurd. Tudjman did not become President of Croatia until 30 May 1990—that is, four years after Milošević rose to the top of the League of Communists of Serbia and only a little over a year before the outbreak of full-scale hostilities in Yugoslavia. Moreover, he inherited a situation which was already on the verge of bloodshed and over which he had little control. Though Tudjman cannot be considered an especially pleasant character, he arrived on the scene too late to be anything more than a scapegoat in the events leading to Yugoslavia's disintegration. It was actually Milan Kučan, the President of Slovenia, who made much of the running in Yugoslavia's twilight years and, in a calculated attempt to boost his own popularity and look after

Slovenia's best interests—though not necessarily those of the rest of Yugoslavia—decided to stand up to Milošević.

Negotiations on Yugoslavia's future never got off the ground because Milošević held all the trump cards and had no need to negotiate. Serbia effectively controlled Yugoslavia's federal institutions and, as communist authority disintegrated throughout eastern Europe and then in Slovenia and Croatia, Milošević was able to forge a close alliance with a disillusioned and increasingly desperate military. Perhaps the most critical single event, as far as the nature of Yugoslavia's disintegration is concerned, was the disarming of the territorial defence forces of Slovenia and Croatia which took place on 17 May 1990, just before the formal transfer of power to the new non-communist authorities. While Slovenia managed to hang on to about 40 per cent of the weapons belonging to its territorial defence force and thus retained the nucleus of a republican army, Croatia found itself completely defenceless. As a result, Milošević and his proxies in Croatia were in a position to wreak havoc throughout the republic, secure in the knowledge that the Croatian authorities could not retaliate. Yet the Serbian media portrayed the growing conflict within Croatia as fundamentally a question of Serb rights, alleging, as earlier in Kosovo, that the republic's Serb minority was subject to genocide.

The tactics which Milošević pursued towards Serb communities outside Serbia during the 1980s and early 1990s were essentially identical to those pursued by Hitler towards the German diaspora across eastern and central Europe in the 1930s. In the same way that Nazi Germany alleged that the German minorities of Czechoslovakia and Poland were being persecuted by their Czech and Polish governments, Serbia alleged that Serbs in Croatia and Bosnia-Hercegovina were victims of Croat and Muslim oppression. However, in both instances the plight of the respective minorities was simply a pretext for intervention. Milošević aimed to destabilise both Croatia and Bosnia-Hercegovina and had no regard for the long-term interests of the Serb communities in the two republics. Had the conflict in Croatia and Bosnia-Hercegovina really been a question of Serb rights, Milošević had ample opportunity to resolve it. Moreover, given the imbalance in firepower between Serbia and the rest of Yugoslavia and the desperation of the Croatian and Bosnian authorities, he could easily have obtained a settlement which was extremely generous to the Serb position. However, the conflict was not a question of Serb rights, and Milošević had no desire to see it resolved.

Another parallel between Yugoslavia in the 1980s and 1990s and central Europe in the 1930s is the international reaction to what was taking place. Far from condemning early Nazi aggression, contemporary Western statesmen and media commentators with a few notable exceptions, including Winston Churchill, generally sought to see the Nazi point of view and justify it. In effect, they were prepared to turn a blind eye to the excesses of Nazism as long as it did not affect them directly, and it was only when Britain saw its own interests as threatened that it changed its tune. Herein lies the great difference between Milošević's Serbia and Hitler's Germany from the point of view of the international community. For the great powers are aware that Serbia can never harm them in the manner that Nazi Germany could. Moreover, since the demise of the Eastern bloc, the West has decided that it no longer has any strategic interests in the former Yugoslavia. While the international community undoubtedly wanted Yugoslavia to remain a single entity, the great powers were not prepared either to invest in democracy there or to intervene to avert tragedy.

When Slovene leaders pressed ahead with an independence declaration, they did so because they felt that they had already exhausted the negotiating process. In the seventeen months of inter-republican talks following the disintegration of the League of Communists of Yugoslavia there had been no progress whatsoever. Moreover, there was no prospect of any breakthrough since, irrespective of what was agreed at the negotiating table, Milošević's proxies had already begun to carve a Greater Serbia out of Croatia and Bosnia-Hercegovina.

In the same way that Chinese intransigence has forced Britain to take unilateral measures in Hong Kong, Slovenia, too, decided that the only option was to act unilaterally and, in retrospect, this would appear to have been the best possible course of action. For Croatia, too, despite the brutality and destruction of the six-month war which followed the independence declaration, it is again difficult to envisage an alternative strategy which would have been less painful. Indeed, the criticism which has been levelled at Tudjman within Croatia is not that he was too belligerent in the run-up to the outbreak of hostilities, but that he was excessively timid and should have sought out weapons more aggressively and, critically, gone to war at the same time as Slovenia.

While the international community could conceivably be forgiven for misinterpreting certain aspects of the war in Croatia, the refusal to protect innocent communities in Bosnia-Hercegovina is unpardonable. In contrast to the governments of Slovenia and Croatia, which defied the international community with their independence declarations, the Bosnian government could not have been more accommodating. Izetbegović and his manifestly multinational government did everything in their power to avoid a war: they attempted to defuse all potential areas of conflict; they refused to arm their people; and they tried to act in accordance with the advice of the European Community. Indeed, as conflicts go, it is virtually impossible to find one which is more black and white than that in Bosnia-Hercegovina. Moreover, the international community had no excuse for not learning in the course of six months of war in Croatia how to distinguish between genuine causes of conflict and pretexts. Nevertheless, the great powers chose to remain on the sidelines and to consider the conflict a purely civil war in which all three belligerents were equally guilty.

The fundamental cause of the war in Bosnia-Hercegovina was not the decision to recognise Slovene and Croatian independence, but the massive imbalance in firepower between Muslims, Croats and Serbs loyal to the Sarajevo government, on the one hand, and militant Serbs, on the other, and the eagerness of those militant Serbs first to threaten and then to use violence. The only way that bloodshed could conceivably have been averted was by massive preventative deployment of UN troops with a mandate to neutralise Serb military superiority. But this was never an option because no country was prepared to commit the necessary troops. Instead, EC mediators aimed to persuade the Bosnian Muslims and Croats to accept the Serb position and worked towards dividing Bosnia-Hercegovina into ethnic territories, even though such entities did not exist at the time and could not come into existence without massive population transfers.

The Yugoslav tragedy

In Bosnia-Hercegovina militant Serbs set out in a *blitzkrieg*-style operation to exterminate the non-Serb population as well as any Serbs who refused to go along with the Greater Serbian vision of the republic's future. Once the killing started there was no way to turn the clock back and no hope of any reconciliation. The burning hatred which

Croats and Muslims now feel towards Serbs is by no means irrational; rather it is an understandable reaction to the atrocities which have been committed against them in recent years, simply on account of their national origins. And it was this premeditated campaign ethnically to cleanse regions earmarked for a Greater Serbia which, after seventy-three years, finally confined Yugoslavia to the dustbin of history.

The savagery of the Yugoslav wars has made it easy for statesmen and commentators opposed to intervention to write the conflict off as essentially 'tribal' and to attribute the slaughter to the Balkan mentality, as if Balkan peoples were somehow predisposed to committing atrocities. However, this interpretation does a gross injustice to all the peoples of the former Yugoslavia and again does not stand up to serious examination.

The key to an understanding of the inhumanity of the Yugoslav wars is the phenomenon of war itself. The state of mind which is capable of committing atrocities is one which has been disturbed by war, not some mythical Balkan mentality. For war is dehumanising; it destroys the very fabric of society and leaves psychologically unstable people in its wake, people who have lost contact with reality and are no longer in control of their own actions. After almost half a century of peace in the Western world, in which time many people have grown up without experiencing conflict, the brutality of war, albeit via a television screen, has come as a nasty shock. But war, and especially a protracted civil war, is brutal. Moreover, Westerners who are sucked into wars, such as the US troops who were engaged in Vietnam, are by no means above committing atrocities themselves.

While Yugoslavia's misery is generally measured in terms of the numbers of dead and wounded and the level of destruction, there is, perhaps, an even greater tragedy, namely the demise of the Yugoslav ideal. It is tragic because, when considered rationally, the Yugoslavia envisaged by the country's intellectual and spiritual founding fathers—that is, a state in which all south Slavs should feel that they belonged—was not only the best formula for national coexistence, it was the only arrangement in which it was possible to reconcile the national ambitions of all Yugoslav peoples. Moreover, contrary to the propaganda currently emanating from both Belgrade and Zagreb, the Yugoslav experiment was by no means an unmitigated failure. Indeed, both before and after the Second World War there were periods of great optimism and excitement, and, until the very end, the country continued to produce visionary leaders with a strong ideological commitment to some form, though not necessarily the same form, of Yugoslavism—from Svetozar Pribičević, King Alexander and Vlatko Maček, to Josip Broz Tito, Milovan Djilas and Ante Marković.

The beauty of the Yugoslav state was that, since all the south Slav lands were in the same country, the various Yugoslav peoples could not fall out over rival claims to ethnically-mixed territories. Though Yugoslavia could never entirely satisfy the nationalist ambitions of every Yugoslav nation, it was a fair compromise and infinitely preferable to the alternative, which is today's carnage. Yet even though the preservation of a Yugoslav state with a commitment to national equality was patently in the interests of virtually all its citizens, the country broke up. But what makes the disintegration especially tragic is that Yugoslavia did not simply fall apart but was systematically destroyed. Moreover, it was destroyed by at of most a handful of people, and to a great extent by a single man, Slobodan Milošević.

Milošević's role in Yugoslavia's disintegration cannot be over-estimated. Indeed, his career is testimony to the impact that an individual can have on the world around him or her, given exceptional circumstances and ruthless ambition, and comparisons with both Stalin and Hitler are not far-fetched. For, like the 20th century's two most notorious dictators, Milošević is essentially an aberration. Though he has played the Serb national card, he is not, and never has been, a Serb nationalist. Moreover, Milošević is no more typical of Serbian statesmen than Hitler was of German leaders, and there is no precedent in Serbia's past either for the man or for the destruction he has sown in his wake.

That Milošević has had such a huge impact on events in Yugoslavia is, in part, due to the nature of communist societies in general, and, in part, a result of the economic malaise afflicting Yugoslavia in the mid-1980s. The Party apparatus in any communist country was an astonishingly powerful mechanism for control, and, from the moment that he became President of Serbia's League of Communists in 1986, in exactly the same manner as Stalin in the Soviet Union, Milošević put it to work shaping Serbian society in his own image. At the same time, Milošević capitalised on the desperate economic climate prevailing in Serbia in the mid-1980s and the frustrations of ordinary people who had seen their living standards collapse during the previous decade. But instead of attempting to correct the deficiencies of the existing economic system, he offered only simplistic solutions and scapegoats to revamp communist authority with nationalism and further his own career.

The key to Milošević's rule and an understanding of modern Serb nationalism is the Serbian media and their sustained campaign to generate national hysteria. Indeed, the Serbian media have played a very similar role in Milošević's Serbia to that played by the Nazi media in Hitler's Germany, though, on account of technological advances in the intervening half century, their influence has been more pervasive and more insidious. At least three years before the shooting war formally began in Yugoslavia, a war psychosis had already set in in Serbia—though, it should be noted, not in the Serb communities of Croatia and Bosnia-Hercegovina, since, at that time, they had not yet been exposed to the media offensive. Irrespective of whether or not Serbs were facing genocide in much of Yugoslavia, as the Serbian media alleged, Serbian society was already gripped by fear and ordinary people genuinely came to believe that they were under siege and, critically, began behaving as if they were surrounded by blood enemies determined to wipe them out.

To anyone who cared to question the allegations of genocide, the image of Yugoslavia portrayed in the Serbian media was a gross distortion of reality. In fact, much like the Nazi propaganda of the 1930s, the Serbian case has never added up, but then arguments do not have to be especially plausible when backed by the kind of military muscle which both Hitler's Germany and Milošević's Serbia could count on. And, irrespective of the relative merits of the Serbian case, Milošević's military alliance and his control over four federal units all but enabled him to dictate terms to the rest of the country. However, the terms on offer, which amounted, at best, to second-class citizenship, were worse than non-Serbs, and especially the Slovenes, were prepared to stomach.

Slovenia was a very different proposition from the rest of Yugoslavia, since, in the absence of a significant non-Slovene minority, Slovenes were in a position to turn their backs on the rest of the country. While the Yugoslav state had generally been good to Slovenes and had certainly fostered the evolution of a modern Slovene national identity, since the emergence of the new Serb nationalism in Milošević's Serbia, Yugoslavia had become a liability. Ironically, by the late 1980s Slovenia—that is, Slovenia's continued presence in Yugoslavia—was in many ways more important to Yugoslavia than Yugoslavia was to Slovenia. For Slovenia was an essential counter-weight to Serbia, and, without Slovenia, Serbs would come close to forming an overall majority in Yugoslavia and conditions for non-Serbs were almost certain to deteriorate. However, as war appeared imminent in the rest of the country and Serbia refused to moderate its hardline position — which included an economic boycott of Slovene products — Slovene leaders decided that their best strategy was to distance themselves as much as possible from the rest of the country.

Although one of the most enduring impressions of the Yugoslav conflict is the degree of hatred on all sides, it actually took many years to erase the Titoist ideal of brotherhood and unity, which had been drummed into all Yugoslavs from an early age, to the point where hostilities could break out. Even then, most Yugoslavs were extremely reluctant to take up arms against their fellow citizens. While Serbia had effectively been at war since 1987, the rest of the country — including the Serb community outside Serbia and out of range of the Serbian media — remained generally tranquil. Where disputes were left in the hands of local people, who were aware how much all sides stood to lose in the event of war, they remained manageable and could be resolved relatively easily. Inter-communal relations proved remarkably durable, to the consternation of nationalist *agents provocateurs*, whose early attempts to tip the country into war failed. And even when war broke out in Slovenia, many in the JNA chose to surrender rather than fight fellow Yugoslavs.

The brutality of the Croatian and Bosnian wars may, in fact, be interpreted as a backhanded tribute to the Titoist vision of Yugoslavia and the genuine bonds which had developed between the country's many peoples since the Second World War. For the atrocities committed by Serb irregulars were necessary to destroy all vestiges of the Yugoslav ideal and formed part of a calculated campaign to shatter, once and for all, relations between Serbs and non-Serbs. What is especially depressing is that, though the impact of the atrocities was enormous, the number of individuals behind the campaign was not great, nor were they representative of the wider Serb community in whose name they claimed to act. The Četniks and *Arkanovci*, who were responsible for the greatest excesses of ethnic cleansing in both Croatia and Bosnia-Hercegovina, were generally outsiders. They were also fanatical nationalists who had been deliberately indoctrinated with a pathological hatred of Albanians, Croats and Muslims.

In the two previous wars which pitted south Slavs against each other this century, the Yugoslav ideal, nevertheless, triumphed on both occasions. This time, however, a Yugoslav state cannot be resurrected in any meaningful form, since the current conflict is very different from its predecessors. Whereas Yugoslavs had little control over events leading to both the First and the Second World Wars and conflict was largely imported from abroad, the present war is a thoroughly home-grown creation. Moreover, in the Second World War in particular, most Slovenes, Croats, Serbs and Muslims actually fought not against each other, but on the same side. For Tito's partisans offered all Yugoslavs an alternative to the parochial nationalism of their respective nations, and, in the aftermath of the Second World War, all opponents — Ustašas, Četniks and anti-communists — were executed without mercy. This time, by contrast, though many Serbs have served in both the Croatian and Bosnian militaries, there has not been a comparable Yugoslav course open to them, allowing them to stand up to Milošević's brand of nationalism, yet retain their Serb identity.

Few Serbs from Croatia and Bosnia-Hercegovina rushed headlong into battle. Despite concerted attempts by nationalist agitators from Serbia to stir up Serb communities in the neighbouring republics from 1988 onwards, the vast majority of Croatian and Bosnian Serbs wished only to steer clear of trouble. Most have been dragged reluctantly into the war and are as much victims as their Croat and Muslim neighbours. Indeed, even those who voted for the nationalist SDS were voting not for the wholesale destruction of their homeland but for security in a period of change. And in most instances their only crime is their backwardness which has made them susceptible to Milošević's propaganda offensive.

Nevertheless, the analogy with Hitler's Germany and the German communities which used to live across eastern Europe is pertinent. In the 1930s, when Nazi propaganda alleged that the German communities of Czechoslovakia and Poland were being mistreated, the allegations were groundless. However, when Nazi Germany was finally defeated in 1945, even though Germans had lived throughout eastern Europe for centuries, they were no longer welcome and their communities disappeared. In the same way, when the Serbian media alleged genocide in the 1980s and early 1990s, the charges were unfounded. But after several years of war the allegations have become self-fulfilling and few Croats or Muslims are still prepared to put up with a Serb neighbour.

Meanwhile, the war goes on and, irrespective of UN involvement, is likely to continue for at least as long as Milošević remains in power. Whereas Serb leaders are now eager for a peace agreement which might cement their gains, their Croatian and Bosnian counterparts are equally determined to prevent them from permanently enjoying the fruits of aggression. Though weapons are coming in more slowly than if the arms embargo were to be lifted, they are, nevertheless, coming in, and the Croatian and Bosnian positions improve by the day. Moreover, Croats, Bosnians and Albanians consider that any agreement requiring Milošević's consent is worthless and are prepared psychologically for the long slog. Given Milošević's record, they all expect him to become embroiled in another conflict and are just waiting for the chance to strike back.

BIBLIOGRAPHICAL NOTE

The best of a rather dated selection of general books on Yugoslav history is probably Stevan Pavlowitch's *Yugoslavia* (Ernest Benn London, 1971). Otherwise, Pavlowitch's more recent work, *The Improbable Survivor: Yugoslavia and its Problems, 1918–1988* (Hurst, London, 1989), is a fascinating collection of historical essays and contains great insight into many aspects of Yugoslav society on the eve of Milošević's rise to power.

Ivo Banac's mammoth *The National Question in Yugoslavia: Origins, History, Politics* (Cornell University Press, Ithaca, NY, 1984) must be the starting point for the early history of the Balkans and Yugoslavia's birth. *The Creation of Yugoslavia, 1914–1918* (Clio Books, Santa Barbara, 1980), edited by Dimitrije Djordjević, is a collection of essays on the Yugoslav idea and the formation of the Yugoslav state which can also be recommended. For an examination of national policy from the foundation of the first Yugoslavia to its destruction, through the Second World War and the formation of the second Yugoslavia, Aleksa Djilas's *The Contested Country: Yugoslav Unity and Communist Revolution, 1919–1953* (Harvard University Press, Cambridge, MA, 1991) is the best. The son of the celebrated dissident and Tito's former right-hand man, Milovan Djilas, Aleksa Djilas published this book on the eve of the outbreak of war in 1991 and it is clearly influenced by the resurgence of national passion in the 1980s. It is especially good on Croat nationalism and the Ustašas.

Of the books specifically on the Second World War in Yugoslavia Jozo Tomasevich's *War and Revolution in Yugoslavia: The Chetniks* (Stanford University Press, 1975) and Walter Roberts's *Tito, Mihailović and the Allies* (New Brunswick, NJ, 1973) can be highly recommended. The two works which tackle the question of the war dead in a scientific manner are both in Serbo-Croat, *Žrtve drugog svetskog rata u Jugoslaviji* (Victims of the Second World War in Yugoslavia) (Naša Reć, London, 1985) by Bogoljub Kočović and *Jugoslavija: manipulacija žrava drugog svjetskog rata* (Yugoslavia: Manipulation of the Victims of the Second World War) (Yugoslav Victimological Society, Zagreb, 1989) by Vladimir Žerjavić. Žerjavić also provides an ethnic breakdown

252

of those killed at Jasenovac, the notorious Ustaša concentration camp, and those summarily executed at the end of the war who were handed over to the partisans by the British army. Though Kočović is a Serb and Žerjavić a Croat, their results are essentially identical.

The formation of a Communist state and the break with Moscow are covered in G.W. Hoffman and F.W. Neal's *Yugoslavia and the New Communism* (New York, 1962). Dennison Rusinow's *The Yugoslav Experiment, 1948–1974* (Hurst, London, 1977) is still probably the finest analysis of the Titoist experiment. Nora Beloff's *Tito's Flawed Legacy: Yugoslavia and the West, 1939–1984* (Gollancz, London, 1985) is worth reading in spite of a number of errors, since it, in effect, amounts to a Serb nationalist critique of Tito and Titoism in the English language. The best book specifically on Tito is Stevan Pavlowitch's *Yugoslavia's Great Dictator: Tito, A Reassessment* (Hurst, London, 1992), a concise and readable account which is generally critical of both the man and his impact on Yugoslavia. Over the years many books have been written about the Yugoslav economy and Socialist Worker Self-Management. Of these, David Dyker's *Yugoslavia: Socialism, Development and Debt* (Routledge, London, 1990) is thorough and the most recent.

Very little of quality has been written about Kosovo in Serbo-Croat and almost nothing has been published in English. In Serbo-Croat, Branko Horvat's *Kosovsko pitanje (The Kosovo Question)* (Globus, Zagreb, 1988) is the only genuine attempt to examine the province from a non-partisan point of view. In English, the best analysis is contained within Branka Magaš's *The Destruction of Yugoslavia: Tracing the Break-up, 1980–92* (Verso, London, 1992).

Several good studies of Milošević and his impact on Serbian society are available in Serbo-Croat. Two contemporaries who tried to thwart Milošević's rise to power both penned prophetic warnings of what the future had in store as early as 1988 and these remain probably the most useful insights into the man. Bogdan Bogdanović's *Mrtvouzice* (Unbreakable Bond) (BST/Cesarec, Zagreb, 1988) is a philosophical analysis of Milošević and his ideology, comparing him to Stalin, written by a former Mayor of Belgrade. Dragiša Pavlović's *Olako obećâna brzina* (Ill-considered Promises) (Globus, Zagreb, 1988) is an account of his own struggles against Milošević within the League of Communists of Serbia during 1987. The now notorious Memorandum of the Serbian Academy of Arts and Sciences has not been published in English, but can be read in French in *Le Nettoyage Ethnique. Documents*

Historiques sur une Idéologie Serbe (Fayard, Paris, 1993), compiled by Mirko Grmek, Marc Gjidara and Neven Simac.

For Yugoslavia's disintegration, Branka Magaš's *The Destruction of Yugoslavia: Tracing the Break-up, 1980–92* (Verso, London, 1992) is a remarkable historical record. It is a compilation of the penetrating writings on Yugoslavia during the 1980s and early 1990s and contains many key documents. Magaš's articles were originally published in a wide range of journals under the pseudonym Michele Lee. However, while the analysis is excellent, Magaš is very much a Marxist historian who examines events through a Marxist prism and this may put off non-Marxists. Chris Cviić's *Remaking the Balkans* (Pinter, London, 1991) is a concise analysis of the entire Balkan peninsula in the aftermath of the demise of communism, published on behalf of the Royal Institute of International Affairs. It examines Albania, Bulgaria, Greece, Romania and Turkey, but focuses on the events which brought Yugoslavia to the verge of disintegration. John Zametica's *The Yugoslav Conflict* (Brassey's, Adelphi Paper, no. 270, 1992) needs to be treated with special caution. The book was commissioned by the International Institute for Strategic Studies and was meant to provide an analysis of the causes of the Yugoslav wars, the policies of the republics and regional and international implications of the conflict. However, Zametica, who has since become an adviser to the Bosnian Serb leader, Radovan Karadžić, was hardly the man to write an impartial account and the book is little better than a work of propaganda. Leonard Cohen's *Broken Bonds: The Disintegration of Yugoslavia* (Westview Press, Boulder, CO, 1993) is a more detached, if rather dull, account of events.

James Gow's *Legitimacy and the Military: The Yugoslav Crisis* (Pinter, London, 1991) examines the role of the military in Yugoslavia's disintegration and is especially good on events in Slovenia leading to that republic's declaration of independence. An analyis by Gow of the diplomatic failure to halt the fighting in the former Yugoslavia is scheduled to appear in a forthcoming book, *Triumph of the Lack of Will: International Diplomacy and the Yugoslav War* (Hurst, London, 1995); and the critical role played by the media in Yugoslavia's disintegration is examined in Mark Thompson's *Forging War: The Media in Serbia, Croatia and Bosnia-Hercegovina* (The Bath Press, Avon, 1994), commissioned by Article 19, the London-based anti-censorship group.

For books specifically on Bosnia-Hercegovina, Noel Malcolm's *Bosnia: A Short History* (Macmillan, London, 1994) and *Bosnia and Hercegovina: A Tradition Betrayed* (Hurst, London, 1994) by Robert J.

Donia and John V.A. Fine can both be recommended. Rabia Ali and Lawrence Lifschultz's *Why Bosnia? Writings on the Balkan War* (Pamphleteer's Press, 1993) is a collection of essays on Bosnia-Hercegovina and the Bosnian war, including powerful analytical contributions by Mark Thompson and Branka Magaš among others, translations of Bosnian literature, and the graphic testimonies of survivors of ethnic cleansing. For Macedonia, Hugh Poulton's *Who are the Macedonians?* (Hurst, London, 1995) is the only study.

Several journalists have penned their own accounts of the war, which are generally a good read, if not necessarily inspired analyses of events. Roy Gutman's *A Witness to Genocide* (Element Books, London, 1993) is a collection of the despatches which won him a Pulitzer Prize. Mark Thompson's *A Paper House: The Ending of Yugoslavia* (Hutchinson Radius, London, 1992) is wonderful travel writing from every Yugoslav republic at the time when Yugoslavia was breaking up. Misha Glenny's *The Fall of Yugoslavia: The Third Balkan War* (Penguin, London, 1992) is an exciting and readable account of what the writer, the then BBC's central European correspondent, was doing as Yugoslavia fell apart. And Ed Vulliamy, the *Guardian*'s award-winning journalist who was among the first reporters to enter a Serb-run detention camp in Bosnia-Hercegovina, tells his story in *Seasons in Hell: Understanding Bosnia's War* (Simon & Schuster, London, 1994).

Many of the participants in the Yugoslav drama have also written books, either about their own role in events or on more general topics which, nevertheless, offer an insight into their personalities. Before becoming President of Croatia, Franjo Tudjman published many historical works which chart the evolution of his career and ideology from partisan to historian to nationalist dissident. His *Nationalism in Contemporary Europe* (Columbia University Press, New York, 1981) reflects his opinions as a nationalist dissident. Dobrica Ćosić, the father of modern Serb nationalism, has also written many books, mainly fiction. *Stvarnost i moguće* (Reality and Possibility) (Belgrade, 1983) is his analysis of national policy in Tito's Yugoslavia. Slovenia's Defence Minister during the independence war and formerly a celebrated dissident, Janez Janša, gives his account of the last years of Yugoslavia in *Premiki: Nastajanje in obramba Slovenske države 1988–1992* (Movements: the Creation and Defence of the Slovene State 1988–92) (Založba mladinska knjiga, Ljubljana, 1992). And Yugoslavia's last President, the Croat Stipe Mesić, went into print with *Kako smo srušili Jugoslaviju* (How we Destroyed Yugoslavia) (Globus, Zagreb, 1992).

INDEX

Abdić, Fikret, 202
Academy of Dramatic Arts, Belgrade, 130
Adriatic Sea, 53, 232
Adžić, General Blagoje, 132, 132n
Afghanistan, 77
Agrokomerc, 69, 99, 202n
Albanalogical Institute, 72
Albania, 18, 31, 43, 72, 87, 88, 154, 212, 217, 219
Albanian: atrocities against Serbs alleged in Kosovo, 161; irredentists, 92; language, 72; minority in Montenegro, 213; nationalism, 30; nationalists, 88; national identity, 88; national movement, 88; education, 87–9; miners, 106
Albanians: 9, 10, 19, 21, 34n, 40, 54–6, 61, 64, 65, 70, 71, 76, 78–81, 86–94, 97, 100, 102, 105–8, 113n, 115, 124, 134n, 140, 142, 144, 151n, 176, 215–19, 241, 242, 249–51; conversion to Islam, 19; religious affiliations, 87; condition in Yugoslavia, 71; proportion living in Yugoslavia, 87; birthrate, 87, 88, 93; League for the Defence of the Rights of the Albanian Nation, 88; relations with Serbs, 92, 93, 94; proportion in the military, 134n; in Macedonia, 218, 219
Alexander the Great, 220, 221
Alexander, King: 29, 30, 33, 38, 39, 54, 220, 247; assassination, 39, 39n, 220
Allman, T.D., 1 and 1n
Anschluss, 116
Anti-bureaucratic revolution, 125, 139
Anti-Fascist Council, 53
Anti-semitism, 129
Appeasement, Franco-British, in 1930s, 41
Arkan, Željko Ražnjatović, 150, 203
Arkanovci, 150, 164, 187, 189, 249

Association for a Yugoslav Democratic Initiative, *see* UJDI
Athens, 219, 221
atrocities: 2, 6, 44, 46, 47, 163, 164, 170, 184, 189, 190, 246, 249; in Second World War, 44, 46, 47; committed by Serb irregulars, 163, 164, 170, 177, 179, 184; committed in Croatia, 177, 179, 184; committed in Bosnia-Hercegovina, 189, 190
Australia, 124
Austria, 18, 28, 50, 113, 116, 210, 212
Austria-Hungary, 23, 25, 27–9, 31, 37
Austro-Hungarian empire, *see* Austria-Hungary
Axis powers, 45, 48, 51, 55
Azra, 65

Babić, Milan, 127n, 130, 136, 145, 148–50, 230
Badinter, Robert, 179
Badinter Commission, 179, 179n, 186
Baker, James, 2, 14, 154–6, 159, 175; attitude towards independence declarations, 2, 14, 154–6, 159, 175; visit to Belgrade, 14, 154, 159, 175
Balašević, Djordje, 65
Balkan culture, 195
Balkan federation, 55
Balkans: 2, 4, 6, 15–21, 23, 26, 31, 36, 41, 80, 87, 156n, 217, 221, 236, 241; 6
Balkan Wars, 23, 30, 40, 213, 218
Baltic republics, 158
Ban, 27, 27n, 40
Banac, Ivo, 16, 16n
Banat, 42
Banija, 41, 161, 167
Banja Luka, 183, 201, 226n
Banovina: 39, 41; ethnic composition, 41

256

Bar, 75
Baranja, 42, 167
Barthou, Louis, 39n
Bassiouni, Cherif, 195n
BBC World Service, 25, 95
Beijing, 106
Belgrade: 13, 22, 29, 30, 33, 41, 42, 44, 46, 49, 52, 57, 61–3, 65, 70, 82, 84, 89, 90, 98–100, 102, 103, 110, 121, 124, 127, 129, 130, 135, 144, 145, 148, 149, 151, 154, 156, 159, 161, 162, 172, 174, 175, 183, 188n, 206, 208, 208n, 209, 211, 212, 214, 216, 217, 227, 230, 239, 246; League of Communists, 82, 83n, 84; University of, 84; University League of Communists, 84; Belgrade-Ljubljana axis, 102
Benkovac, 129, 130, 135
Beobanka, 83, 84
Berisha, Sali, 217
Berlin, Congress of (1878), 22, 23, 213
Berlin Wall, 1
Bihać, 202
Bijelo Dugme, 65
Bijeljina, 187, 189
Bismarck, Otto von, 35
Boban, Mate, 199, 200, 227
Bogdanović, Bogdan, 98
Bogomil Church, 18, 19
Bogomils, 17, 20
Bohemia, 77
Boka Kotorska, 213n
Bolshevik Revolution, 57
Borba, 97n, 208
Borders, 1945 creation of, 53
Borovo Selo, 62, 151, 161, 164, 168
Bosnia: 17–19, 53, 131, 179, 183, 194n, 199, 202, 230; early Bosnian state, 17, 18; heretical tradition, 19; link with Hercegovina, 19n
Bosnia-Hercegovina: 1–4, 9, 11–15, 19, 20, 23, 25, 28, 30, 31, 36, 40, 41, 43, 45–9, 52, 53, 55, 59, 62, 63, 69, 72, 76–8, 80, 99, 102, 113, 115, 116, 120, 122, 126, 131, 138, 139, 142, 144, 146, 147, 151, 152, 154, 157, 171, 173, 176, 177, 179–92, 194–210, 213–15, 218, 221–30, 232, 233, 237, 238, 240, 241,

243–5, 248, 249; international recognition 2, 9, 173, 181, 187–9, 196, 221; annexation (1908) 23; Slav conversion to Islam, 19; land reform, 40; dead in Second World War, 45; League of Communists, 69; arms industry, 77; 1990 election, 120, 182; mediation, 180, 181; ethnic composition, 180; outbreak of war, 180, 181, 187, 188; referendum, 180, 186; territorial defence force disarmed, 183; Bosnian independence, 2; UN deployment, 4; anti-Serb pogroms (1914), 31; Serb republic, 185n, 186; cantonisation, 186, 187, 189; arms embargo, 188
Bosnian army, 191, 199, 201, 225, 226, 230
Bosnian Church, *see* Bogomil Church
Bosnian Croats: 23, 54, 63, 180, 184–92, 194, 198–201, 204, 227, 230, 245; proportion of total population of Bosnia-Hercegovina, 180
Bosnian election, 120; federation, 227; independence, 185; media, 184; Muslim landowners, 37
Bosnian Serbs: 3, 23, 45, 48, 49, 54, 62, 63, 116, 126, 136, 146, 151, 180, 183, 184, 188, 189, 192, 195–204, 208, 209, 222, 223n, 224, 226, 227, 245, 248, 249; army, 131, 184, 197, 204, 226; dead in Second World War, 45; police domination, 63; armed by Serbian Interior Ministry, 136, 183; proportion of total population of Bosnia-Hercegovina, 180; referendum, 185n; military tactics, 190; parliament, 198
Bosnians, 182, 183, 185, 193, 195, 196, 223, 237, 239, 251
Boutros-Ghali, Boutros, 195
Bratstvo i jedinstvo, see brotherhood and unity
Brezhnev, Leonid, 77
Brioni Accord, 159, 160, 170, 175, 234
Britain, *see* Great Britain
British Army, 205n
Broek, Hans van den, 175, 177
Brotherhood and unity (*bratstvo i jedinstvo*), 10, 53, 95, 126, 131, 140, 249

Broz, Josip, *see* Tito
Brussels, 176
Budapest, 27, 33
Budiša, Dražen, 73, 232
Bulatović, Momir, 213, 214
Bulgaria: 23, 24, 26, 42, 43, 49, 218,
    220; Turkish minority, 24
Bulgarian, 31
Bush, President George, 108, 131, 174n,
    203, 225
Byzantium: 17; split with Rome, 17

Cable News Network, *see* CNN
Canada, 124, 199n
Čanak, Nenad, 171
Cankarjev Dom: 106, 162; meeting, 106;
    press centre, 162
Carrington, Lord: 176, 177, 179, 180,
    181, 186, 189, 191, 193; opposition to
    recognition of Slovenia and Croatia,
    181
Castro, Fidel, 67
Catholic(s): 5, 16, 17, 20, 34n, 39, 44,
    87; minority among Albanians, 87
Catholic Church, 18, 44, 52, 142n
Cavour, Camillo di, 35
Cazinska Krajina, 201, 202n
Census: 1910 Austro-Hungarian, 23;
    1921, 34n; *1981*, 80, 90, 113; *1991*,
    8, 113n, 218, 219
Četniks, 22, 22n, 47, 150, 151, 164, 183,
    207, 208, 249
Channel Four, 191, 193, 194
Chernobyl, 103n
Christendom, 19
Christian Europe, 20
Christianity: 16, 17, 184; Slav conversion
    to, 17
Christopher, Warren, 203
Churchill, Winston, 42, 244
CIA, 173
Civil society, 139, 189
Clinton, President Bill, 203
CNN, 161
Coalition of National Agreement, see
    KNS
Cold War, 61, 153, 205
Cominform, 37n, 57–59

Comintern, 57, 81
Committee for the Protection of Human
    Rights, 105, 106
Communism: 4, 8, 11, 12, 51, 80, 106,
    109, 112, 114, 123, 135, 139, 184;
    Yugoslav, 11, 109; demise of, 11, 12,
    106, 135, 139; failings of, 103; Croa-
    tian, 123
Communist(s): 11, 38, 48, 51, 52, 54,
    55, 57, 58, 60, 62, 67, 68, 72, 78, 90,
    100, 101, 104, 105, 109, 111, 119,
    123, 127, 130, 132, 133, 153, 220n;
    armed forces, 132; Party: 12n, 52, 54,
    63, 85, 247; apparatus, 63, 85, 247;
    Party of Yugoslavia, see CPY; revolu-
    tion, 54; rule, 49, 109; society, 132;
    Yugoslav, 11, 48, 51, 52, 54, 55, 57,
    58, 60, 62, 67, 68, 104, 109, 119;
    Bosnian, 111; Croatian, 72, 78, 133;
    former, 123, 127, 130; Greek, 57,
    220n; Macedonian, 111; non-Serbian,
    100; Serbian, 90, 101, 133; Slovene,
    101, 104, 105, 107, 111, 119, 132;
    Slovenia's former, 153; Tito's, 38;
    Vojvodina, 75
Concentration camps, 3
Concordat, 39n
Conference (Helsinki) on Security and
    Disarmament in Europe (CSCE), 175
Conscientious objection to military
    service, 103
Consensus economics, 68
Constitution: 1921, Vidovdan, 36, 37;
    1931, Alexander's, 38, 39; *1946*, 53,
    109n; *1974*: 13, 70, 74, 81, 90, 109n,
    134, 137, 143, 217; details and length,
    74; Croatian, 141; new Yugoslav,
    138; Stalin's 1936, 143
Ćosić, Dobrica, 79, 80, 80n, 81, 208
Council for the Rights of National and
    Ethnic Groups in Montenegro, 214
Coup d'état: 23, 42, 116, 133; Milošević's
    in Montenegro, 116; 1903 in Serbia, 23;
    1941 in Yugoslavia, 42; 1991 in Soviet
    Union, 133
CPY, Communist Party of Yugoslavia,
    57–60
Crna Ruka (Black Hand), 31

264 *Index*

League of Communists (*contd*)
Komunista — Pokret za Jugoslaviju (SKPJ), 133, 134
League for the Defence of the Rights of the Albanian Nation, 88
Lebanon, 3
Leopold I, King, 21n
Lika, 41
Ljubljana: 33, 42, 52, 102, 105–7, 144, 155, 160, 174; Belgrade-Ljubljana axis, 102
Ljubičić, Nikola, 133
Lokar, Sonja, 110
London, 36, 50, 170n, 191, 192, 193, 195, 222
London: 191, 192, 193, 195, 222; 1992 conference, 191, 192, 195, 222; agreement, 193
Luxembourg, 158, 159n

Maastricht Treaty on European Union, 179
Macedonia: 3, 4, 12, 13, 16, 18, 21, 21n, 23, 24, 40, 42, 53–5, 69, 72, 78, 87, 99, 115n, 151, 156n, 175, 176, 179, 184, 185, 218–21; Aegean, 218, 220; Albanian minority, 99, 218, 219; economic reform, 221; ethnic composition, 218; land reform, 40; Pirin, 218; potential for future conflict, 3; terrorism, 24, 39n; trade embargo, 221; UN deployment, 4; Vardar, 218, 220
Macedonian(s): 5, 9, 17, 21n, 22, 34n, 40, 51, 53, 56, 65, 71, 76, 134n, 218–21; proportion in the military, 134n, conscript killed in Split, 152; irredentists, 220; nationalism, 219; Orthodox Church, 219n; question, 215, 218; Slav identity, 218
Maček, Vlatko, 38, 39, 40, 41, 43, 49, 247
MacKenzie, Gen. Lewis, 194n
Major, John, 191
Mamula, Branko, 104, 133
Manolić, Josip, 123n, 232
Market socialism, 68
Marković, Ante: 8, 115–22, 136, 137, 142, 151, 156, 175, 247; economic

stabilisation programme, 8, 118, 137, 142; formation of political party, 120
Marković, Draža, 84
Marković, Mihailo, 81
Marković, Mirjana, 84, 133
Martić, Milan, 136n
Martićevci, 136, 136n
Marx, Karl, 60
Marxism-Leninism: 7, 11, 51, 52, 57, 60, 101, 109; failings of, 11; on national question, 51, 52
Marxist-Leninist edifice, 132
Maslenica bridge, 229, 229n
Maspok, see Croatian spring
Media: 3–6, 9, 10, 42, 56, 64, 78, 79, 89, 91, 94, 95, 96, 97, 98, 103, 114, 115, 116, 121, 122, 124, 125, 126, 130, 135, 136, 140, 141, 145, 146, 147, 148, 149, 161, 162, 163, 169, 184, 185, 190–93, 195–7, 207, 208, 213, 214, 224, 225, 229–31, 236, 238, 239, 242, 243, 248–50; international, 3, 9, 42, 161, 169n, 190–3, 195–7, 214, 224, 225, 229, 236, 238, 239; local, 4, 5, 6, 56, 78, 79, 89, 163n, 184, 185, 192, 230, 231; neglect of Yugoslav affairs, 9, 12; Serbian, 10, 79, 91, 95, 96, 97, 98, 114, 115, 116, 121, 122, 124, 125, 126, 130, 134, 135, 136, 140, 145, 146, 147, 148, 149, 161, 162, 163, 184, 207, 208, 213, 214, 248–50; traditional role in Yugoslav society, 10, 64, 95; coverage of Tito, 56; Slovene, 79, 103, 148, 161, 162; Croatian, 78, 95, 130, 141, 148, 161, 162, 169, 230, 231; Yugoslav media and Kosovo, 89; Serbian media attempts to criminalise Albanians, 91; media-generated hysteria in Serbia, 122; media war, 130, 147, 148, 149, 161, 162, 163; Bosnian, 184, 185; Montenegrin, 213
Mediation: 2, 15, 190, 202, 203; EC, 2; UN, 2, 15, 202, 203; mediators, 195, 198, 224, 225, 238, 245
Mediterranean Games, 1979, 65
Medjimurje, 42
'Meeting of Truth', 107

Index

Kosovo Serbs, 87, 88, 89, 90, 91, 92, 93, 94, 161; proportion of Kosovo population, 90; proportion in military, 105, 134; Milošević's loan from, 108

Serbs, Croats and Slovenes, kingdom of, 32, 34, 35, 38, 40, 81, 241

Šešelj, Vojslav, 150, 151, 183, 203, 207, 208, 213

Šibenik, 126, 152; anti-Serb rampage, 152

Siberia, 59

Sidran, Abdulah, 112

Skopje, 87, 219, 220, 221

SKPJ, *see* League of Communists – Movement for Yugoslavia

Slavs, 113, 221

Slavonia, 21, 22, 25, 40, 42, 62, 63, 125, 149, 161, 164, 165, 169, 171, 228; land reform, 40; ethnic composition, 62; eastern, 125, 149, 161, 164, 165, 169, 171; western, 149, 171

Slobodna Dalmacija, 231

Slovakia, 20

Slovaks, 21, 210

Slovene(s), 5, 9, 17, 25, 26, 33, 34, 48, 50n, 55, 56, 76, 79, 81, 101, 102, 105–8, 113, 132n, 134n, 137, 142, 160, 161, 166, 233–5, 237, 241, 248; handed over to partisans by British Army and executed at end of Second World War, 50n; proportion in military, 134n; artists, 103; cultural identity, 102; delegation at the 14th Congress of the LCY, 110; electorate, 137n; independence, 2, 137; national identity, 101, 103, 248; nationalism, 101, 103; nationalists, 158; independence referendum, 137

Slovenia: 1, 2, 4, 5n, 7, 9, 11–14, 16, 26, 36, 42, 53, 57, 63, 69, 72, 75, 77, 79, 86, 101–6, 108, 109, 113, 115–20, 122, 126, 133, 137–9, 142–4, 146, 147, 151, 152, 154–61, 166, 171–9, 181–6, 188, 205n, 206, 209, 221, 228, 232–5, 237, 242, 243, 244, 245, 248, 249; EC recognition, 1, 2, 4, 172, 178, 179, 188, 221; US recognition 2, 173; international recognition, 9, 245; independence declaration, 2, 12, 13,

14, 143, 152, 154, 155, 156, 157, 175, 178, 245; outbreak of war, 2, 14, 42, 155, 156, 157, 159n, 176; relative wealth, 5n; traditional alliance with Serbia, 7; challenge to Serbia, 11, 101; multiparty elections, 12, 118; territorial defence force disarmed, 14, 19, 139, 144; territorial defence force, 157; division in Second World War, 42; economic expansion, 75; relative wealth, 102; communist leadership, 103, 118; League of Communists, 107; multiparty elections, 120, 138; impact of Marković's reforms, 122; lobbies international community, 14, 152, 153; economy, 233

Slovenia's opposition, 106

Slovenia's Youth Organisation, 104, 105; media, 79, 104, 105

Socialist Worker Self-Management, 60, 67, 68, 107, 234

Solzhenitsyn, Alexander, 236

Soros, George, and Foundation, 195n

South Slavs: 16, 17, 19, 22, 25, 26, 28, 30–2, 241, 246, 249; migrations, 17

South Slav lands, 247

South Slav nationalists, 28

Soviet: aggression, 75; bloc, 59; bogey, 59, 111; camp, 56; Empire, 57, 59; influence, 67; intervention, 205; invasion of Czechoslovakia, 76; military, 133, 158; support, 109; threat, 58–60, 77; yoke, 111

Soviet Union: 11, 42, 47, 49, 51–4, 57–60, 77, 85, 103n, 111, 113, 132, 143, 158, 174, 247; demise of communist authority, 11

Spanish Civil War, 48

Špegelj, Martin, 144, 145, 145n, 157, 166, 167

Split, 42, 134, 152

Sporazum, *see* Cvetković-Maček agreement

Srbobran, 27, 28

Srebrenica, 197

Srpski pokret obnove, Serb Renewal Movement, 122, 207

Stalin, Joseph: 51, 53, 55–60, 74, 77, 85,